Teaching in the Pandemic Era in Saudi Arabia

Teaching in the Pandemic Era in Saudi Arabia

Edited by

Amani Khalaf Alghamdi

BRILL

LEIDEN | BOSTON

All chapters in this book have undergone peer review.

The Library of Congress Cataloging-in-Publication Data is available online at https://catalog.loc.gov

Typeface for the Latin, Greek, and Cyrillic scripts: "Brill". See and download: brill.com/brill-typeface.

ISBN 978-90-04-52165-0 (paperback)
ISBN 978-90-04-52166-7 (hardback)
ISBN 978-90-04-52167-4 (e-book)

Copyright 2022 by Koninklijke Brill NV, Leiden, The Netherlands.
Koninklijke Brill NV incorporates the imprints Brill, Brill Nijhoff, Brill Hotei, Brill Schöningh, Brill Fink, Brill mentis, Vandenhoeck & Ruprecht, Böhlau and V&R unipress.
All rights reserved. No part of this publication may be reproduced, translated, stored in a retrieval system, or transmitted in any form or by any means, electronic, mechanical, photocopying, recording or otherwise, without prior written permission from the publisher. Requests for re-use and/or translations must be addressed to Koninklijke Brill NV via brill.com or copyright.com.

This book is printed on acid-free paper and produced in a sustainable manner.

To all those who lost their fight against COVID-19 and to all teaching staff, and parents in Saudi Arabia and around the world. There are no words to describe what teachers and parents have to overcome to ensure continuity of education for our children and young people during the pandemic.

Contents

Preface IX
List of Figures and Tables XI
List of Abbreviations XII
Notes on Contributors XIV

Introduction   1
   Amani Khalaf Alghamdi

1   COVID-19 Emergency Remote Education Curriculum: Saudi Higher Education – Same or Adjusted?   3
   Reima Al-Jarf

2   Reflections of a Saudi Female Practitioner: As a Mother, Instructor, Researcher, and Instructional Technology Specialist in Distance Learning during the COVID-19 Pandemic   22
   Fawzia Omer Alubthane

3   Post-COVID e-Learning in Bahrain: Where Are We in Meeting the Educational Reform Objective of Sustainable Development?   39
   Nina Abdul Razzak

4   How Students Were Engaged during the Second Wave of COVID-19 by EFL, Linguistics and Translation Instructors in Distance Learning   61
   Reima Al-Jarf

5   When Learning Was Disrupted in Saudi Arabia: Full-Scale Distance e-Learning as a Solution to Face COVID-19   82
   Amani Khalaf Alghamdi and Wai Si El-Hassan

6   Equity and Inclusion in Saudi Education during the Pandemic   105
   Mohammed Alharbi

7   Comparative Study of Alternative Teaching and Learning Tools: Google Meet, Microsoft Teams, and Zoom during COVID-19   120
   Kamran Ahmed Siddiqui and Shabir Ahmad

8   Reorientation of Teaching/Teachers about Education and
    Pandemic   130
        Sami Ghazzai Alsulami

9   Students' Satisfaction with e-Learning in Saudi Higher Education during
    the COVID-19 Outbreak   154
        Chaudhry Kashif Mahmood, Tayyiba Khalil,
        Aseel Fuad Ali Al-Karasneh and Talha Sarfaraz

10 Impact on Teaching Strategies in Saudi Arabian Universities Owing to
    COVID-19 Pandemic   168
        Maqsood Mahmud, Hoda M. Abo Alsamh, Talha Sarfaraz,
        Mohd Anuar Arshad, Arshad Mahmood and Bala Raju Nikku

11 It's Time to Rethink Teaching! Bloom's Pyramid of Higher Order
    Thinking Skills Revisited   181
        Randa Hariri

Preface

In March 2020, as the world was still baffled with the unknowns of the COVID-19 pandemic, I decided to have a book published, which is about how teaching and learning in higher education changed its face as a result of this global health outbreak. The outbreak of the novel coronavirus (SARS-CoV-2) was first reported from Wuhan, China, on December 31, 2019. By contrast, teachers across the world and in Saudi Arabia in particular were undertaking the plethora of on-the-ground work to combat and alleviate the impact of the pandemic. The focus of this volume, as I witnessed first-hand the effect of COVID-19 on education, excited me. I wanted to respect and document the shift from face-to-face education to emergency online education. The world was unprepared for this government-mandated mode of learning, yet people felt they had no choice but to accept it for the sake of everyone's health and continuity of learning.

Decades earlier, distance education was given as a choice to Saudi Arabian university educators. The Saudi Ministry of Higher Education spent millions to train faculty, to hold conferences, and to obtain online platform licenses. But its efforts did not fully convince university leaders and faculty members to implement an authentic distance education delivery mode. In many cases, it was not fully put to use. As a faculty member myself, I was once called upon for using a learning management system (LMS) to assess my postgraduate students' academic performance. However, no one expected to live to a point when online learning and assessment was the only choice available. It took about a year for life to return to some semblance of normalcy. I started discussing the effect of online teaching with my postgraduate students, and I had a few papers published on distance education, before inviting my fellow colleagues and faculty members to participate in this volume.

I was motivated and inspired to learn from Google that there were more than 70,000 publications, in Arabic and English, about teaching in this "new world order" in Saudi Arabia. This new educational reality, in which students are no longer in the physical classroom, yet are fully and seriously engaged in education, inspired me to edit this collection about Teaching and Learning in the Pandemic Era: Perspectives from Saudi Arabia.

Many faculty members from my network positively responded to the call for chapters, which reached many scholars in the Arabian Gulf region. Although targeting the Saudi context, I could not resist including chapter three, which is from a colleague from Bahrain (a neighboring country of Saudi Arabia) that has an interesting perspective about teaching during the COVID-19 pandemic.

On November 26, 2021, the World Health Organization (WHO) designated B.1.1.529 as a variant of concern, and they named it Omicron. This happened while I was editing this book. Because of this voracious virus mutation development, learning may have to return to complete distance and online schooling. Endless variants of the coronavirus seem to be emerging, further compelling me to discern lessons learned for the future.

This collection presents to educators, parents, and other interested readers a variety of perspectives, challenges, and highlights of the teaching methods that could be useful. Its purposes are to not only document an important time of human history, education, and the outbreak of unknown pandemics but also outline strategies to serve as insights into and predictions of the unknown future of humanity, diseases, and human learning.

Figures and Tables

Figures

5.1   Technical issues with emergency distance education and possible solutions.   89
5.2   Crises as a catalyst for change in Saudi higher education.   96
9.1   Demographics of students.   160
10.1 University students' statistics (pre-training).   173
10.2 Technology and community engagement during COVID-19 pandemic (pre-training).   174
10.3 University community engagement: becoming a change agent in the digital era (pre-training).   174
10.4 University students' statistics (post-training).   175
10.5 Technology and community engagement during COVID-19 pandemic (post-training).   175
10.6 University community engagement: becoming a change agent in the digital era (post-training).   176
11.1 Ladder of higher order thinking skills.   192

Tables

4.1   Some flower names in English and Arabic.   70
5.1   Major emergency distance education concerns expressed by Saudi students and faculty members (N = 2,009 tweets from 8 Twitter feeds).   88
7.1   Comparative account of Meet, Teams, and Zoom for systems requirements.   122
7.2   Comparative account of Meet, Teams, and Zoom for teaching and learning features.   124
7.3   Comparative account of Meet, Teams, and Zoom for security features.   126
9.1   Categories for instrument items.   160
9.2   Means, standard deviation, and the category for all instrument items (N = 345).   162
9.3   Means, standard deviations, and ANOVA test of students' satisfaction level toward e-learning.   164

Abbreviations

α	statistical significance
μ	the population mean
df	degree of freedom
F	ratio of two variances
SD	standard deviation
Sig.	significance
4G	fourth generation of mobile networks
4IR	The Fourth Industrial Revolution
ACT	American College Test
A Level	Advanced Level
AMO	ability-motivation-opportunity
ANOVA	analysis of variance
AS Level	Advanced Subsidiary Level
BEDB	Bahrain Economic Development Board
BQA	Bahrain Education & Training Quality Authority
CAP	content-assessment-pedagogy
CDI	course design intelligence
CIE	Cambridge International Examinations
Coop	cooperative training program
COVID-19	coronavirus disease 2019
DeL	distance e-learning
DL	distance learning
DSR	deanship of scientific research
EFL	English as a Foreign Language
ESD	education for sustainable development
GCC	Gulf Cooperative Council
GPA	grade point average
HEIS	higher education institutions
HOTS	higher-order thinking skills
HRM	human resources management
HyFlex	hybrid flexible
ICT	information communication technology
IGCSE	International General Certificate of Secondary Education
IELTS	International English Language Testing System
iEN	Saudi national educational portal
IT	information technology
K-12	kindergarten through 12th grade or Year 13

ABBREVIATIONS

KPIS	key performance indicators
LMS	learning management system
MoE	Ministry of Education
OECD	Organization for Economic Co-operation and Development
O Level	Ordinary Level
PISA	Program for International Student Assessment
RBV	resource-based view
SAT	Scholastic Aptitude Test (previously known)
SOP	standard operation procedures
SPSS	statistical package for the social sciences
TED	Technology, Entertainment, and Design
TESOL	Teaching English to Speakers of Other Languages
T&L	teaching and learning
TNA	training needs analysis
TOEFL	Test of English as Foreign Language
UES	The Unified Education System
UIS	UNESCO Institute for Statistics
UN	United Nations
UNESCO	United Nations Educational, Scientific and Cultural Organization
UNICEF	The United Nations Children's Fund
USM	Universiti Sains Malaysia
VLE	virtual learning environment
WHO	World Health Organization
ZPD	zone of proximal development

Notes on Contributors

Nina Abdul Razzak
is an academic consultant at the Bahrain Education and Training Quality Authority (BQA). Before this, she was an assistant professor of educational psychology and educational leadership at the Bahrain Teachers' College of the University of Bahrain. In her long educational career in Saudi Arabia and Bahrain, Dr. Abdul Razzak has held various positions at the K-12 level, and undergraduate and postgraduate levels in higher education. Dr. Abdul Razzak has several publications in international scientific journals and her research interests include best practices and technology integration in education, and the effects of child maltreatment. She is also the founder and managing editor of her own international peer-reviewed scientific journal: *The Journal of Teaching and Teacher Education*.

Shabir Ahmad
is a faculty member at the College of Business Administration, Imam Abdulrahman Bin Faisal University, Saudi Arabia. He earned a Ph.D. in Management with distinction from UTM, Malaysia, and an MBA in International Business from Cardiff Metropolitan University, UK. His research focuses on corporate sustainability, family businesses, innovation, entrepreneurship, and CSR. His work has been published in various reputed journals including Journal of Family Business Management, Journal of Small Business and Enterprise Development, Journal of Entrepreneurship in Emerging Economies, and Sage Open Journal. He serves as article editor for *Sage Open Journal* and as a reviewer for *Business and Society Review, Journal of Law and Management*, and *Journal of Asian Business and Management*.

Amani Khalaf Alghamdi
is a professor at Imam Abdulrahman Bin Faisal University (IAU) in Dammam, Saudi Arabia. She is an award-winning scholar who is widely published with more than 40 Scopus publications. She is well-known in the field of education in Saudi Arabia and abroad. Her research interest is multifaceted and includes education and curricula in Saudi Arabia, analytical and critical thinking and their infusion in teaching, online education and cultural manifestations, higher education, narrative research, and critical multicultural education. Dr. Alghamdi has over 28 years of national and international teaching experience. She has presented at various international conferences and is published in American, Canadian, Saudi, and Australian high-impact factor journals.

Dr. Alghamdi is the founder and first vice dean of the female section at IAU's Faculty of Education.

Mohammed Alharbi
gained a Ph.D. from the College of Education and International Services, Andrews University. He earned his doctoral degree in curriculum and instruction in 2020. Dr. Alharbi is now a teacher at the Ministry of Education in Saudi Arabia. He has more than 10 years of experience in teaching mathematics for middle school students. His area of interest is Multicultural Education and Equity in Education. Dr. Alharbi cooperated with the Center of Teachers Professional Development to present training sessions to inform teachers about the role of multicultural education in developing the education system. ORCID: https://orcid.org/0000-0003-1486-7687

Reima Al-Jarf
is a professor of ESL, ESP, linguistics, and translation. She has 700 publications and conference presentations in 70 countries. Some of her articles are published in Web of Science and Scopus journals. Since the outbreak of the COVID-19 pandemic, she has written and published 12 book chapters and journal articles. She reviews Ph.D. theses, promotion works, conference and grant proposals, and articles for numerous peer-reviewed international journals including some Web of Science and Scopus journals. She won 3 Excellence in Teaching Awards, and the Best Faculty Website Award at her university. Her areas of interest are foreign language teaching and learning, technology integration in education, and translation studies. ORCID: https://orcid.org/0000-0002-6255-1305

Aseel Fuad Ali Al-Karasneh
is lecturer in Pharmacy Practice and Clinical Pharmacy in Clinical Pharmacy College at Imam Abdulrahman Bin Faisal University (IAU), Dammam, Saudi Arabia. Her research focuses on the social and administrative pharmacy policies and epidemiology. She received her master's and bachelor's degrees from Jordan University of Science and Technology. Before joining IAU, she worked as a teaching and research assistant for one year at College of Pharmacy, University of Science and Technology.

Hoda M. Abo Alsamh
is Vice Dean of Postgraduate Studies and Research, College of Business Administration, Imam Abdulrahman Bin Faisal University, Dammam, Saudi Arabia. She published several international articles in the area of her research

interest. Her research interests include human resources management, organizational behavior and community services.

Sami Ghazzai Alsulami

is assistant professor of Educational Leadership at the Islamic University of Madinah, Saudi Arabia. Dr. Sami is currently in charge of the Vision 2030 realization office at the university and he is Dean for Research and Consultation. He earned his doctorate degree with honors at Texas Tech University. Besides advising freshman year students at the Islamic University of Madinah, Dr. Sami does the teaching activities that employ the Socratic philosophy of pedagogy where students are encouraged to think critically and challenge the status quo. Dr. Sami's research interests are of relevance to the contemporary literature strands of educational management, education policy, and faculty development.

Fawzia Omer Alubthane

is a Saudi assistant professor who graduated from the Department of Instructional Technology, Ohio University, USA. She teaches a number of courses in the field of education, such as Instructional Technology, Scientific Research, Instructional Computer, Education Media, Independent Study, and other courses. She is the head of the e-Learning Unit in the college as well as a member in a number of committees. Additionally, she participated in conferences in Saudi Arabia and the USA, such as The Clute International Conference on DC and The First Virtual Forum for e-Learning and Distance Learning held by Shaqra University. She conducted a number of training courses on e-learning and technology in education and published five research papers in both languages (Arabic and English). ORCID: https://orcid.org/0000-0002-1952-6569

Mohd Anuar Arshad

is a senior lecturer at School of Management, Universiti Sains Malaysia. His areas of interests are in HRM, OB, OD and HRD. His current program of research focuses on HRM and OL. He holds a Ph.D. in Commerce from Murdoch University, Perth, Western Australia. He has an industrial working experience for almost eight years in various positions ranging from production operator, production supervisor, assistant manager and human resources officer. He has also been attached with various industries in the past, such as manufacturing, services and plantation. His research interest focuses on human resources development and he is currently looking into the area of Intelligence Quotient (IQ), Emotional Quotient (EQ) and Spiritual Quotient (SQ).

Wai Si El-Hassan

(BA (Hons.), MA) is Lead Job Coach, SEND, Guildford College of Further and Higher Education, Surrey, UK. She is an alumnus of the University of East Anglia, Norwich, UK, and the Education University of Hong Kong. Wai Si has ample international teaching experience in teaching English in Hong Kong, the UK, Saudi Arabia and Jordan, and her research encompasses sustainability education, language teaching, special education and higher education. Some of her papers appeared in Scopus journals and other prestigious international journals covering areas of pedagogy of empowerment, assessment and accreditation, sustainability education, energy literacy, distance education, entrepreneurship education, financial literacy, teaching of 21st century skills and so on. Wai Si is also a regular reviewer of the *Journal of Australian Educational Researcher*. ORCID: https://orcid.org/0000-0002-5920-6076

Randa Hariri

is Associate Professor, Master Program of Educational Leadership. Founder and former Director of the Center of Excellence in Teaching and Learning. Former Director of Strategic Planning, and Performance Evaluation Department in Dar Al Hekma University, Jeddah, Saudi Arabia. She has a Ph.D. in Education, "Teaching Excellence and Quality in Higher Education", awarded by the University of Sheffield, UK. Dr. Hariri has obtained an M.A. in Educational Administration and Policy Studies, and a postgraduate diploma in Educational Leadership and Management from the American University of Beirut. She also has licentiate in Psychology: Educational Psychology, and is a certified KPIS professional and practitioner, strategic planning professional, curriculum and academic program developer, teacher trainer, policy and procedures writer, accreditation and quality reviewer and consultant, theses supervisor, and reviewer in Scopus indexed Q1 journals. Dr. Hariri won excellence awards for teaching and leadership and has over 16 publications.

Tayyiba Khalil

is a lecturer at College of Business Administration, Imam Abdulrahman Bin Faisal University, Dammam, Saudi Arabia. She completed her master's and MSc in Management from University of Central Punjab, Pakistan. She holds a certificate in Career and Academic from Indiana University, USA – Council for Adult and Experiential Learning (CAEL). She also has a marketing specialization certificate from Virtual University in Pakistan. She has more than 10 years of teaching experience at a number of prestigious higher education institutions. Her expertise is mostly concerned with digital marketing, consumer behavior, service quality, and business education. She has multiple research articles at major conferences as well as Scopus and ISI-indexed journals.

Arshad Mahmood
has a Ph.D. and he is a Post-Doctoral Fellow at School of Management, Universiti Sains Malaysia. Dr. Arshad has published his research works in different international journals, such as *Journal of Management, Spirituality and Religion*, *Management Research Review*, *Sustainability*, *Journal of Cellular Physiology*, *Journal of Human Values*, *International Journal of Ethics and Systems*, as well the *Journal of Chinese Economic and Foreign Trade Studies*. His research interests are in the areas of organizational behavior, training and development, spirituality, organizational learning and entrepreneurship. School of Management, Penang, University of Science Malaysia, Malaysia.

Chaudhry Kashif Mahmood
is a faculty member at College of Business Administration, Imam Abdulrahman Bin Faisal University, Dammam, Saudi Arabia. He completed his Ph.D. in Management with distinction at Universiti Technologi Malaysia, Malaysia. He has over 13 years of teaching experience at several prestigious educational institutions. Consumer behavior, business education, digital marketing, and entrepreneurship management are among his research interests. He has numerous research publications published in prestigious conferences, Scopus and ISI-indexed journals.

Maqsood Mahmud
is an assistant professor at Department of Management Information Systems, College of Business Administration, IAU, Dammam, Saudi Arabia. He is also Director of Business Re-enforcement Intelligence and Cybersecurity Lab (BRICS-Lab). He earned his Ph.D. at University of Technology Malaysia in the field of Information Security Management in 2013 and did a PostDoc at King Saud University. He published more than 50 research articles in reputed conferences and ISI-SCi indexed journals. He has served as reviewer/editor of various international conferences and journals. He worked on five funded projects in which two were from projects of King Abdulaziz City of Science and Technology (KACST), Riyadh, and three from DSR, IAU, ENTRA, Saudi Arabia. He is certified ToT for Web of Science (WoS) Clarivate Analytics. Furthermore, he is a holder of two US Patents on commercialization of biometric data/templates security and natural language processing.

Bala Raju Nikku
joined the School of Social Work and Human Service, Thompson Rivers University, as an assistant professor in 2018. He served in the academia and grassroots social work practice in India, Nepal, Malaysia and held adjunct positions in the UK and Thailand. He has been a social work and social policy teaching faculty, researcher and practitioner for the last 20 years. Dr. Nikku worked in the area of disasters management, health, poverty and their framing and implementation on the ground. He is currently part of a research collective (www.canada-asia-researchcollective.org) and interested in applying rights-based approaches to human displacement. His research interests include international social work, green social work, disasters and epidemics, community engagement, Health Equity Action Framework, scholarship of teaching and learning, decolonization, intercultural studies, race and immigration, comparative social policy, and curricular innovations.

Talha Sarfaraz
is a faculty member at College of Business Administration, Imam Abdulrahman Bin Faisal University, Dammam, Saudi Arabia. He has worked in academia for the last 10 years. His interests include digital marketing, consumer behavior.

Kamran Ahmed Siddiqui
works at Imam Abdulrahman Bin Faisal University as an associate professor of Marketing and Entrepreneurship. He received his Ph.D. (Business Administration) from Manchester Business School, UK, and his master's degree is in marketing from the University of Bradford, UK. He also holds an MBA-MIS from IBA, Karachi, Pakistan. He has more than 30 years of experience in the corporate and education sectors. He has expertise in marketing, branding, advertising and marketing research, information systems, project management, and leadership development. Dr. Siddiqui is a seasoned trainer for Microsoft, Novell, Oracle, and Project Management. He is also a member of Project Management Institute, USA, and American Marketing Association, USA. He has more than 50 article publications in reputable scientific journals and 20 international conference papers to his credit.

Introduction

Amani Khalaf Alghamdi

Teaching in a pandemic era calls for a reorientation of the aims of teaching and teacher education, so that educators can begin to imagine multiple futures in which children, youth, and families can thrive amidst a myriad of pandemic-related challenges. To that end, this edited collection contains 11 peer-reviewed chapters from the Pan-Saudi context that are focused on the pursuit of an education in the COVID-19 pandemic era and the shift in teaching modes that is called for in these precarious times. Together, the contributors confront the very thought of teaching and teacher education in the face of a global health crisis with almost no end in sight.

The collection confronts three overall themes. Foremost is the *social context* and what accounts for the disavowal of the pandemic in Saudi national and local school improvement discourse. Some authors highlighted educators' success stories of teaching during the pandemic. Others discussed about what was distracting Saudi higher education actors in teaching and teacher education programs. This thread accounts for and addresses the emotional paralysis on a societal scale that is preventing a significant reorientation to teacher education praxis as a result of the pandemic.

Second, the collection addresses the *consequences* of shifts in teaching mode on educational and emotional well-being especially with regard to pandemic teaching and learning, the virtual realm as it relates to social cohesion and fragmentation during the teaching and learning processes.

Third, the collection addresses the *reorientation* of teaching and teachers about education and the pandemic. Some authors focused on positive and effective teaching narratives related to teaching in this era in diverse fields but namely in social science, humanities, and social justice. The issue of cosmologies in teaching and teacher education during and after a pandemic was also discussed as was how parents and teachers dealt with the anxiety that surfaces as one confronted the challenges of attendant crises during a pandemic (e.g., the climate crises). The chapters related to this thread highlighted one or more of the following thoughts:

- Using education to reinvigorate education and/or reimagine new learning landscapes that help students deal with the impact of pandemic change – teaching to challenge post pandemic systems.
- Co-creating educational encounters with students that foster solidarity and collective responses to human suffering caused by the pandemic.

– Cultivating imaginative community-based solutions of pandemic-related issues especially educational issues.
– Unmasking information and/or the ethics of information sharing (e.g., science literacy, social media, fake news, etc.); traversing (negotiating and navigating) social media territories during the pandemic as they pertain to learning.

In conclusion, the hope of scholars contributing to this collection was the Saudi education system would overcome various challenges that it had experienced (suffered) during the pandemic. The topics herein emerged from the contributing authors' experience with and reflections on the intersection of the Saudi education system with the pandemic. Their scholarship highlights opportunities to continue the conversation around the impact of the pandemic era on teaching and learning in Saudi Arabia.

CHAPTER 1

COVID-19 Emergency Remote Education Curriculum

Saudi Higher Education – Same or Adjusted?

Reima Al-Jarf

Abstract

This chapter aimed to find out whether instructors, departments and/or colleges of education, computer science, language, linguistics, and translation at Saudi universities have adjusted, or reconstructed their curricula in the distance learning (DL) environment during the first 3 semesters of the COVID-19 pandemic and how those departments are carrying out the teaching practicum and graduation projects in DL. No changes have been made in curricula in DL during the pandemic have been reported because the program courses and course descriptions cannot be easily modified or changed as these are usually approved by the departments, colleges and academic councils, not individual instructors. Numerous options for completing the teaching practicum and graduation projects in translation and computer during the pandemic are reported.

Keywords

COVID-19 – pandemic curriculum – college curriculum – distance education – remote education

1   Background

The term curriculum refers to the academic content, units, and lessons that teachers have to teach in a specific course, program, or school. It is usually comprised of the learning goals, objectives, or standards that the students are expected to meet; the skills and knowledge that they are expected to acquire; the topics and content to be covered; the books, materials, readings, presentations, projects and assignments to be given to students; technologies to be used in a course such as videos; and the assessment techniques for evaluating students' learning such as quizzes, tests, rating scales, checklists, scoring rubrics, and others. Thus, a course curriculum would consist of specific learning goals or objectives of the course an instructor is teaching, the material to be covered, the topics, assignments, and projects that the students need to complete in order to achieve the end-of-course goals. In addition, the students must be provided with practice during the course.

To achieve educational goals, school and college stakeholders need to plan, design, and organize the instructional units, lessons, learning activities, readings, and assessment techniques in the course, show how the course topics will be taught and in which order and what the students will be doing in the course. This process is called curriculum design. Curriculum design[1] is the systematic organization of a curriculum, which involves creating an overall course blueprint, matching the course content to learning objectives, developing a course outline, course descriptions, and building the whole course or program. For each learning objective, the course content, subject matter, exercises, activities, and assessment techniques are identified.

There are three types of curriculum design[2]: subject-centered which focuses on a specific area of study; learner-centered which focuses on the students' abilities, skills, interests, and goals; and problem-centered design which focuses on specific social, economic, medical, educational, and psychological issues and how to come up with solutions for those issues.

In designing and implementing a particular curriculum, Chaudhary (2015) emphasized that the curriculum developer/designer should take some factors into consideration like the learners, teachers, the school environment, school budget, culture and ideology, resources, materials, facilities, instructional supervision, and assessment. In educational practice, these factors interact with each other and create influences that cannot be attributed to a single factor. Schweitzer (2019) added that the curriculum developer/designer should identify what will be done in the course, who will do it, how and according to which schedule in order to improve students' learning. The developer/designer should make sure that the learning goals are aligned and complement each other especially when the students move from one stage or level to the next.

To manage the curriculum design process, Schweitzer (2019) pointed out that the curriculum developer/designer should do the following: (1) identify the needs of the students, (2) make a list of learning objectives and outcomes, (3) identify constraints that will affect curriculum design, (4) create a curriculum map, i.e., curriculum matrix to evaluate the sequence and coherence of instruction, (5) identify the instructional methods that will be used throughout the course and consider how they will work with the students' different learning styles, and (6) *define the evaluation techniques* (placement, aptitude, achievement, diagnostic, formative, summative, norm-referenced or criterion-referenced) that will be used during and at the end of the academic year to assess learners, instructors, and the whole curriculum. *Curriculum design is not a one-step process.* It is an on-going process. There is always a need to review, modify, change, adapt, adjust and reconstruct the curriculum of a particular course or program to meet the learning requirements of students and the requirements of the labor market.

Curriculum design is not only essential for face-to-face instruction, but is also essential for other modes of teaching such as blended, distance and online education. In this respect, Chugh et al. (2017) declared that the design of the distance learning (DL) curriculum should meet institutional and industry requirements, reflect educational objectives, and take into consideration elements of pedagogy and engagement. To ensure that the distance education curriculum meets contemporary educational practices, the authors proposed a triad consisting of pedagogy, technology, and an engaged community of learners.

2 Literature Review

Before the outbreak of the COVID-19 pandemic in early 2020, most university courses all over the world were delivered face-to-face, with some courses delivered online, and some instructors using blended learning as a supplement to in-class instruction. But due to the COVID-19 pandemic, there was a sudden switch from face-to-face instruction to DL, which was mandated in all countries, at all levels of education, and for all kinds of courses during school closures starting in March 2020. Studies reviewed by Al-Jarf (2020b) showed that students in most countries were not satisfied with the new course delivery mode, i.e., online DL, due to numerous challenges such as accessibility, connectivity costs, technical problems, lack of staff training and confidence, limited social contact, lack of student engagement, communication, interaction and cooperation with each other and with their instructors, absence of traditional classroom socialization and long response time from instructors. Likewise, the teachers reported that online teaching during the pandemic required new skills. They were not instructionally nor technologically trained in DL. Learning resources and materials suitable for DL were inadequate and they were not able to use interactive resources.

In addition, both students and instructors preferred face-to-face instruction to DL, because more content is covered. Collaboration and interaction among students in face-to-face instruction is greater. The students' contact with their classmates and instructors is present in face-to-face but missing in DL. Unlike DL, face-to-face, in-class instruction develops the dynamics of group work. Social interaction on campus and in the classroom strengthen students' identity as members of a community. Lack of classroom and on-campus socialization in DL made it difficult for students to participate in group projects (Al-Jarf, 2020b).

For the above reasons, some researchers such as Adnan & Anwar (2020) called for the improvement of the higher education curriculum and the design of appropriate content for online lectures and DL during the pandemic. As a result, emergency DL in some countries triggered some curriculum change, curriculum redesign, and curriculum adjustments in online DL in numerous disciplines such as chemistry, engineering, mathematics, science, early childhood education, physical education, social studies, and language learning.

In chemistry courses in particular, the social distancing measures introduced to prevent the spread of COVID-19 led to the rapid redesign of undergraduate-level chemistry instruction in higher education from face-to-face to online delivery. For example, Easdon (2020) adjusted the topics covered in a biochemistry course. This adjustment included covering the life cycle of SARS-CoV-2 and switching to the chapters covering nucleic acid topics. This change promoted students' engagement in the online version of the course for the remainder of the semester. In a course on catalysis in which 188 students were enrolled, Sarju (2020) used a blended multimedia instructional approach, informed by equality, diversity, inclusion, and cognitive load theories. Information was chunked and delivered online through short videos, supported by a written course handout, small group tutorials and banks of multiple-choice questions. Usage statistics, autobiographical critical reflections, and student feedback showed that the course received overwhelmingly positive feedback from students who appreciated the course format, accessibility, and delivery. At a large public university in the USA, general and organic chemistry laboratory courses have always had curricular, administrative, logistic, and high enrolment challenges. To meet those challenges in the transition from face-to-face to remote teaching during the COVID-19 pandemic, Howitz et al. (2020) utilized their existing web-based course content, made additions and alterations to their curriculum, and replaced experimental work with videos.

At a large southwestern university, Chernosky et al. (2021) redesigned an engineering course for adult learners. First, the researchers identified the key components of satisfaction, student engagement strategies and key course characteristics, which could increase satisfaction and reduce dropout rates. Those included faculty interaction, authenticity, student-to-student engagement, feedback, multimedia, and homework. Then, the researchers developed an equitable instructional design model, which was a learner-centered engineering course of value.

In New Zealand, Nguyen et al. (2020) designed an Early Childhood Education and Care (Level 4) Program delivered fully online. The new course design focused on instruction that empowers learners in an online flexible DL environment, innovative teamwork, and initial feedback from stakeholders, the integration of sociocultural and constructivist theories with information communication technology and an assessment approach. The re-designed pedagogy and innovative teamwork resulted in very positive initial feedback from stakeholders. In another study, Metscher et al. (2021) reported adaptations made by three teacher educators in an early childhood teacher-preparation program in New York City to facilitate student engagement. Those included the use of breakout groups, an interactive whiteboard, an interactive agenda, and community-building activities.

In social studies, Helmsing and Noy (2020) integrated key concepts about global health during the COVID-19 pandemic and offered social studies educators an approach to support lessons on COVID-19 across sociology, geography, and other fields within social studies education. They provided select digital resources for students and teachers to use in teaching and learning about the COVID-19 pandemic through a global health perspective aligned with the National Council for the Social Studies Thematic Standards.

Moreover, Stahl (2021) redesigned a mathematics curriculum using available technology to implement approaches that incorporate the findings of learning theories, collaborative learning, computer mediation, student discourse and feedback. The proposed model used an existing dynamic-geometry technology to translate Euclidean geometry study into collaborative learning by small groups of students who study together, facilitated by a teacher or supervisor. The dynamic-geometry technology allowed teachers and students to interact with the same material in multiple modes. This dynamic-geometry technology proved to be beneficial for online students, co-located small groups, and school classrooms, with teachers and students having shared access to materials and students' work across all interaction modes.

In implementing a data science curriculum, Berg and Hawila (2021) used R and R-related tools. Readers were directed to helpful R resources. Then they used R in exploring COVID-19 data, and ethnic/racial distributions and COVID-19 death rates. Supplementary R markdown files were also included, which allowed all graphics to be easily reproduced.

Due to the lack of commercially developed, online-based textbook packages for distance language learning courses, and the distance separating students which seemed to hinder the provision of language learning experiences that focus on social and cultural contexts, Noriko (2013) utilized online learning communities as networks of social relationships, engagement, and interaction. In addition, students enrolled in a first-year Japanese DL course developed basic communication skills and increased their awareness of cultural differences through the instructor's intervention and collaborative work with peers and using a combination of synchronous and asynchronous DL.

A second line of research in the literature focused on creating flexible and adaptable course content and procedures in curriculum redesign to cope with DL and make it more effective. For instance, Watkins et al. (2020) created an inclusive design of diverse learning experiences, individualization and adaptation of learning materials, open education practices and flexible digital resources to optimize learning opportunities for all students. Likewise, Pulker and Kukulska-Hulme (2020) proposed a model for reusing open educational resources in language learning. They found that reuse/adaptation of resources had a positive effect on students and it was the main factor in enhancing students' learning.

In South Africa, Mendy and Madiope (2020) described what colleges did as they responded to the need for curriculum reform in Open Distance e-Learning in South Africa. Results revealed reforms in the following areas: student support, technology-enhanced teaching and learning, alternative assessment systems, excellence in quality assurance, student retention, rate of students completing a course, and student accessibility. The reforms were narrowed to three areas, namely curriculum content, curriculum responsiveness, and practical pedagogy.

In Australia, a cross-curriculum priority that stresses Australia's engagement with Asia was mandated by the Australian government. This means that Asian beliefs, cultures, environments, and Australia-Asia relationships should be embedded in the learning processes at Australian schools especially during the COVID-19 pandemic, which affected the whole world so significantly (Guo, 2021).

A student-centered pedagogy and course transformation, which affected more than 600 courses at Purdue University in the USA, was carried out to accumulate knowledge on effective teaching, to facilitate student learning, improve outcomes, and change the institutional culture around teaching and learning. Focus was on self-determination theory, which stimulated faculty's motivation and creativity and shaped the setup and transformation of the program from a course redesign to a professional faculty development program. The faculty was given autonomy to build on their expertise in the discipline, pursue their interests and preferences according to a guided framework, and maximize their interaction with colleagues through faculty learning communities (Levesque-Bristol, 2021).

Some Departments of Education such as the Kentucky Department of Education (2020) addressed the knowledge gaps due to school closure and extended remote learning during the COVID-19 emergency DL. Their reports provided guidance on initial steps for how educators can plan and bridge the knowledge gaps. They analyzed their 2019–2020 curriculum to be able to make adjustments in the 2020–2021 curriculum, and to be able to address potential knowledge gaps due to extended remote learning in incoming students. They identified areas for potential gaps in 2019–2020 students to share in vertical conversations and drafted an adjusted curriculum for the 2020–2021 school year.

Another course design used during the COVID-19 pandemic was the Content-Assessment-Pedagogy (CAP) triangle, which provides a framework for making curriculum design decisions about what content must be emphasized, what might be omitted or added, what content components should be assessed, and how to design learning activities that maximize students' learning. A critical feature of the CAP framework is the alignment of content, pedagogy, and assessment with each other and placing what instructors want learners to retain long after instruction in the center. It was concluded that pedagogy and assessment need to relate to the learning outcomes with feedback, not grades, as the most important aspect of assessment, and practice as the essence of pedagogy (Streveler & Smith, 2020).

Moreover, Chugh et al. (2017) recommended utilizing a mixture of synchronous and asynchronous environments in DL. They proposed the integration of pedagogy, technology, and an engaged community of learners. Before designing a curriculum, specific contexts and needs should be identified. The curricula should define competencies that students need to display and the content that should be delivered. In general, it may not be possible to design a curriculum that suits one cohort of students; hence, curriculum design should accommodate and serve the needs of both DL students and those in the traditional classroom setting. Curriculum design practices should focus on learning, connecting, and engaging the students and should support the needs of DL students, demands of the labor market and educators as well.

Regarding the Saudi context, students and instructors at some Saudi universities reported some problems with school closure and the sudden transition to DL, which started in March 2020 (spring semester 2020). Fifty-five percent (55%) of Saudi students majoring in languages, linguistics and translation were dissatisfied with DL, found it ineffective and frustrating and preferred face-to-face instruction. Since DL was a new mode of learning, the students had difficulty understanding online lectures especially in courses that require practice. It was not possible for the students to follow the lecture and chat, and respond to queries and comments at the same time. Sixty-nine percent (69%)

of the students surveyed had problems communicating with their instructors and classmates. Students' most common concern was exams and passing their courses with high grades (Al-Jarf, 2020b).

Similarly, translation and interpreting instructors were dissatisfied with DL during the first semester of the pandemic (spring 2020). The new DL environment was a new mode of teaching and delivering lectures to students. They did not know how to adapt the course material to the new DL environment. They had difficulty communicating with a large number of students registered in their courses and give feedback to each student on their translation of the assigned texts. They added that the students were not interested in online learning, were not enthusiastic, were demotivated and disappointed. The online course attendance was not as high as in face-to-face classes. The students refused to give oral presentations online, did not ask questions, many did not participate in online discussions, and did not do assignments. There was little interaction in the new DL environment (Al-Jarf, 2020b).

Since summer 2020, Saudi universities have taken numerous steps towards solving platform problems, improving internet connectivity and access, providing devices to disadvantaged students who did not have devices in spring 2020 (Al-Jarf, 2021d). They have set new online exam procedures and standards and offered training workshops for teachers. In spring 2021 (the third semester of the pandemic), language and translation instructor surveys showed that the instructors went beyond lecturing and using PowerPoint in DL. They started to use new online activities for increasing students' engagement such as: searching for linguistic and translation key terms and concepts, answering problem-solving questions, using online debates, summarizing a research paper, attending a thesis defense online, inviting specialized guest speakers online, giving project-based assignments, connecting writing and speaking topics with Saudi Arabia's Vision 2030, collecting and analyzing translation errors, translating Wikipedia articles from English to Arabic, online interpreting contests, analyzing family speech, a video, and talk shows in the light of some pragmatic and linguistic theories and concepts, student-created digital stories, and podcasts. In online speaking courses, the students gave online oral presentations, answered problem-solving questions orally, participated in listening and speaking activities and online debates. They integrated new technologies such as Slido, Padlet, and Kahoot in DL (Al-Jarf, 2021, 2022).

3   Aims of Study

The above literature review has revealed lack of studies in Saudi Arabia about whether universities, colleges, departments, or instructors have made any changes, modifications or enhancements in their course curriculum while teaching online during the pandemic. Therefore, the current study aims to find out whether instructors, departments and/or colleges at Saudi universities have changed, reviewed, modified, adapted, adjusted, or reconstructed the curriculum content taught at a sample of colleges (languages, linguistics, translation, English Literature, Education and Computer Science) in the DL environment during the first 3 semesters of the pandemic (Spring 2020, Fall 2021, and Spring 2021). Specifically, the study will find out whether any changes have been made in the following aspects of the curriculum: (1) set of courses offered by the program; (2) course titles; (3) number of credit hours allocated to each course; (4) the topics taught; (5) amount of material covered in DL courses during pandemic; (6) the course material (books, readings, resources) used; (7) any new training courses offered to equip the students with new interpersonal and technological skills needed for the pandemic and post-pandemic labor markets; (8) delivery of teaching practicum courses and graduation projects in the DL environment during the pandemic. The study will not focus on other components of the curriculum such as learning activities, students' engagement, and assessment in DL during the pandemic as they were the subject of other studies by the author (Al-Jarf, 2020b, 2021, 2022). However, occasional reference will be made to these studies when necessary.

4   Significance of Study

The current study will help stakeholders at Saudi universities gain insights into online curriculum and course design for DL learners during the COVID-19 pandemic era. It will show them how to enhance existing DL courses and the different ways for converting traditional courses to courses that are suitable for both DL and face-to-face instruction. It shows the need to reconsider how to teach subjects in the pandemic online environment. It will help them upgrade teaching and learning in the DL environment. It aims to promote understanding of curriculum design practices and understanding of how to update, modify pedagogy and technology, and engage the community of learners as a basis for ensuring that the curriculum meets contemporary practices in the 21st century.

5   Methodology

5.1   *Participants*
The participants in the present study consisted of 125 Saudi students and 80 instructors from different colleges, such as: English Language Centers, Colleges

of Languages, Translation, Linguistics, English Literature, Education and Computer Science from 7 public universities and 1 private university included: King Saudi University, Princess Noura University, King Abdul-Aziz University, Umm Al-Qura University, Ta'if University, and Imam Abdulrahman Bin Faisal University, Tabuk University and Prince Sultan University (a private university). Fifty percent (50%) of the students and 55% of the instructors were from Colleges of Languages, Translation, Linguistics and English Literature, 30% of the students and 25% of the faculty were from Colleges of Education; and 20% of the students and 20% of the instructors were from Colleges of Computer Science. Ninety percent (90%) of the instructors and 80% of the students were female. Fifty-two percent (52%) of the instructors had a Ph.D. degree; 38% had an M.A., and 10% were teaching assistants. Eighty-seven percent (87%) of the students were undergraduate (sophomore, junior and senior); and 13% were M.A. and Ph.D. students. Students and instructors were from different departments (sub-specialties) at Colleges of Education and Computer Science.

5.2   Data Collection

All instructors and students in the samples responded to a survey with the following open-ended questions that asked them about the curriculum in their DL courses during the COVID-19 pandemic (Spring 2020, Fall 2021, and Spring 2021). Questions also asked whether any changes, modifications or additions had been made. Those questions included: (1) set of courses offered by the program; (2) course titles; (3) number of credit hours allocated to each course; (4) the topics taught – if yes, give examples; (5) amount of material covered in DL courses during the first three semesters of the pandemic and whether it is the same, less or more than that covered in face-to-face instruction before the pandemic; (6) the course material (books, readings, handouts, videos, podcasts digital resources) used, and whether any digital resources have been added – if yes, give examples; (7) whether new training courses have been offered to equip the students with new interpersonal and technological skills needed for the pandemic and post-pandemic labor markets; and (8) how the teaching practicum courses and graduation projects are carried out in the DL environment during the pandemic.

5.3   Data Analysis

Instructors and students' responses to the surveys were compiled, sorted out according to each question, and then quantified. Responses to a question from all students and those from all faculty were pooled separately. Where applicable, percentages of instructors and students giving the same response were calculated. Instructors and students' responses are also reported qualitatively.

Where necessary, quotations of some instructors and students' responses are given. Instructors and students' responses to each question were not classified in terms of instructors and students' gender, area of specialization, instructors' degree, students' educational level, type of college, or university.

6 Results and Discussions

6.1 *The DL College Curricula during the Pandemic as Reported by Instructors*

All of the instructors in the sample reported that no adjustments have been made in the languages, translation, linguistics, literature, education or computer science course curricula in the DL courses offered to students during the first three semesters of the pandemic (Spring 2020, Fall 2021, Spring 2021). The set of courses offered in each college program, course titles, credit hours allocated to each course, course content, topics taught, amount of material covered, types of material used by the students are the same as those offered before the pandemic, when classes were held face to face. The only difference is in the delivery mode.

In addition, the instructors indicated that the set of courses in the college/department program and the course description of each cannot be easily modified, changed, or added to as these are usually approved by the department, college and academic councils, not individual instructors. Any changes to be made in the curriculum have to be approved by the aforementioned councils. Since the council members were working remotely, it was not easy, nor possible to make any changes or adjustments in the curriculum even if those adjustments are necessary.

At Saudi universities, instructors are not given the freedom, nor the choice to change or add new topics to the course content they are teaching without getting the approval of at least their department, or college councils, which was not possible because of the disruption that the pandemic has created. However, instructors at Saudi universities have the choice and freedom to select the learning activities to be given to the students even when they are using textbooks assigned by the department as in the listening, speaking, reading, writing, grammar and vocabulary courses

As for the Teaching Practicum courses that senior students at colleges of education or English departments have to complete, before the pandemic student-teachers would go to elementary, junior or senior high schools, observe teachers and practice teaching the students in the classroom (face-to-face). But during the pandemic, when all courses were delivered online, there were several options. The following are examples mentioned by the participants.

An instructor at a college of education reported:

> Before the pandemic, the students used to practice teaching in the real classroom, but during the pandemic, the Teaching Practicum shifted to online microteaching.

Another practicum instructor at another college of education commented:

> There is a Teaching Practicum at our department during the pandemic. Our student-teachers practice distance teaching. They use *Madrasati* (the Ministry of Education's platform) to practice teaching. They borrow the class teacher's username and password to access the courses delivered on *Madrasati* and teach the students (*Madrasati*; مدرستي means "My School").

An instructor at an English department wrote:

> In face-to-face instruction before the pandemic, senior students at the English department were required to take a Teaching Practicum course for a whole semester where they practiced teaching English face-to-face. During the pandemic the students attended their Teaching Practicum twice a week as it was before the pandemic.

An instructor at an English language center said:

> Before the pandemic, we had a teacher mentoring program, in which new instructors and graduates received training in the principles of teaching, how to interact with students, how to use Blackboard in language teaching, and how to design tests and homework-assignments. The program is still operating during the pandemic, but the training period has been reduced to one month only instead of a whole semester.

An instructor at a private university indicated:

> Before the pandemic, we had a face-to-face Cooperative Training Program (Coop) for students majoring in linguistics and translation. During the pandemic, this Coop is still required although training opportunities for senior students are very limited. Working face-to-face or remotely (during the pandemic) depends on where the student is doing her training.

A translation instructor added:

> Graduating seniors have a choice to translate a book or go for field training in translation. Some translation students used to go to King Abdullah Bureau for Translation and Arabization, the Deanship of Research, the Ministry of Municipal and Rural Affairs, the Ministry of Foreign Affairs, some marketing firms, some hospitals, and others for training. But during the pandemic, the students were asked to translate 14,000 words at home (i.e., remotely) instead of going to the office and working on their translation face to face.

A computer instructor declared:

> During the pandemic, some places that offered training for computer science students such as Makkah Municipality allowed the students to complete their practicum during the summer to maintain social distancing. The students also had the option to attend 135 hours of online training courses in computer, IT and technological skills.

6.2 The DL College Curricula during the Pandemic as Reported by Students

Graduate and undergraduate students in the sample confirmed what the instructors mentioned about the college curricula. The set of courses offered in program, number of credit hours allocated to each course, course content, topics taught, amount of material covered, material, textbooks, handouts are the same as those mentioned in the course outline and course description. No digital resources have been added, uploaded, or required. They also revealed that they had not received any instruction or extra training in interpersonal skills, digital skills, computer skills, remote communication, and so on.

However, the students mentioned one difference between face-to-face and DL instruction during the pandemic which is lecture recording by the platform used in DL such as Zoom and Blackboard. They added that with lecture recordings, they did not need to attend online lectures synchronously as they can re-play lecture recordings (asynchronously) any time and as many times as they wish, especially when they miss a class. They did not have this advantage in face-to-face instruction before the pandemic, where lectures were *not* recorded, therefore, they had to take notes by hand during the lecture, and if they missed a lecture, they had to borrow lecture notes from a classmate or read the lecture material/handout at home.

7 Discussion

Findings of the present study have shown that no changes, modifications, or enhancements have been made in the curricula of a sample of college majors (languages, translation, linguistics, literature, education, and computer science) at a sample of Saudi universities in DL during the COVID-19 pandemic. The college curricula, i.e., the set of courses offered by the departments, course titles, number of credit hours, course content and topics taught, amount of content covered and course material, and resources in DL during the pandemic are the same as those in face-to-face instruction before the pandemic. The only change was in the delivery mode, in the teaching practicum and graduation projects, in addition to the recordings of the online class lectures by the DL platform. These findings are partially inconsistent with findings of prior studies such as Easdon (2020); Sarju (2020); Howitz et al. (2020); Chernosky et al. (2021); Nguyen et al. (2020); Metscher et al. (2021); Helmsing and Noy (2020); Stahl (2021); Berg and Hawila (2021); Watkins, Treviranus and Roberts (2020); Pulker and Kukulska-Hulme (2020); Streveler and Smith (2020); and Chugh et al. (2017), in which instructors made adjustments and enhancements in the online chemistry, engineering, mathematics, science, early childhood, social studies, physical education and language learning courses during the pandemic.

Saudi students' preference for lecture recordings and asynchronous learning, in the present study, is similar to findings of other studies by Chung et al. (2020) and Al-Nofaie (2020). In the former study, Malaysian college students preferred online learning via pre-recorded lectures uploaded to Google Classroom and YouTube, but the biggest challenge was for diploma students who had difficulty understanding the course content. As in the present study, Al-Nofaie (2020) reported that Saudi students preferred learning via an asynchronous rather than a synchronous learning environment due to its flexibility.

8 Conclusion

The outbreak of the COVID-19 pandemic in early 2020 has forced many schools and universities around the world to shift from face-to-face to remote teaching and learning using a variety of platforms such as Zoom, Microsoft Teams, Google Meet, WebEx, Blackboard and others without prior notice and without prior training in online instruction. The pandemic has also posed an urgent need to redesign college curriculum in terms of the content and topics taught, the redesign of activities, the utilization of technology in delivering classes to students with emphasis on collaborative learning, student engagement, interaction and online assessment and feedback. Since the subjects in the present study have reported no official changes made in the languages, translation, linguistics, English literature, education, and computer science curricula at Saudi universities during the first three semesters of the pandemic, the present study recommends the integration of current global issues (topics) related to the COVID-19 pandemic from different perspectives depending on the students' major. For example, students majoring in languages, translation, linguistics, and English literature may read articles, watch videos, write essays, give presentations, or participate in online debates about some issues related to COVID-19. They may practice critical thinking skills through the reading of articles or watching videos about the pandemic. The students may share and propose digital material on the COVID-19 from the World Health Organization, UNICEF and other websites, or digital resources that they can read or watch. (Al-Jarf, 2022a, 2022b, 2022c). Students and instructors from different backgrounds may enter into a dialogue with each other using a blog, online discussion forum or social media page to gain knowledge of the reality of the coronavirus pandemic or distance learning and reflect on them critically (Al-Jarf, 2020a).

Students majoring in education may discuss the impact of COVID-19 on students' psychology and well-being. They may practice teaching children online using the *Madrasati* Platform, designed and supervised by the Saudi Ministry of Education, learn how to motivate schoolchildren to communicate and interact in the DL environment. Graduate and senior students may work as a teacher aide where they can help teachers at elementary, middle, or high schools and special education centers in providing online assistance to students, help in grading, leading small group online instruction, supervise virtual field trips and prepare digital materials for the students. They can attend seminars and thesis defenses online as well.

Students majoring in computer science may create certain apps related to the pandemic. They can design robots to be used in hospitals, airports, restaurants, factories and other locations to help doctors and nurses in treating coronavirus infected patients, help passengers at airports, help serve food and drinks at restaurants and coffee shops, and help workers in the factories. In data mining courses, students may collect and analyze pandemic statistics from around the world. They can conduct some learning analytics,[3] i.e., collecting, analyzing, measuring, and reporting data about students in DL contexts in Saudi Arabian schools and universities, in order to understand and optimize learning, and improve the DL environment. They may help in solving faculty and students' connectivity problems and access and train instructors and students in using the different DL platforms. They may collect data about students while using LMS's, DL platforms, social media, or other online tools. They may track students' clicks, time on task, navigation patterns, information flow, social interaction, and concept development through discussions and make these data available for analysis.

Higher education institutions in Saudi Arabia should be encouraged to utilize learning analytics about teaching practices in DL, analyze, compare, and link those to learning processes and learning outcomes, in addition to gathering instructors' views about online learning and engaging them in the development of learning analytics for learning designs.

Finally, this study recommends that future researchers investigate other aspects of the curriculum, such as comparing the amount of material covered in courses before the pandemic and in online instruction during the pandemic (Al-Jarf, 2021c). Issues such as assessment and engagement in DL during the pandemic; assessing students' achievement (using placement, achievement; formative or summative assessment); evaluating instructors' performance in DL; evaluating the curriculum content and course topics to find out their relevance to DL; difficulties encountered during online delivery of the course content; and evaluating the effectiveness of the new teaching practicum and graduation project alternatives used during the pandemic are still open for future research studies. Student assessment can be conducted from different angles: self-assessment, quizzes, exams, rating scales, and/or checklists. Assessment of instructors' performance can be conducted through observations, interviews, and/or surveys. The suitability of the curriculum from the students and instructors' perspectives and its relevance to the program goals can be assessed as well. The evaluation of student engagement, communication and experiential learning activities in DL during the pandemic is still open for further investigations in the future. Such new areas of research are needed to explore the effectiveness of different aspects of DL and to help students achieve the desired learning outcomes, program, and course goals.

Notes

1 https://tophat.com/glossary/c/curriculum-design/#:~:text=Curriculum%20design%20is%20the%20planning,assessments%20that%20achieve%20educational%20goals.&text=These%20include%20subject-centered%20design,design%20and%20problem-centered%20design
2 https://www.thoughtco.com/curriculum-design-definition-4154176
3 Learning analytics – Wikipedia.

References

Adnan, M., & Anwar, K. (2020). Online learning amid the COVID-19 pandemic: Students' perspectives. *Journal of Pedagogical Sociology and Psychology*, 2(1), 45–51.

Al-Jarf, R. S. (2020a, September 24–25). *Building cultural bridges through social media networks: A case study* [Paper]. 9th International Conference Building Cultural Bridges (ICBCB), Almaty, Kazakhstan. https://files.eric.ed.gov/fulltext/ED611746.pdf

Al-Jarf, R. S. (2020b). Distance learning and undergraduate Saudi students' agency during the Covid-19 pandemic. *Bulletin of the Transylvania University of Braşov Series IV: Philology and Cultural Studies*, 13(62), 2, 37–54. https://doi.org/10.31926/but.pcs.2020.62.13.2.4

Al-Jarf, R. S. (2021a). EFL speaking practice in distance learning during the coronavirus pandemic 2020–2021. *International Journal of Research – GRANTHAALAYAH*, 9(7), 179–196. https://doi.org/10.29121/granthaalayah.v9.i7.2021.4094

Al-Jarf, R. S. (2021b). ESL teachers' professional development on Facebook during the Covid-19 pandemic. *European Journal of Education and Pedagogy (EJ-EDU)*, 2(6), 75–81. https://doi.org/10.24018/ejedu.2021.2.6.220

Al-Jarf, R. S. (2021c). How much material do EFL college instructors cover in reading courses? *Journal of Applied Linguistics and Language Research (JALLR)*, 8(1), 65–79. https://www.jallr.com/index.php/JALLR/article/view/1151/0

Al-Jarf, R. S. (2021d). Investigating equity in distance education in Saudi Arabia during the COVID-19 pandemic. In *Proceedings of the 17th international scientific conference on eLearning and software for education*, Bucharest, Romania (Vol. 1, pp. 13–21). https://proceedings.elseconference.eu/

Al-Jarf, R. S. (2022a). Blogging about current global events in the EFL writing classroom: Effects on skill improvement, global awareness and attitudes. *British Journal of Teacher Education and Pedagogy (BJTEP)*, 1(1), 73–82. https://doi.org/10.32996/bjtep.2022.1.1.8

Al-Jarf, R. S. (2022b). Blogging about the COVID-19 pandemic in EFL writing practice. *Journal of Learning and Development Studies (JLDS)*, 2(1), 1–8. https://doi.org/10.32996/jlds.2022.2.1.1

Al-Jarf, R. S. (2022c). Developing students' global awareness in EFL reading and speaking. *South Asian Research Journal of Arts, Language and Literature (SARJALL)*, 4(1). doi:10.36346/sarjall.2022.v04i01.00X

Al-Jarf, R. S. (2022d). How students were engaged during the second wave of COVID-19 by EFL, linguistics and translation instructors in distance learning. In A. K. Alghamdi (Ed.), *Teaching in the pandemic era in Saudi Arabia*. Brill

Al-Nofaie, H. (2020). Saudi university students' perceptions towards virtual education during COVID-19 pandemic: A case study of language learning via Blackboard. *Arab World English Journal*, 11(3), 4–20.

Berg, A., & Hawila, N. (2021). Some teaching resources using R with illustrative examples exploring COVID-19 data. *Teaching Statistics: An International Journal for Teachers, 43*(1), S98–S109.

Chaudhary, G. (2015). Factors affecting curriculum implementation for students. *International Journal of Applied Research, 1*(12), 984–986.

Chernosky, J., Ausburn, J., & Curtis, R. (2021). Students as consumers: Retaining engineering students by designing learner-centric courses of value. *Journal of Continuing Higher Education, 69*(2), 100–120.

Chugh, R., Ledger, S., & Shields, R. (2017). Curriculum design for distance education in the tertiary sector. *Turkish Online Journal of Distance Education-TOJDE, 18*(2), 4–15.

Chung, E., Subramaniam, G., & Dass, L. (2020). Online learning readiness among university students in Malaysia amidst COVID-19. *Asian Journal of University Education, 16*(2), 46–58.

Easdon, J. (2020). Adjusting a biochemistry course to cover SARS-CoV-2 topics. *Journal of Chemical Education, 97*(9), 2738–2741.

Guo, K. (2021). Australia's engagement with Asia in the national curriculum. *Frontiers of Education in China, 16*(1), 60–78.

Helmsing, M., & Noy, S. (2020). Teaching global health in the time of COVID-19: Key concepts for social studies classrooms. *Journal of International Social Studies, 10*(2), 103–112.

Howitz, W., Thane, T., Frey, T., Wang, X., Gonzales, J., Tretbar, C., Seith, D., Saluga, S., Lam, S., Nguyen, M., Tieu, P., Link, R., & Edwards, K. (2020). Online in no time: Design and implementation of a remote learning first quarter general chemistry laboratory and second quarter organic chemistry laboratory. *Journal of Chemical Education, 97*(9), 2624–2634.

Kentucky Department of Education. (2020). *COVID-19 considerations for reopening schools: Academic re-entry, stage one – drafting an adjusted curriculum.* https://education.ky.gov/comm/Documents/Reopening%20Guidance%20%20051520kf_tkt%20421pm%20TM.pdf

Levesque-Bristol, C. (2021). *Student-centered pedagogy and course transformation at scale: Facilitating faculty agency to IMPACT institutional change.* Stylus Publishing.

Mendy, J., & Madiope, M. (2020). Curriculum transformation: An ODeL case in South Africa. *Perspectives in Education, 38*(2), 1–19. https://doi.org/10.18820/2519593X/pie.v38.i2.01

Metscher, S., Tramantano, J., & Wong, K. (2021). Digital instructional practices to promote pedagogical knowledge during COVID-19. *Journal of Education for Teaching: International Research and Pedagogy, 47*(1), 121–124.

Nguyen, N., Everiss, L., Rosewarne, S., Vladinova-Aylor, K., Ippel, J., & Boyd, M. (2020). Environment: Stories from designing and developing the New Zealand certificate in early childhood education and care (level 4) programme. *Journal of Open, Flexible and Distance Learning, 24*(2), 56–70.

Noriko F. I. (2013). Designing a curriculum for a distance learning class: An example of a first-year Japanese course. *Theory and Practice in Language Studies, 3*(10), 1717–1725. http://www.academypublication.com/issues/past/tpls/vol03/10/01.pdf

Pulker, H., & Kukulska-Hulme, A. (2020). Openness re-examined: Teachers' practices with open educational resources in online language teaching. *Distance Education, 41*(2), 216–229.

Sarju, J. P. (2020). Rapid adaptation of a traditional introductory lecture course on catalysis into content for remote delivery online in response to global pandemic. *Journal of Chemical Education, 97*(9), 2590–2597.

Schweitzer, K. (2019). *Curriculum design: Definition, purpose and types.* https://www.thoughtco.com/curriculum-design-definition-4154176

Stahl, G. (2021). Redesigning mathematical curriculum for blended learning. *Education Sciences, 11,* art. 165, 1–12. https://doi.org/10.3390/educsci11040165

Streveler, R., & Smith, K. (2020). Opinion: Course design in the time of coronavirus: Put on your designer's CAP. *Advances in Engineering Education, 8*(4), 1–19.

Watkins, C., Treviranus, J., & Roberts, V. (2020). *Inclusive design for learning: Creating flexible and adaptable content with learners* (Knowledge series: A Topical Start-Up Guide to Distance Education Practice and Delivery). Commonwealth of Learning, ERIC Number ED610734.

CHAPTER 2

Reflections of a Saudi Female Practitioner

As a Mother, Instructor, Researcher, and Instructional Technology Specialist in Distance Learning during the COVID-19 Pandemic

Fawzia Omer Alubthane

Abstract

This chapter is an auto-ethnographic narrative provides an insight into my experience as a mother, instructor, researcher, and instructional technology specialist regarding distance education during the COVID-19 pandemic. I aim to shed light on my experience of performing those roles during the period of school suspension due to the pandemic. Reflecting on my experience in the first person and quoting several reflections and comments from others in the same field will describe the experiences of various people in the context being studied. These reflections and comments revealed different perspectives on distance education, including the positives and negatives, advantages and disadvantages, facilities, and difficulties. According to these results, I developed several implications for practice.

Keywords

COVID-19 – distance learning – reflections – instructional technology – instructor

1   Introduction

Have you heard of the butterfly effect? Approximately 45 years ago, Edward Lorenz posed the following question: "Does the flap of a butterfly's wings in Brazil set off a tornado in Texas?" "The purpose of his provocative question, he said, was to illustrate the idea that some complex dynamical systems exhibit unpredictable behaviors such that small variances in the initial conditions could have profound and widely divergent effects on the system's outcomes" (Vernon, 2017, p. 130).

The idea here is that constant changes are the law of the universe, and these changes can occur from small and unexpected events or sparks that have been underestimated. Moreover, rapid changes and shifts not only test human beings' ability to adapt but also their ability to modify, improve, and revise. The process of adjusting during the transitional phase requires deep reflection, purposeful thoughts, accurate studies, well-made plans, and informed decisions.

The COVID-19 pandemic has resulted in sudden transformations and unprecedented changes globally in all fields, such as education, society, economy, policy, and psychology. Many daily activities were disrupted and affected in these sectors, which required officials to adapt to the new developments and find solutions and alternatives to ensure the continuation of activities in these sectors in safe environments (Technology Center Foresight, 2020).

In the educational sector, schools have been suspended globally. On Sunday, March 8, 2020, the Ministry of Education in the Kingdom of Saudi Arabia announced the temporary suspension of face-to-face classes in schools in all governmental and private educational institutions in all regions and governorates of the Kingdom. The Minister of Education issued an order to activate virtual schools and distance education during the suspension period to ensure the effective continuation of the educational process. As a result of this unprecedented transformation, many changes occurred that directly and indirectly affected the society of Saudi Arabia educationally, economically, socially, and psychologically. To investigate these impacts, various studies have been conducted.

In this article, I use an auto-ethnographic narrative to present a self-reflective case study of my experience regarding social and educational interactions during the schools' suspension period due to the COVID-19 crisis. This is intended to provide the readers with insights into an individual's experience as a mother, university instructor, researcher, and instructional technology and e-learning specialist regarding distance learning.

2   Methodology

As indicated above, I will use an auto-ethnographic narrative to present a self-reflective case study of my experience of distance learning during the COVID-19 crisis. "Autoethnography is an approach to research and writing that seeks to describe and systematically analyze personal experience in order to understand cultural experience. This approach challenges canonical ways of doing research" (Ellis et al., 2011, p. 273). Mortari (2015) suggested that reflection is a significant mental activity that "allows people to engage into a thoughtful relationship with the world-life and thus gain an awake stance about one's lived experience. Reflection is a crucial cognitive practice in the research field" (Mortari, 2015, p. 1).

"As a method, autoethnography combines characteristics of autobiography and ethnography. When writing an autobiography, an author retroactively and selectively writes about past experiences" (Ellis et al., 2011, p. 275). Delany (2004), Didion (2005), Goodall (2006), and Herrmann (2005) noted that when the author writes an autoethnography, he or she might also interview others and review texts, such as photographs, journals, and recordings, to assist with recall.

I will reflect on my experience from multiple angles and provide insights into my role as a mother, instructor, researcher, and e-learning specialist. Each of these roles tells stories and experiences that are not only personal but also include the human and social interactions that were experienced by both me and the surrounding individuals who lived in the same situation, played the same role, and had similar experiences. These interactions include interviews, observations, and discussions that took place between those individuals and me.

3   Context

I live in Riyadh, the capital city of the Kingdom of Saudi Arabia. I am married and have three boys between the ages of 11 and 18. One is in primary school, and two are high school students. They attend international private schools in Riyadh. My family is a conservative Saudi Muslim family. Most families in our society are characterized by strong social cohesion and stable and interconnected families, as social communication (the connection of the kinship) represents important Islamic and social values. Economically, my family belongs to the middle class, according to the economic levels and standards in the Saudi society.

I am an assistant professor. My major is educational technologies, which is a specialization that deals with multiple educational aspects, including instructional design and technologies, educational theories, distance learning, e-learning, and communication skills in the educational process. Currently, I work in the kindergarten (early childhood education) department, where I teach courses that are centered on educational technology, research, and educational computers for female students at the College of Science and Human Studies in Huraymila, which is 75 km from Riyadh. The journey to the college from home takes approximately an hour.

The area where the college students live varies. The female students are spread out across Riyadh, Huraymila, and other cities and villages around

Huraymila. Many students use private buses to travel to the college. The social and economic status of the students is diverse, as some of them are married and have children.

Distance learning and e-learning represent a new and unusual experience for the College of Science and Human Studies in Huraymila. Before the pandemic, the college's class delivery was solely based on face-to-face lessons, so it did not offer any online courses. The use of technology in teaching and learning in the college is limited to electronic presentations in the classroom and communication via email and various forms of social media. In addition, there were several attempts and commitments made by some departments to use educational platforms and websites, such as Acadox, Edmodo, Google Drive, and miscellaneous mobile apps. Before the COVID-19 crisis, the electronic platform of the university, to which the college is affiliated, was being developed. However, progress regarding the development of the platform advanced significantly and quickly after the crisis and suspension of the college.

4 Reflecting on My Experience during the School Closure Period

4.1 *As a Mother*

For mothers, schools represent a place that helps them with their children. For housewives, schools may provide them with time to catch up on chores or get some rest. For female employees, schools provide them with a safe environment for their children to learn during working hours. Before the school closure due to the pandemic, the role of the parents was limited to helping the children with school homework, reminding them to study, and explaining some lessons.

Because of the school closure, the adoption of distance learning, and the aftermath of the pandemic, the role of parents has become bigger. Students are learning and attending their classes online at home. Most mothers have become responsible for watching their children during class time; helping them with homework and learning activities; and watching them during online tests. One of the working mothers told me that she had to take time off from work so that she could stay with and support her children during their distance learning lessons. For some families, the situation was less burdensome, as they had either housemaids or the father and mother who shared the responsibility, especially when they had several children in primary schools.

The financial burden causes another difficulty for some families, as there are not enough devices available for all the children in the family. One mother told me that she and her husband gave their mobile devices to their children to attend their school's virtual classes because they were unable to provide one for each child. Nevertheless, social cohesion in our societies is a wonderful asset, as some families, schools, institutions, and charities cooperated in providing equipment for families in need. Furthermore, there were several initiatives that contributed to alleviating the suffering of many families, which demonstrated the cooperation and social cohesion in our community.

As a mother of three students, I had no issues with my older sons because as they are both in high school, they are more independent. Although there was a need for follow-ups, monitoring, and reminders, it was a bearable burden. It was more difficult with the younger child, who is in the fifth grade of a primary school. For a child with Asperger's syndrome, which is one of the disorders on the autism spectrum, attending school is an opportunity for him to interact with others and acquire the necessary social skills. This quiet child does not like school very much. Although distance learning was comfortable for him, it was not so for me because he constantly needs to be reminded about virtual lessons, assignments, and exams. His interaction with the teacher and peers during the virtual classes was limited.

One of my students is married and has a daughter with Down syndrome. She told me the following:

> I cannot tell you that distance learning has many positives for her. I do not think that it is a positive environment for kids with Down syndrome because they like to engage with others, they like to socialize, they learn from others, and they imitate other children. The negative aspect is that she became less involved with other children and this is not good for her. Also, there is an important point: in the first term, the school placed kids with special needs in individual classes without mixing with normal children. This matter was negative, but, thank God, it was modified in the second term and she took virtual classes with normal children, so her achievement and performance improved.

Another college student has a daughter who suffers from visual problems and needs to learn Braille. The mother told me that although the teachers helped her, she was very tired because the little girl did not know anything, and she needed a lot of patience and effort to learn Braille, especially since they live in a small city.

Distance learning during the COVID-19 pandemic, however, has many advantages, especially for mothers. I found distance learning less stressful than traditional education, which involves waking up early, preparing for school, catching the bus, and being held up in traffic. One mother, who is also a student, told me the following:

> Distance learning saves us from taking the buses and making journeys. We feel more comfortable with this current situation. To us, it is a relief from worries keeping asking – Why are they late? Why haven't they come home yet?

One positive of distance education is about children's health. Children sometimes catch infectious diseases from their schoolmates. During the school closure, I felt more comfortable that my children were safe from infectious diseases. As indicated by one mother:

> Now, even the spread of infectious diseases has slowed down… I mean, in traditional face-to-face education, infectious diseases spread among students, especially in primary schools.

Another positive is about bullying, which is one of the main reasons that some parents choose homeschooling in many societies. Many mothers are worried that their children will be bullied. Although my older children have not been bullied a lot, I was particularly worried that my little boy with Asperger's Syndrome would be bullied at school. His teachers had to give me constant reassurance. When the school was closed during the lockdown, I felt more relieved since no physical class attendance was needed. Another student of mine is also a mother, and she told me that her son, who has special needs, was constantly bullied at school and that it sometimes led to physical bullying. Because of distance learning, she felt relieved since his son's situation had become much better than before.

Although there is a risk of cyberbullying during virtual classes, both the teacher and the mother who stays online with her son during the virtual class can protect the child from this type of bullying and defend him/her. In such situation, the mothers would say to themselves, "my kids are near me now, I watch them, and I will protect them." This is how I felt, and it was comforting.

Another positive aspect is that mothers can encourage their children to participate and interact with their teacher and classmates. While observing my son during the virtual lessons, I noticed that when I encouraged him to participate, he would be more willing to engage with the lesson. However, this requires a lot of patience, especially with children who are not interested in participating.

In addition, it is a good opportunity for parents to observe how teachers treat their children, how much they care about them and interact with them, and whether they encourage them to participate. I appreciated the teachers who supported and encouraged the children. One mother who has a child with special needs found that distance learning allowed parents to help their children, especially if they have special needs, to supervise their learning, and to observe how teachers treat them. She indicated that distance learning provides an opportunity for her to see how the teacher deals with her son, supports him, and motivates him to participate.

On the other hand, it is not convenient for teachers to be watched by parents the whole time. One teacher told me that some parents strictly monitor the teacher and sometimes interfere during the virtual class, which disrupts the lesson. One educational supervisor stated the following:

> Some parents say no one talks to my son... no one talks to my daughter... Also, one of the mothers was watching the teacher, then she said to the teacher that 'you made my daughter read this passage and not the others.... You hold my daughter accountable and correct her mistakes, but you did not do that to others!

During the COVID-19 crisis, distance education became a mixture of formal and informal education, as schools and universities switched to 'home-based' mode, the mother could supervise the learning of her children, attend lessons, and listen to the teachers' presentations of the lessons. Additionally, parents could attend lectures on topics in which they are interested. I was excited to review math lessons with my son in his virtual classes. One of my relatives told me that she reviewed all the courses and lessons of the fourth grade of primary school with her young son since she attended these lessons virtually with him and help him with his homework. One of my university students told me that her mother is keen to attend some virtual lectures with them to benefit from those lessons. This means that lessons are now available to mothers as well.

Spending more time with my sons is one of the advantages of distance learning. In traditional education, I usually come back from work exhausted, and then I start doing my housework as a mother and duties as an instructor. My sons return from school and become busy with their homework. By the time we have finished, it is bedtime. The next day, my sons go to school, while I go to work. By contrast, distance learning gives me the opportunity to spend more time with them. With face-to-face learning, mothers, who are teachers or mothers, need to either find someone to take care of their children and take them to the nursery, or leave them with a housemaid or relative. One of my students told me that she used to look for someone to take care of her child while she attended face-to-face lectures. However, due to the virtual classes, she can now attend her lectures and take care of her young child. Another student told me that she sometimes breastfeeds her baby during the lectures, especially since we often do not turn on the camera.

In general, mothers' experiences with distance learning may be unique. Mothers are accustomed to traditional education that shapes their life in a certain pattern, system, arrangement, and daily schedule. The changes caused by the pandemic were sudden and swift and represented a quantum leap that overturned the normal school day in our society. We adapted to these new situations, discovered some of the advantages, and faced several challenges. We shared opinions, experiences, advice, and reflections on these unusual situations, which became the focus of our conversation and the heart of our interests and concerns as both members of society and mothers. In all cases, in crises and sudden changes, mothers continue to convey their own experiences that no one can emulate, especially when it comes to their sons and daughters.

4.2 *As an Instructor*

My experience as a university professor may be different from that of a teacher in a public school (K-12). However, there are several general commonalities between teachers. Distance learning in virtual classrooms represents an unusual experience for many teachers, even university professors. Distance learning is a completely different environment with new details, designs, and strategies, and the rapid transition from a traditional environment to this new environment may have created a kind of imbalance, especially in the beginning. As an e-learning specialist, the idea, concept, and experience of virtual classrooms and distance e-learning are not entirely new to me. The process of teaching and learning in these environments requires additional skills to help teachers to deal with the elements and circumstances of these new educational environments properly and carefully.

Some people may point out that as university students are more responsible and interested in learning during virtual lectures, dealing with them may be easier than K-12 students. Moreover, many parents play a key role in helping teachers by supervising their children in K-12 schools during the virtual lessons. This may facilitate the task of teachers and make it easier for them to encourage student interaction and participation. In higher education, the students should take responsibility for their learning, and many university students shoulder this responsibility well. Nevertheless, there are several university students, who require follow-ups, encouragement, and effort from the professors to arouse their interest, encourage their interaction, and hold their attention.

It was not easy for me to encourage my students to interact and engage during the lessons, especially with so many distractions around them, such as social media. To be honest, sometimes I am not sure whether all my students are paying attention. I used to ask them questions constantly and encourage them to participate; however, now, I am unsure whether all of them stay focused, especially when I stop asking questions or explain a certain point without any interruptions.

In one of the virtual lectures, I called on one of my students to ask her a question. The student did not reply, although I repeated my attempts. Her name was on the screen, which indicated that she was online and was attending the lesson. Although I asked her again to turn on the microphone and answer the question, she did not reply. At the end of the virtual class, I told my students that they could leave, except for those who had a question. All the students left except that student. I thought that she had a question or wanted to apologize or explain her behavior. I asked her to respond but she did not answer. I had to leave and end the class. The following day, she apologized for her behavior and explained that she was in fact asleep. Therefore, she was considered absent from that lesson.

Some may think that a simple solution, such as turning on the camera, may be sufficient to monitor the students and keep them attentive. However, this solution is not appropriate in our society and does not suit us as women. Turning on the camera means that the female students must be wearing *hijab* (i.e., a head covering and loose-fitting clothes worn by some Muslim women) all the time, which may be inconvenient for them. Moreover, our society is characterized as a conservative society that values privacy, which is an important principle. Many female students and teachers do not want their homes, families, and personal lives to be exposed to others, even if they are classmates or teachers. I fully understand this because it represents my feelings, thoughts, values, and principles as well.

Physical presence is a necessity that is deeply rooted in our culture. It is a key value in our religious, social, and educational lives. Attending the mosque daily and weekly to pray is a religious duty. In our communities, physical presence holds great importance since it plays an effective role in social interaction. In social events, such as visits, parties, celebrations, and funerals, physical presence is highly appreciated. In education, physical presence is a significant educational value. Therefore, traditional face-to-face classes are popular in Saudi education.

In face-to-face classes, the teacher can use body language that effectively influences communication and the achievement of goals. Virtual classes lack this feature, especially when the camera is turned off. As a teacher, I missed the use of body language in distance learning. Some of my students told me that they were missing it as well, as body language enriches educational presentations and facilitates communication. Moreover, some students told me that they missed the communication, social presence, and direct interaction in traditional education. One of my students pointed out the following:

> For me... I mean, I do not like distance education... I like to go... walk... see my classmates and friends at the university... I like to have people around me... so that I can ask for help whenever I do not understand something, so that I do not need to focus too much... I like to learn from someone who is there with me. I feel that distance education does not make these things possible... I feel that distance learning is boring... we cannot physically be there or interact with our peers like regular classes.

The school atmosphere and university environment are full of life, such as morning sunshine, the smell of coffee, the laughter of students in the corridors, peers' gatherings, morning greetings, and the noise of teaching in the halls. Those are the magnificent moments that I missed in distance learning. Those beautiful memories that breathe life into rigid college buildings, halls, and corridors are unforgettable.

In our universities, men and women are often separated, so we do not need to wear hijab at the university. Therefore, the scent of morning perfumes, the simple touches of make-up on the faces of the female students and teachers, and their morning elegance are among the most wonderful scenes that provide the college with the colors of beauty mixed with the seriousness of academic pursuit. I really missed all those moments.

In contrast, some teachers found that distance learning and teaching has many advantages. For example, it is more comfortable and convenient, especially for married female teachers. It saved them time and effort and provided them with the opportunity to develop and improve their skills while taking care of their home and children. One teacher stated the following:

> First of all, distance education from my point of view is so wonderful. It saves me time and effort. I have time... I can do research, enroll in courses, and expand my knowledge... It is more comfortable... There is no huge effort in distance education unlike traditional one in terms of morning shifts, classes, activities, and extra classes... At work, I feel that it consumes my energy and expends my effort, and when I come home, I feel drained. I feel tired all day long. I feel that I am negligent in performing my household chores, especially as I go back and complete my school duties, such as preparing new lessons and marking exams. The day is full of work. As for distance education, I am able to reconcile between my life and work,

and I was psychologically comfortable. Even if I am tired, I can teach the lesson and then get some rest, while in traditional education, when I am tired or sick, I will be absent, and the lesson will be canceled.

As a married teacher and a mother with a home and children to take care of, I somewhat agree with this teacher's opinion.

4.3 As a Researcher

The COVID-19 pandemic is a phenomenon that has attracted the attention of researchers in various fields, including fields of economy, sociology, education, religious studies, politics and psychology. This phenomenon opened the door for researchers in those fields to study such new phenomenon and investigate the repercussions of its effects on the present and future. Researchers may have benefited and profited from the crisis, as there are many topics that are related to COVID-19 and its effects have emerged that deserve to be discussed and studied.

The educational field is an important one that has been significantly affected by the COVID-19 pandemic. The rapid spread of the coronavirus infection necessitated the closure of schools and the implementation of the distance learning system through the internet, electronic tools, media, and online platforms. Distance learning is not a modern concept, as it was founded in the last century. However, its application was limited, especially in public education (K-12 schools).

Traditional face-to-face education is the most common and approved system in the educational field in Saudi Arabia in particular, as it has gained people's confidence and been adopted for many years. However, distance learning represented a huge shift in educational practices and imposed unusual methods and strategies in the educational system. These transformations produced new research topics in the educational field, which were addressed by researchers using various research methods.

As a result, a large amount of educational research has been conducted from multiple angles to address distance learning, teaching, and e-learning during the COVID-19 pandemic. Specialized scientific journals have released special issues for research and studies that focus on education in the lockdown period during the COVID-19 pandemic. As a researcher, I have conducted research, and I am currently working on additional research alongside this article.

As a researcher, I undertook studies during the COVID-19 crisis that had taken a broader and more comprehensive approach in terms of topics, environments, sample categories, and data sources. I turned to public school, where I addressed some of the issues associated with e-learning in K-12 schools, such as the *Madrasati* platform, which is used in public schools in Saudi Arabia for distance learning. Additionally, I am interested in studying the pros and cons of distance learning and education and its impact on various groups in our society. Moreover, my research samples are no longer limited to faculty members or university students; they have become more extensive and they include teachers in public education, parents, and employees.

The data sources have become more diverse. They are no longer limited to questionnaires or interviews, as they now include multiple resources, such as social media, jokes and anecdotes related to distance learning, observations, and the news. Everything around me could become a resource of data, such as people, situations, visits, discussions, and moments of entertainment and simple conversations that surround us. I now deal with many situations and events as a researcher, and even the minor ones will no longer go unnoticed. I have improved my skills as a researcher, become more profound, and acquired the sense of a curious researcher.

4.4 *As an Instructional Technology Specialist*

Many people think that distance learning in educational institutions during the COVID-19 crisis is limited to e-learning or online learning courses. However, this is not true. Since I am specialized in instructional technology, where e-learning environments and online learning courses serve as an important focus, I thought that this was the right time for e-learning specialists to take the lead and clarify the designs and strategies of e-learning, which is completely different from traditional mode of learning. Unfortunately, there was confusion regarding emergency distance education, which resulted from the school closure due to the pandemic and the e-learning environment, structure, elements, methods, and designs.

E-learning and online courses depend on accurate educational planning and design using a systematic model on which decisions are built. Additionally, e-learning depends on an integrated environment of interconnected factors and elements that affect the quality of e-learning class structures. In this regard, Hodges et al. (2020) referred to the distance learning applied in the COVID-19 era as "emergency remote teaching" (Hodges et al., 2020, p. 3). The authors noted, "well-planned online learning experiences are meaningfully different from courses offered online in response to a crisis or disaster. Colleges and universities working to maintain instruction during the COVID-19 pandemic should understand those differences when evaluating this emergency remote teaching" (Hodges et al., 2020, p. 1).

The transition from face-to-face education to distance learning using the internet and electronic devices was rapid, as it was a necessary and fast solution for the school closure problem. As a result, traditional education, with all its tools, methods, and strategies, was transferred to an e-learning environment, which is fundamentally different from the traditional teaching and learning environment. Furthermore, many teachers and faculty members lack the skills that are required to design and develop high-quality online courses. In addition, developing and producing high-quality online courses according to reliable and adopted quality standards require time and effort.

Many training courses were held to develop the technological skills of teachers and faculty members to help them to lead online classes. Computer application specialists, educational presentation trainers, and technologists competed to provide various training courses via interactive video applications, such as YouTube videos and social media. I believe that these courses contributed to the development of teachers' technological skills. However, the following questions remain: What about design skills? What about the educational skills that are required for an online learning environment? What are the best educational strategies for online courses? How do you design electronic courses correctly?

Although some training courses were conducted on these aspects, in my opinion, they were not enough. Personally, I think that teachers and faculty members need a complete qualification program rather than limited training courses. Additionally, these integrated qualification programs should be conducted by educationalists who are specialized in e-learning and designing online courses.

4.5   As an e-Learning Specialist

As an e-learning specialist, I feel uncomfortable when people around me think that the educational processes that took place in emergency distance teaching during the COVID-19 crisis represent e-learning courses and refer to them as e-learning. What bothers me most is that people judge the success and quality of e-learning courses based on the practices and results of emergency distance teaching. One of my colleagues, who is specialized in instructional technology, expressed the following opinion on this issue:

> Distance education in our societies is not desirable… and people do not have enough confidence in it… also because distance education over the pandemic was not, in fact, a true integrated model of e-learning, distance learning during this crisis did not sufficiently strengthen people's confidence in e-learning.

The distinction between e-learning and emergency distance teaching during the COVID-19 crisis does not mean that emergency distance teaching is ineffective. On the contrary, it was enough to fill the gap where great efforts were made to contain the situation. Distinctive and interactive electronic platforms were developed to help students to learn and teachers to teach, such as the *Madrasati* platform. In private schools and universities, the appropriate educational electronic platforms were used. Although emergency distance education was able to succeed regardless of the circumstances and obstacles, its environment and design differs from the design and environment of true e-learning and online classes.

5 Results and Discussion

The COVID-19 pandemic has greatly affected various aspects of societies globally. This influence was not limited to a specific group or levels, and it has had various positive results and negative repercussions. In the disrupted educational environment and with the closure of schools, a new educational system that might not have been popular before has emerged and it was proposed as the best solutions under those circumstances. Although distance education was not a desirable option in many societies, especially for the early educational stages and K-12 schools, it has become a new reality and a feasible solution.

Many parents, teachers, researchers, and experts believe that this new, unique, and unusual experience has had an unforgettable impact on different communities. It has shown both positives and negatives, and opened the door for experts, stakeholders, and specialists to revise the plans, processes, and methods that have been taken for granted for a long time. Before the pandemic, it was difficult to change some educational practices, despite all the attempts, experiments, and suggestions that were made by numerous studies.

The circumstances of school closures during the pandemic have given researchers the opportunity to discuss and study many diverse issues related to the education process during this crisis. Additionally, it allowed them to present new suggestions and plans to improve, modify, and revise some of the traditional procedures in the educational system.

Despite the pressure that parents suffered to follow up with and monitor their children's learning in distance learning, they felt that this type of education could keep their children safe and help them to avoid physical bullying or contracting disease. Moreover, distance learning allowed parents to spend more time with their children and encouraged them to participate during online classes.

Teachers found themselves in a new environment that requires different technological and teaching skills. Stimulating students' interactions and encouraging them to participate requires greater effort and a higher level of skills. Teachers have adapted to this new situation, enrolled in a variety of training courses, and developed their technological skills. Nevertheless, they still require training courses to promote the necessary skills to design and develop effective distance e-learning courses. Although distance education may help teachers to save time and effort and spare them from some routine tasks related to shifts and traditional school activities, they have become subject to constant monitoring by parents and educational supervisors.

Although remote emergency education helped to overcome the obstacles and difficulties of sudden school closure, its structure and design are different from e-learning environments. This is an important point that has been pointed out by researchers and specialists in the fields of instructional technology and e-learning, who should have a more prominent position and role in the design, guidance, and training regarding online courses.

6   Implications for Practice

6.1   *Blended Online Learning*

The experience of distance learning during the crisis shows that this educational system can be successful if it is properly designed. Such experience also revealed the problems that should be addressed to improve distance learning courses. This type of education has a lot of potential that should be taken into consideration.

Based on that, I believe that blended online courses that combine distance online learning with traditional face-to-face education could be a reliable educational method. Through blended online learning, it is possible to bridge the gaps and address the negatives of the two systems. Additionally, it can strengthen and enhance the advantages and positives that each system includes.

In blended online courses, 30–80% of the course content is delivered online (Allen & Seaman, 2015). This percentage can vary according to the school stage. I would suggest that 10–20% of the course content could be delivered online in primary education and 20–30% in middle and high schools. In higher education, this could increase to 40–50%.

6.2   *Promote Cooperation and Communication between the Home and School*

During distance learning, school activities and educational practices took place in the home, and parents actively participated in the teaching process. This experience has shown that cooperation and communication between parents and schools is no longer limited. Instead, their communication is continuous and it has become stronger, and more effective.

6.3 *Emergency Remote Teaching*

Hodges et al. (2020) suggested that teaching and learning practices should not simply return to how they were before COVID-19, as we should not forget what we learned during the period of school closure and the experience of emergency remote teaching. Additionally, emergency remote teaching should be included in the professional development programming for any personnel involved in the instructional mission of colleges and universities.

I agree with Hodges et al. (2020) in this regard. Experience has shown that emergency remote teaching, when implemented during a crisis, can be properly designed according to the elements, conditions, strategies, standards, and tools and applied appropriately when schools are closed during crises and disasters. Emergency remote teaching is expected to be one of the teachers' and faculty members' skills.

6.4 *Conduct More In-Depth Research on the Effects of the Pandemic*

Many studies were conducted to address the effects of the COVID-19 pandemic in various fields. However, our society in Saudi Arabia requires more in-depth research. I would suggest conducting more qualitative research that is directed toward different and diverse groups in the community, such as children, parents, administrative staff, and even bus drivers, who provide transport to pupils and students.

Applying multiple methods and instruments for data collection, such as observations; analyzing comments, jokes, tweets, and posts in social media; and conducting interviews with different samples, could provide more diverse and in-depth data. Analyzing this qualitative data would produce comprehensive perspectives from the cultural, social, and psychological aspects, and educational influences generated because of the crisis. Moreover, I would suggest writing reflections and articles about the future expectations and changes caused by this pandemic and how they can be used to reconsider many of the traditional methods and approaches that are applied in various fields.

6.5 *Hiring Educational Specialists to Design Effective Online Courses*

To design effective educational environments for online learning, blended learning, and remote emergency teaching, qualified educational experts, who are specialized in instructional technologies, curricula, and teaching methods, and content experts should lead the mission. Focusing on technological tools, software, and applications would not be sufficient to design and produce effective and high-quality online courses that contribute to achieving educational goals.

References

Allen, I. E., & Seaman, J. (2015). *Grade level: Tracking online education in the United States.* https://files.eric.ed.gov/fulltext/ED572778.pdf

Delany, S. R. (2004). *The motion of light in water.* University of Minnesota Press.

Didion, J. (2005). *The year of magical thinking.* A.A. Knopf.

Ellis, C., Adams, T. E., & Bochner, A. P. (2011). Autoethnography: An overview. *Historical Social Research/Historische Sozialforschung,* 273–290. https://doi.org/10.12759/hsr.36.2011.4.273-290

Goodall, B. H. L. (2001). *Writing the new ethnography.* AltaMira.

Herrmann, A. F. (2005). My father's ghost: Interrogating family photos. *Journal of Loss and Trauma, 10*(4), 337–346.

Hodges, C., Moore, S., Lockee, B., Trust, A., & Bond, A. (2020). *The difference between emergency remote teaching and online learning.* https://er.educause.edu/articles/2020/3/the-difference-between-emergency-remote-teaching-and-online-learning

Mortari, L. (2015). Reflectivity in research practice: An overview of different perspectives. *International Journal of Qualitative Methods, 14*(5). https://doi.org/10.1177/1609406915618045

Technology Center Foresight. (2020). *Post-COVID-19-new reality: The unprecedented transformation digital.* Ministry of Technology Information and Communications, Saudi Arabia. https://www.mcit.gov.sa/sites/default/files/pandemic_final.pdf

Vernon, J. L. (2017). Understanding the butterfly effect. *American Scientist, 105*(3), 130. https://www.americanscientist.org/article/understanding-the-butterfly-effect

CHAPTER 3

Post-COVID e-Learning in Bahrain

Where Are We in Meeting the Educational Reform Objective of Sustainable Development?

Nina Abdul Razzak

Abstract

This chapter reports on a research study that investigated the question, "How has progress toward sustainable development in the Kingdom of Bahrain been impacted by the COVID-19 transition to e-learning?" The study was qualitative in nature in the form of a small-scale inquiry of a specific case, where aspects of e-learning in higher education institutions in the post-COVID Bahrain were analyzed. An Education for Sustainable Development (ESD) model was used to frame the analysis. The results of the study indicated that progress toward the achievement of the sustainable development objective in Bahrain has been slightly expedited by the transition to e-learning. There were several persistent barriers, which were in need of addressing. Such examples include the absence of an overarching e-learning strategy aligned with the requirements for achieving sustainable development, and the lack of capacity-building opportunities targeting e-course instructional design that incorporates ESD components. Such instructional design includes higher-order thinking skills (HOTS) integration, interdisciplinary critical reflections, and knowledge transfer.

Keywords

e-learning – post-COVID – sustainable development – educational reform – higher-order thinking skills – ESD

1   Introduction

The author's work (in the form of a dissertation) completed in partial fulfillment of the requirements for her recent academic pursuit of a Ph.D. by Prior Publication in the field of education (Abdul Razzak, 2020) inspired this chapter. In that work, she focused on the educational reform in the Kingdom of Bahrain, covering themes related to various aspects. They include opportunities and limitations of research in Bahrain; challenges to educational improvement efforts and reform initiatives; predominant teaching and learning (T&L) methods in the educational institutions of the Kingdom; and pedagogies related to student-driven learning and deep learning that may mitigate existing challenges to reform. Many of the ideas included in that work, thus, are reflected in this chapter because of their relevance to the main aim and scope of the research study. In particular, information that accounts for the contextual background, literature review, and conceptual framework of this study relies considerably on research conducted for the previous work, where the contextual background is mainly one of various educational reforms in the Gulf Cooperative Council (GCC) region, including the Kingdom of Bahrain.

Over the last two decades, many of the GCC countries have undergone major national educational reforms. Such reforms generally take into account, in their attempts to transform public education, the changing needs of these countries' economies and societies; they also tend to emphasize science education and the integration of information communication technology (ICT) in instruction (Wiseman & Anderson, 2012). As reflected in the main concepts and key initiatives of the national visions of the GCC countries, the changes targeted by the GCC educational reforms are expected to have significant returns for the status of individuals socially, professionally, and economically or financially, as well as for their general well-being (Bahrain Economic Development Board [BEDB], 2009; Oman Vision 2040, 2019; Vision 2030 Kingdom of Saudi Arabia, 2019).

These reforms originated as a response to the pivotal aim of the GCC countries' governments and regulatory bodies to develop educational systems of high quality that can support national economies while improving them and enabling them to compete globally. This is in addition to the expectation from such educational systems to enhance durable (Filho, 2000) or systematic and long-term sustainable development in these countries, by accompanying strong relationships between societal and environmental security with economic progress (Montebon, 2018). As the 1993 Agenda 21 of the United Nations emphasized, sustainable development depends on "our ability to balance economic, social, and environmental concerns" (Mossman, 2018, p. 38), with education playing a key role in this process (UNESCO, 2010). The question here is, "What type of education provided by educational systems can foster students capable of balancing economic, social, and environmental concerns, thus leading to sustainable development?" Some questions that are more relevant to the GCC region in general and to the Kingdom of Bahrain in particular – and that will be tackled later on in this chapter – are, "Where are we in meeting the educational reform objective of sustainable development? And how has progress toward sustainable development been affected by the COVID-19 transition to e-learning?"

In response to the first question, researchers (Bates, 2010; Castells, 2000) argue that the type of education that can lead to sustainable development is one that prepares students for dealing with the global predominance of ICTs, which have contributed to the formation of new social structures and a global economy. "Social structures" here refer to the human relations arrangements that coordinate social ties, production or consumption relationships, experiences, and power. Additionally, the "global economy" refers to the network of financial transactions and production sites, markets, and labor groups driven by businesses, money, and information across the world (Castells, 2000). These new social structures underlying society are electronically/network based and have resulted in a global economy based on knowledge. In this economy, knowledge is a key determinant in the competitiveness, growth, and prosperity of nations. The networks contributing to such an economy are beneficial for many reasons, such as providing flexibility, adaptability, and speed in executing and managing tasks, away from controlled and hierarchical forms of organization, in a rapidly changing world. More important, in this context, their value lies in their potential to bring together many minds that work collaboratively to develop radically new products or services that could possibly solve complex social, environmental, or scientific problems (Iacobucci & Hoeffler, 2016; Khatib et al., 2011; Jonsson, 2010).

Information in its diversity and immensity, as the world is witnessing in the current information age or knowledge society, can sometimes be overwhelming and misleading. As Kirtiklis (2017) explained, this is not just because much more information is available now but also because information in its generation, processing, and transmission has become the fundamental source of productivity and power thanks to modern technological developments. This implies that, if sustainable development is to be achieved, education should empower people to make the utmost use of this valuable technologically conceived resource in innovative and creative ways – and not solely for economic purposes. However, the ability to absorb and apply knowledge in productive ways requires extensive and interactive learning processes, experience, and skill development and acquisition, especially higher-order thinking skills (HOTS), as well as strong networking among researchers, commercial organizations, and other institutions (Bramwell & Wolfe, 2008). For this reason, it has become a fundamental necessity in this age for individuals to develop what

Barnett (2004) called human dispositions, which can hone their critical evaluation skills and selection of information sources and empower them to integrate and manipulate large and diverse amounts of information, to generate more innovative forms of data and products. This carries implications for the types of educational experiences that individuals must go through to be able to develop such human dispositions. Scholars such as Castells (2014) and Romer (2007) have included herein experiences that provide students with ample opportunities for assessing and judging information sources before utilizing them; for critically synthesizing and manipulating data to produce new and innovative ideas, including producing new ICTs that are crucial for evolving into knowledge-based economies; for actively learning in ways that promote independent self-driven learning; and for employing innovative aptitudes to better respond to the challenges and prospects the latest developments in technology have brought about.

This helps explain why, in GCC countries' reforms, curriculum and pedagogical transformation focusing on developing students' critical thinking, communication, problem-solving, digital literacy, creativity, and innovation, is a government priority (Baporikar & Shah, 2012; BEDB, 2009). It also highlights the significance of such competencies for learning, professional excellence, and success in today's networked society and global economy in general. The main issue, nonetheless, is identifying the educational paradigm that could be a good fit, if not the best one, for promoting critical competencies (better known as 21st-century skills) that are essential for achieving success in today's world and for facing unpredictable challenges in the future. The constructivist student-centered paradigm of T&L has been dominating the educational scene for some time now in comparison to teacher-centered models that rely heavily on lecturing and teacher-led demonstrations (Bell, 2010; Goldman, 2017). However, many scholars have recently found that the predominance of student-centeredness is not sufficient for producing generations of graduates with 21st-century skills who can adeptly balance economic, social, and environmental concerns and challenges while sustaining development in their countries given the rapid speed at which the world is moving today. Rather, scholars are leaning toward a more targeted T&L paradigm that aims specifically at sustainable development, better known as "Education for Sustainable Development" or ESD. What exactly ESD entails is the next point of focus in this chapter, which delineates the conceptual framework of the research study and provides the lens and road map for tackling the main research components. The conceptual framework will be followed by the study's research problem, methodology, main findings and discussion, concluding remarks, and recommendations.

2   Conceptual Framework

Digital technologies are vital to contemporary societies, and with the global trend moving toward greater interconnectedness, it is essential that today's students be educationally prepared to embrace the technologies of the future and benefit from their positive rather than their negative aspects. This again means that students must acquire and develop the tools (e.g., technical, social, cognitive, ethical) needed to enhance sustainable development. These tools allow technology to advance while enriching the economy as well as other vital life aspects, such as family ties, friendships, and positive cultural coexistence. Technology should not be allowed to progress at the expense of these aspects and of other important life dimensions, such as individual and environmental health. Hence, there is a need for the focus on educational reform initiatives in the GCC and elsewhere to be channeled specifically in this direction.

To develop the tools referred to above, students must receive ESD, which UNESCO (2018) defined as education that "empowers learners to take informed decisions and responsible actions for environmental integrity, economic viability and a just society, for present and future generations, while respecting cultural diversity." Scholars (Bursztyn & Drummond, 2014; Hughes, 2018) view ESD as one of the results of the major paradigm shift of the 21st century. This shift is due to rapid changes in almost every life aspect. These changes are diverse in nature (i.e., social, economic, demographic, technological, political, and environmental) and add to the complexity of the world, not because of the changes themselves but because of their character and intensity and the scope of their impact (Barnett, 2004). Given the world's greater connectedness, one challenge or problem in one part of the globe can now more easily affect the other parts because of the greater ease in transportation, communication, and dissemination of information. This ease is due to rapid and massive technological advances and networks (Castells, 2014). The spread of the coronavirus globally and the various responses to it are a clear demonstration of this fact.

In sum, ESD involves judicious decision-making and purposeful problem-solving in the face of 21st-century changes and challenges, which because of their rapid nature leave us uncertain of whether knowledge and skills that previously worked will continue to do so for meaningful engagement in the future (Barnett, 2004). ESD does not just target the development of existing knowledge and skills because these cannot take us very far. Rather, ESD aims at the development of a certain type of being (self, trait, or disposition) who is capable of withstanding incessant challenges to our understanding of things and the world and who also can act purposively and judiciously, employing new and innovative strategies in the face of such challenges. ESD, thus, offers a way forward and is not just focused on the present. Neither is it just focused on employability of graduates. In simple words, ESD prepares students for not only current jobs and life challenges but also future ones. It is therefore far from being an economically driven model of education, which by definition mainly supports 'education for employment' and which some scholars (e.g., Mossman, 2018 and the author included) consider to be unbalanced and thus incapable of leading to sustainable development. Rather, ESD is more holistic in approach, to the point where it comes very close to Ancient Greek philosophers' views on education, particularly Aristotle's. Education in Aristotelian terms is an all-round and well-balanced process of development; involving experience (learning by doing); contemplation (critical reflection); practical reasoning; and an integration of theories for the simultaneous development of students physically, cognitively, and spiritually (Barnes, 1982).

The question that comes to mind at this point is what other than problem-solving and decision-making strategies does ESD entail? Above, the author referred to the learning of new technologies in addition to active learning (i.e., learning by doing), self-driven learning, and critical evaluation, synthesis, and reflection. These strategies, however, constitute mainly pedagogy or the methodology of teaching, whereas education also comprises curriculum content focusing on transferable knowledge and skills as well as skills for learning, in addition to pedagogy. Learning by doing in ESD, thus, along with the other pedagogies, is not undertaken in abstraction but rather in connection with content to be learned. More precisely, scholars (Fullan & Scott, 2014) have argued that ESD involves knowledge and skills acquired in context and coupled with action leading to deep and meaningful learning and graduate students, who are literate with respect to sustainability in various life aspects, savvy about implementing change, and inventive and creative, and who have clear positions about tacit assumptions driving the 21st-century agenda. Learners with such qualities, according to Fullan and Scott (2014), are "naturally capable and competent under all conditions" (p. 8) and can rely on themselves in a complex and uncertain world and can help others do the same. Next, the author identifies what counts as "content" when it comes to ESD.

Content, according to ESD proponents, should not be related to just one disciplinary area. Researchers have argued that subject-specific or disciplinary knowledge is no longer enough for graduates to rely on, especially in rapidly changing and publicly accountable fields (MacDougall, 2012; Moore, 2011). As such disciplines/fields advance and as new information technologies continue to transform decision-making, students will have to develop expertise in new technologies and acquire new strategies of decision-making and problem-solving that take into account multiple inputs, frameworks, and disciplines (MacDougall, 2012; Moore, 2011). ESD proponents, thus, propose an interdisciplinary problem-oriented approach to learning (Beachy, 2011; Fullan & Scott, 2014; Mossman, 2018) that empowers students to tackle authentic problems mirroring the complexities of real life (e.g., Bursztyn & Drummond, 2014; Wagner, 2011). Such interdisciplinary education accomplishes this by developing in students a multidimensional skill foundation consisting of critical, constructive, and systems thinking; communication; and teamwork and collaboration as well as other skills with tangible applications (Mossman, 2018; Tarrant & Thiele, 2016). By consistently using such skills to tackle authentic problems that mirror real complexities and experiences through the course of their education, students begin to find such complexities and experiences more natural and manageable with time. This helps them transfer their knowledge and skills to real-world settings and problems with greater ease (Brown & Calnan, 2011; Repko et al., 2017).

In light of the above, interdisciplinarity has the potential to empower students to prosper in work and life and become global citizens capable of coping with and adjusting to changes irrespective of time or place, rather than just being social and professional actors or citizens at the national level (Okogbaa, 2017). Further, reflection is a vital component of interdisciplinary education because interdisciplinarity involves not only the integration of disciplines (Repko et al., 2017), but also the integration of the insights formed from different disciplines – that is, the integration of one's and others' reflections about a certain issue. This integration aims at establishing common ground among the different disciplinary insights about the objects or concepts under study to understand them more comprehensively. Interdisciplinary integration, thus, is a metacognitive process where one reflects on (i.e., critically analyses and evaluates) their own insights (i.e., reflections) and those of others belonging to different disciplines, to reach a more holistic and higher level of comprehension.

This view of education results in university graduates, who are well-equipped to not only fit into the existing social, economic, and political systems, but also actively influence these systems' directions (Spring, 2006). They are also capable of making decisions that are relevant to both foreseeable and unforeseeable future issues (Martin, 2007). Such skills and competencies are significant because they are exactly the ones today's employers seek out and value given the increasing demand for broad skill sets that will facilitate achievement of economically driven targets in the competitive global economy (Bancino & Zevalkink, 2007; Jacobson-Lundeberg, 2016; Mossman, 2018).

3   Research Problem and Question

Going back to the question, "Where are we in meeting the educational reform objective of sustainable development?" which was raised earlier in relation to the context of Bahrain. Several research studies (Al-Ammary et al., 2016; Al-Sulaimani, 2010; Luckin, 2008; Wiseman & Anderson, 2012), including the current author's, over a period of 10 years pre-COVID (e.g., Abdul Razzak, 2016a, 2016b), have indicated the existence of a number of barriers to achieving this objective. This is despite the fact that the strategies of the regulatory bodies as well as those of the higher education institutions (HEIs) in Bahrain generally emphasize the employment of instructional methods that can enhance the skills needed for knowledge acquisition, creation, and implementation, contributing to sustainable development of innovation at the national level (Abdul Razzak, 2018). The intention and guiding principles are, thus, in place in the Kingdom; however, the main issue is one of misalignment between the intended and actual use of instruction that leads to sustainable development.

When it comes to actual implementation, the most significant barrier that researchers have identified, and that almost all GCC education systems share, is the inability of these systems to build "knowledge production capacity." It is this capacity that creates opportunities for innovation, which typically require active, HOTS-enhancing inquiry-based instruction available via ICT (Luckin, 2008; Wiseman & Anderson, 2012). Knowledge production capacity refers to the development of subject-area expertise and its transferability to new contexts to support research development and innovation in real-world situations beyond the classroom (Abdul Razzak, 2018; Wiseman & Anderson, 2012). This barrier is evident despite the availability of, and access to, state-of-the-art ICT resources, including the latest e-learning systems.

Based on relevant research findings (Abdul Razzak, 2016a; Bahrain Education & Training Quality Authority [BQA] Annual Report, 2018), this barrier seems to be attributed partly to teachers' uncertainty about, and lack of expertise in, effective methods for promoting HOTS, such as critical thinking and other deep learning skills, namely, critical reflection, which are crucial for knowledge production and innovation. This unpreparedness of teachers is found at all levels of education from elementary school to higher education. Evidence of this can be found, for example, in the published findings of quality reviews conducted by BQA of public schools in Bahrain. The findings identified inconsistent use of effective teaching, learning, and assessment strategies by teachers, in addition to limited opportunities to develop students' HOTS (BQA Annual Report, 2018, p. 29; BQA Annual Report, 2020, p. 23). Similarly, when it comes to HOTS' integration in HEIs, the author found that out of 119 university academic programs reviewed by BQA in its first cycle of "programs-within-college" reviews, only 79 (i.e., 66%) satisfied the requirements of the academic standards of the graduates and related assessments (BQA Annual Report, 2018). This was generally attributed in the BQA review reports to assessment tools and methods that are unsuitable for assessing the intended learning outcomes, especially those related to the acquisition of HOTS and analytical and problem-solving skills. The BQA reports also stated that the assessment tools designed by the faculty members tended to focus mainly on recall and retrieval of information instead of stimulating students to employ HOTS. Finally, the findings of one author's study (Abdul Razzak, 2016a) confirmed teachers' need for guidance when trying to integrate HOTS with classroom instruction. These findings highlighted several challenges teachers face in the process, such as the inability to integrate HOTS without simultaneously shifting focus away from the main lesson content and the mismatch between the selected instructional activities and the targeted HOTS.

The unpreparedness of teachers to integrate HOTS, as a factor leading to the inability to build knowledge production capacity, is only one side of the story. The need of schoolteachers and higher education faculty for special e-learning guidance is another (Abdul Razzak, 2016b; Al-Ammary et al., 2016). E-learning or online learning with its special characteristics positively affects learners' performance and development of HOTS, in addition to providing them with ample opportunities for critical reflection on their learning (e.g., Chang, 2012; Lopez-Perez et al., 2013). However, designing online activities, even basic ones, is not always easy for all teachers. This was especially the case before COVID-19 and became more evident during the sudden transition to e-learning after the outbreak. Years before the pandemic, one author (Abdul Razzak, 2016b) learned that university faculty found designing simple and basic online activities challenging. They thought it was difficult to create complex e-lessons, such as those capitalizing on students' HOTS. Another study conducted around the same time in Bahrain discovered similar challenges and very limited usage of e-learning features when it came to the faculty (Al-Ammary et al., 2016).

This unpreparedness of teachers, whether in terms of HOTS integration or e-learning design, is not unique to Bahrain or the GCC; several international studies have also confirmed it (Cheong & Cheung, 2008; Mandernach, 2006; Ramdiah et al., 2019). It constitutes a challenge in the development and teaching of 21st-century skills and, consequently, the fulfilment of the educational reform objective of sustainable development in the Kingdom. What makes it a greater concern in the eyes of the author is her realization that none of the educational reform initiatives in the Kingdom of Bahrain (e.g., Ministry of Education school improvement projects, BQA frameworks, Bahrain Teachers College guiding principles) include interdisciplinary approaches even though values of holistic education are embedded throughout these initiatives. In the author's view, this absence of interdisciplinarity, therefore, may constitute a critical gap in the Kingdom's educational reform, acting as an additional barrier to achieving the sustainable development objective.

In sum, for ESD to lead to knowledge production capacity, three main conditions or components are necessary: HOTS integration in instruction; opportunities for deep and meaningful critical reflection on learning, where learners' insights drawn from different disciplines are integrated; and ICT integration in instruction, where e-learning lessons and activities are designed in such a way that they not only capitalize on students' HOTS but also create opportunities for innovation, knowledge production, and/or knowledge and skill transfer. Based on what was mentioned above, the Kingdom of Bahrain before COVID-19 was in need of improving its HOTS and e-learning/ICT integration processes in education to move closer toward achieving the sustainable development objective. As for the integration of insights/reflections from different disciplines in learning to tackle problems and issues, that was and continues to be formally/officially nonexistent in terms of both policy and procedures. In light of all this, and given the different challenges and opportunities COVID-19 has brought about, is it possible that with the transition to e-learning and the increased shift of attention, time, and resources to online environments and modes of learning and assessment, education in Bahrain could be beginning to take a leap, no matter how small, toward achieving the Kingdom's objective of sustainable development?" Such complex question is crucial because it constitutes the foundation for the study's main research question: "How has progress toward sustainable development been affected by the COVID-19 transition to e-learning?" To answer this question, it is necessary to first identify and discuss the status of e-learning post-COVID so as to shed light on how it has changed, if at all, and explore whether these changes help support sustainable development in any way.

4 Methodology

To address the main research question, a qualitative research method was adopted. The main objective was to fully understand a phenomenon in context and provide an in-depth account of it (Leininger, 1992). Thus, this study aimed to investigate the issue of e-learning in HEIs in Bahrain post-COVID and evaluate its practices in regard to how much they may be contributing to ESD. The study is consequently social context dependent and a "small-scale inquiry" of a specific case, to use Flyvbjerg's (2001, p. 392) expression. Such an inquiry was selected because of the researcher's interest in thoroughly analyzing some aspects of e-learning within HEIs in Bahrain that can eventually provide an interpretivist perspective and understanding in terms of knowledge. The researcher was not concerned with establishing any generalizations or causal or temporal connections; instead, she mainly sought an in-depth understanding of "behaviour in its specific social context" (Bryman, 2004, p. 53). Because gaining direct access to HEIs in Bahrain for conducting empirical research and collecting data was not permissible for the researcher, considering her occupational position, she decided instead to rely on sets of relevant data that had already been officially collected and analyzed through her workplace (BQA). However, instead of taking the analyzed data and working with it as is, she went one step beyond and reflected on the data, thus making her own reflections the object of analysis and study.

Given that reflections on field experiences have been proven to provide a great depth of understanding (Babbie, 2013), the researcher decided to rely on an analysis of her own reflections regarding the results of the 2020 BQA evaluation of e-learning practices and applications in HEIs in Bahrain after the COVID outbreak. To collect data, the BQA evaluation utilized a variety of sources:

– HEIs' self-evaluation results regarding their own e-learning practices
– HEIs' faculty and students' e-learning experience surveys
– A review of e-learning practices in a sample of HEIs
– A benchmarking exercise of BQA institutional and program review frameworks against local and international guidelines related to e-learning

The data collected from these different sources and analyzed formed the basis of the researcher's reflections. Using the research strategy of analyzing her own reflections proved to be advantageous for the researcher because, in addition to providing her with an in-depth understanding of e-learning aspects and practices in HEIs, it aligned well with her research purpose and intention.

To analyze her reflective narratives, the researcher first collated them into one document and then categorized the data into clusters of meaningful ideas, focusing on interpreting single instances giving special attention to any discrepant cases and then identifying patterns and underlying themes. Several themes emerged from the analysis. Some were not quite relevant to the aim and scope of this study and thus were left out. The pertinent ones, however, are presented and discussed in the subsequent section; they were interpreted through a process of synthesis and generalization to arrive at conclusions that had implications with respect to e-learning in HEIs in Bahrain in general and sustainable development in particular.

5   Findings and Discussion

This section includes the main themes that emerged from the analysis of the reflective narratives and that are pertinent to this study's focus. Each theme is coupled with its corresponding description and with the implications it may bear for achieving the sustainable development objective in Bahrain.

5.1 Theme One: Rationale for e-Learning Adoption within Academic Programs

This theme relates to the reasons behind the adoption of e-learning in the academic programs BQA reviewed and whether it was adopted as a matter of an institutional policy, strategy, or plan.

After the COVID outbreak, a governmental resolution at the national level was taken for all educational institutions in Bahrain to adopt remote T&L as an alternative to the traditional face-to-face instructional approaches. In response, HEIs developed special emergency transition plans and set procedures to organize the complete shift to online education and assessment of students in a time of crisis. Since then, HEIs have been operating in accordance with these special plans, with some institutions just beginning to offer a HyFlex model of education. This model allows for hybrid learning in a flexible course structure, giving students the option of attending face-to-face classes, participating in classes online, or doing both.

The fact that e-learning implementation in HEIs is being carried out in response to a national strategy implies that there is alignment between both; however, this does not necessarily mean that there is alignment between the e-learning implementation and the national strategy concerning sustainable development. This is because such an alignment depends on the quality of what is being offered through e-learning and how much it can integrate the three components of ESD (i.e., HOTS integration, critical reflection on insights drawn from different disciplines, and e-learning instructional design that capitalizes HOTS and creates innovation and knowledge transfer opportunities, as an area of improvement for most HEIs, the need to develop a comprehensive e-learning strategy covering related T&L and assessment policies, procedures, and plans as well as practical components in terms of field training (internship) and practical courses in case of the continuation of the COVID-19 crisis, its recurrence, or the emergence of similar crises in the future. This area of improvement indicates the e-learning that has been taking place in HEIs is most likely still far away from a well-designed and structured framework of standards. Such a framework would guide e-learning's implementation in such a way that ESD components, which by nature require extensive planning, could be intentionally and systematically incorporated. The lack of such a framework is not surprising because, in the early days of the pandemic, the sudden shift to e-learning occurred as an emergency transition and HEIs were too busy "firefighting" (i.e., managing the crisis) to plan ahead.

An overarching and comprehensive e-learning strategy, if developed, would replace the emergency transition plan and would add better direction, structure, and quality to the e-learning implementation irrespective of time and circumstance. Further, if developed in alignment with the sustainable development objective, such a strategy would have the potential to enrich the e-learning implementation with the necessary ESD components.

5.2   Theme Two: E-Learning Platforms Being Used

This theme focuses on the e-learning platform or learning management system that the academic programs BQA reviewed have been using, and which of their features are being utilized.

The data analysis indicated that the two most common e-learning systems used in HEIs are Moodle and Blackboard, with some institutions also using communication platforms such as Zoom and Microsoft Teams. The features of these systems primarily aid in live broadcasting of lectures in audio and video, recording of lectures, and uploading of educational materials and resources. These systems also include features that allow for direct interaction, providing students with opportunities to participate in question-and-answer sessions, share ideas, present and discuss their work, and attend virtual office hours and meetings with faculty members. Despite the availability and utilization of these features, however, the data indicated limited responsiveness or interaction of some students with their instructors and peers in the virtual learning environment (VLE) and poor participation in required academic tasks and duties. There is also a need for students to strengthen their effective communication with their peers in the VLE, especially during collaborative group work. This deficiency in online interaction and engagement is not unique to Bahrain, as the findings of several international research studies indicate. These studies identified the absence of essential personal interactions as one of the most noticeable drawbacks of e-learning (Al-Rawashdeh et al., 2021; Arkorful & Abaidoo, 2015; Islam et al., 2015) and as a detrimental factor negatively affecting collaborative learning (which usually enriches students' knowledge and ideas). This issue also bears serious implications in relation to achieving the sustainable development objective. Poor interaction or engagement implies limited active learning, which is one of the necessary pedagogies for ESD. This limits the chances of successful achievement of the objective of sustainable development.

5.3   Theme Three: E-Learning Capacity-Building and Training

This theme focuses on the e-learning capacity-building opportunities HEIs provide to the relevant stakeholders, namely, the faculty and students.

From the beginning of the pandemic, HEIs have worked hard to equip their faculty and students with the skills needed to function as smoothly as possible online. Several training workshops were organized relating to e-learning, and these were electronically delivered to students, faculty members, and administrative staff. Many of the HEIs also collected feedback on the effectiveness of the workshops for improvement purposes, although this was not done regularly in all the institutions. Additionally, HEIs relied on several informative tools (e.g., user manuals, educational videos, and links to training materials) to help guide faculty members in the use of the e-learning platforms. In an exceptional case, one HEI invited external parties to provide technical and academic training workshops and seminars on remote education and e-learning for its employees and faculty members.

A close examination of the type of capacity-building opportunities HEIs have provided showed that most of them focus on the use of technology tools. Nothing in the collected data referred to training related to instructional design of e-courses, so it is safe to conclude that almost no special training on any of the three components necessary for ESD (e.g., HOTS integration in e-lessons and activities, interdisciplinarity, knowledge transfer) was provided. Nevertheless, it is important to note the clearly improved awareness in recent years within HEIs in Bahrain. The awareness is about the importance of diversifying intended learning outcomes, T&L strategies, and assessments, and not restricting them to the basic levels of cognitive thinking in Bloom's taxonomy irrespective of the T&L mode being implemented (i.e., whether online or face-to-face or hybrid or HyFlex). Such awareness can be mainly attributed to the BQA quality assurance frameworks and standards that these HEIs and their academic programs comply with, and to the relevant capacity-building opportunities that the Directorate of the Higher Education of BQA regularly provides them with. Nevertheless, the absence of capacity-building opportunities targeting the incorporation of components necessary for ESD can slow down the achievement of the educational reform objective of sustainable development. This is further confirmed through two areas of improvement identified through the data analysis process:

- The need for faculty members to be trained on how to conduct more meaningful online formative assessments; and
- The need for mechanisms assessing faculty members' ability to design e-courses that contribute to students' achievement of intended learning outcomes and that help develop students' HOTS.

Formative assessments are of relevance here because they tend to encourage students to participate in class and can increase cooperation among students

(Bell & Cowie, 2001). When well-designed and conducted, they can serve as active learning catalysts contributing to ESD. The second area of improvement is obviously relevant because of its direct relation to the significant ESD components of ICT integration in instruction and HOTS development through effective e-course design. The data analysis of the BQA reviews indicated that faculty are not receiving training in those areas.

5.4 Theme Four: Instructional Processes Carried out via the e-Learning Systems

This theme relates to the different ways e-learning systems are being used for instruction within the HEIs.

The data analysis indicated the utilization of electronic systems for a multiplicity of purposes: uploading course materials; monitoring students' attendance and faculty members' presence and interaction in the VLE; carrying out virtual office hours and academic advising sessions; delivering lessons synchronously that students can record; supervising students' research work; and so on. An additional purpose is covering practical components of courses through simulations, virtual labs, and role-playing skits. As for student assessments, these are being implemented through various strategies, including research assignments, projects, case studies, problem-solving, and open-book tests, in addition to online quizzes and examinations.

From the data analysis, it is clear that students are satisfied with the types of online assessment taken place. They even reported finding the assessments more varied and often more meaningful than those previously used in the face-to-face classes. This is not surprising at all–going online forced faculty members to be more creative in their T&L and assessment methods and to move more toward performance-based assessments and activities than they normally would in a face-to-face classroom. In a face-to-face classroom, they could easily get by with mostly lecturing and pencil-and-paper quizzes and examinations. In most cases, faculty members feel apprehensive about online assessments in general and online examinations in particular because of the higher chances of cheating (Jara & Mellar, 2009). Therefore, they view performance-based assessments as a safer option. These help in ensuring that students' works are their own. Additionally, such assessments can help resolve the issue of poor student engagement online, especially when they take the form of group projects or assignments.

In this context, moving to performance-based assessments and tasks is a step in the right direction. It is well known that such activities are more authentic than other forms of learning experiences (Pratiwi et al., 2018). They promote deep and meaningful learning while encouraging transfer of knowledge and skills from one context to the other (Fullan & Scott, 2014). They also have the potential to reinforce independent self-driven learning on the part of students, encourage them to set personal learning goals and manage their learning processes to achieve certain targets (Kallick & Zmuda, 2017). As active learning experiences, performance-based assessments and activities constitute a part of the main pedagogies needed for ESD, namely, self-driven and active learning, and thus contribute to achieving the sustainable development objective.

Nevertheless, it is important to note that the data analysis pointed to the need for the academic programs BQA reviewed to better ensure that student workload in terms of study time and assessments is appropriate. Students had reported feeling somewhat overloaded with work because of poorly coordinated scheduling of assessment tasks by their professors. This is an area of improvement in need of serious consideration mainly because student overload can impede their critical reflection on their own learning. Such reflection requires time and space to be meaningful and effective. The main issue here is that critical reflection, being one of the components of ESD, cannot be compromised if sustainable development is to be realized.

6 Concluding Remarks and Recommendations

The research study focused on the Kingdom of Bahrain and aimed at answering the question, "How has progress toward sustainable development been affected by the COVID-19 transition to e-learning?" The research question was examined by discussing the status of e-learning post-COVID and assessing how it contributes to achieving the sustainable development objective at the national level. After establishing how ESD can be the best educational paradigm for producing generations of graduates capable of adeptly balancing economic, social, and environmental concerns and challenges and thus sustaining development in their countries, this ESD model was used to frame the researcher's analysis of her reflections on the data collected and analyzed through the BQA reviews of HEIs' e-learning practices.

Based on this analysis, it is safe to conclude that progress toward achieving the sustainable development objective in Bahrain has been slightly expedited by the COVID-19 transition to e-learning. This is due to the increase in opportunities this transition has created for performance-based assessments and activities to be experimented with and implemented in instruction, which is an increase that happens to align well with ESD. HEIs should continue with and reinforce this approach, along with other active learning strategies that promote self-driven learning, irrespective of the mode of learning adopted in the near future – even if it means HEIs going back to total face-to-face instruction.

Nevertheless, many more steps need to be taken on the path toward achieving the sustainable development objective. As the data analysis indicated, several barriers or areas of improvement remain:
- The issue of students' poor participation and engagement in online classes.
- The lack of capacity-building opportunities targeting e-course instructional design in general and instructional design that incorporates ESD components (i.e., HOTS integration, interdisciplinary critical reflections, and knowledge transfer) in particular.
- Student overload due to lack of coordination and poor scheduling of assessments by faculty members, which impedes critical reflection on their learning; and above all.
- The absence of an overarching and comprehensive e-learning strategy that is aligned from the beginning with the requirements for achieving the sustainable development objective.

These areas of improvement yield important recommendations for HEIs in Bahrain, some at the institutional level and others at the faculty level. First, at the institutional level, an overarching e-learning strategy aligned with sustainable development should be developed in every HEI to ensure that ESD components are incorporated in the T&L and assessment processes taking place within its academic programs. This strategy can also help in guiding whatever capacity-building plans the HEI develops in the direction of providing greater professional development opportunities for the design of structured activities and tasks that capitalize on students' HOTS development, independent self-driven learning, and ability to transfer their newly acquired knowledge and skills to different contexts. Second, at the level of the faculty members, it is recommended that they get harder and smarter on being more creative and innovative in their implementation of e-learning and utilization of e-learning systems' features in ways that would create a more interactive and meaningfully engaging VLE for students. They should also train and educate their students about the different features of the e-learning system(s) they adopt to empower students to become more independent in their learning. At the same time, they should be more considerate and organized in how they assign students' work, taking into consideration the fact that giving students time to reflect on their learning experiences is more important than the learning itself. John Dewey's famous quote validates this notion: "We do not learn from experience. We learn from reflecting on experience" (1933, p. 78). Undeniably, students infusing their critical reflections with insights drawn from different disciplines would meet the conditions required for ESD and would, therefore, bring Bahrain closer to meeting its objective of sustainable development through education. However, because interdisciplinarity is not yet (at least explicitly and officially) on any of the national agendas, the main recommendation of this study is that Bahrain add it as an item of strategic planning at both the national level and the level of HEIs in the Kingdom.

References

Abdul Razzak, N. (2016a). Teachers' experiences with school improvement projects: The case of Bahraini public schools. *Cogent Education, 3*(1). https://doi.org/10.1080/2331186X.2016.1229898

Abdul Razzak, N. (2016b). Strategies for effective faculty involvement in online activities aimed at promoting critical thinking and deep learning. *Education and Information Technologies, 21*(4), 881–889. http://dx.doi.org/10.1007/s10639-014-9359-z

Abdul Razzak, N. (2018). Bahrain. In A. Weber & S. Hamlaoui (Eds.), *E-learning in the Middle East and North Africa* (pp. 27–53). Springer International Publishing AG.

Abdul Razzak, N. (2020). *Practitioner research: Nation-wide educational reform for school improvement in the Kingdom of Bahrain* (Publication No. 48240) [Doctoral dissertation, Kingston University]. Eprints Kingston.

Al-Ammary, J., Mohammed, Z., & Omran, F. (2016). E-learning capability maturity level in the Kingdom of Bahrain. *The Turkish Online Journal of Educational Technology, 15*(2), 47–60. https://www.semanticscholar.org/paper/E-Learning-Capability-Maturity-Level-in-Kingdom-of-Al-Ammary-Mohammed/391310f981f14d73b5e849d3e18348d93e5218e3

Al-Rawashdeh, A. Z., Mohammed, E. Y., Al Arab, A. R., Alara, M., & Al-Rawashdeh, B. (2021). Advantages and disadvantages of using e-learning in university education: Analyzing students' perspectives. *The Electronic Journal of e-Learning, 19*(3), 107–117.

Al-Sulaimani, A. A. (2010). *The importance of teachers in integrating ICT into science teaching in intermediate schools in Saudi Arabia: A mixed methods study* [Unpublished doctoral dissertation]. RMIT University.

Arkorful, V., & Abaidoo, N. (2015). The role of e-learning, advantages and disadvantages of its adoption in higher education. *International Journal of Instructional Technology and Distance Learning, 12*(1), 29–42.

Babbie, E. R. (2013). *The practice of social research*. Wadsworth Cengage Learning.

Bahrain Economic Development Board. (2009). *From regional pioneer to global contender: Our vision – The economic vision 2030 for Bahrain*. https://i2g4c9h4.rocketcdn.me/app/uploads/2021/12/Vision-2030-English.pdf

Bahrain Education & Training Quality Authority. (2018). *Annual report 2018*. https://www.bqa.gov.bh/En/Publications/AnnualReports/13%20jun%20FINAL%20English%20Annual%20Report%202018.pdf

Bahrain Education & Training Quality Authority. (2020). *Annual report 2020*. https://www.bqa.gov.bh/En/Mediacenter/Documents/Annual%20Report%202020.pdf

Bancino, R., & Zevalkink, C. (2007). Soft skills: The new curriculum for hard-core technical professionals. *Techniques: Connecting Education and Ccareers, 82*(5), 9–18.

Baporikar, N., & Shah, I. (2012). Quality of higher education in 21st Century – A case of Oman. *Journal of Educational and Instructional Studies in the World, 2*(2), 9–18.

Barnes, J. (1982). *Aristotle: A very short introduction*. Oxford University Press.

Barnett, R. (2004). Learning for an unknown future. *Higher Education Research & Development, 23*(3), 247–260.

Bates, T. (2010). New challenges for universities: Why they must change. In U. D. Ehlers. & D. Schneckenberg (Eds.), *Changing cultures in higher education* (pp. 15–26). Springer.

Beachy, R. (2011, February 24). *Addressing the grand societal challenges requires change in conduct of research: The role of NIFA in "assisting" the change* [Conference keynote address]. Third biennial Midwest summit on leadership in interdisciplinarity, networking & collaboration (LINC), St. Louis, MO, United States.

Bell, B., & Cowie, B. (2001). The characteristics of formative assessment. In *Formative assessment and science education* (Science & Technology Education Library, Vol. 12). Springer. https://doi.org/10.1007/0-306-47227-9_4

Bell, S. (2010). Project-based learning for the 21st century: Skills for the future. *The Clearing House: A Journal of Educational Strategies, Issues and Ideas, 83*(2), 39–43.

Bramwell, A., & Wolfe, D. A. (2008). Universities and regional economic development: The entrepreneurial University of Waterloo. *Research Policy, 37*(8), 1175–1187. https://doi.org/10.1016/j.respol.2008.04.016

Brown, P., & Calnan, M. (2011). The risks of managing uncertainty: The limitations of governance and choice, and the potential for trust. *Social Policy and Society, 9*(1), 13–24.

Bryman, A. (2004). *Social research methods* (2nd ed.). Oxford University Press.

Bursztyn, M., & Drummond, J. (2014). Sustainability science and the university: Pitfalls and bridges to interdisciplinarity. *Environmental Education Research, 20*(3), 313–332.

Castells, M. (2000). Toward a sociology of the network society. *Contemporary Sociology, 29*(5), 693–699.

Castells, M. (2014). *The impact of the internet on society: A global perspective*. OpenMind. https://www.bbvaopenmind.com/en/articles/the-impact-of-the-internet-on-society-a-global-perspective/

Chang, Y. S. (2012). Student technological creativity using online problem-solving activities. *International Journal of Technology and Design Education, 13*(2), 1–32.

Cheong, C. M., & Cheung, W. S. (2008). Online discussion and critical thinking skills: A case study in a Singapore secondary school. *Australasian Journal of Educational Technology, 24*(5), 556–573.

Dewey, J. (1933). *How we think: A restatement of the relation of reflective thinking to the educative process.* Heath & Co Publishers.

Filho, L. W. (2000). Dealing with misconceptions on the concept of sustainability. *International Journal of Sustainability in Higher Education, 1*(1), 9–19.

Flyvbjerg, B. (2001). *Making social science matter: Why social inquiry fails and how it can succeed again.* Cambridge University Press.

Fullan, M., & Scott, G. (2014). *New pedagogies for deep learning.* Collaborative Impact SPC. https://www.michaelfullan.ca/wp-content/uploads/2014/09/Education-Plus-A-Whitepaper-July-2014-1.pdf

Goldman, D. (2017). *Cultivating engagement through student-centered learning in a high school media art class* (Publication No. 5-2017) [Masters' thesis, Dominican University of California]. Dominican Scholar. https://scholar.dominican.edu/masters-theses/261

Hughes, C. (2018, November 18). *Seven global challenges for 21st-Century education.* International School Parent. https://www.internationalschoolparent.com/articles/seven-global-education-challenges/

Iacobucci, D., & Hoeffler, S. (2016). Leveraging social networks to develop radically new products. *Journal of Product Innovation Management, 33*(2), 217–223.

Islam, N., Beer, M., & Slack, F. (2015). E-learning challenges faced by academics in higher education. *Journal of Education and Training Studies, 3*(5), 102–112.

Jacobson-Lundeberg, V. (2016). Pedagogical implementation of 21st-century skills. *Educational Leadership and Administration: Teaching and Program Development, 27*, 82–100.

Jara, M., & Mellar, H. (2009). Factors affecting quality enhancement procedures for e-learning courses. *Quality Assurance in Education, 17*, 220–232.

Jonsson, P. (2010, July 15). BP oil spill: 'Mystery plumber' may be brains behind containment cap. *The Christian Science Monitor.* https://www.csmonitor.com/Environment/2010/0715/BP-oil-spill-Mystery-plumber-may-be-brains-behind-containment-cap

Kallick, B., & Zmuda, A. (2017). Orchestrating the move to student-driven learning. *Educational Leadership, 74*(6), 53–57.

Khatib, F., Dimaio, F., Cooper, S., Kazmierczyk, M., Gilski, M., Krzywda, S., Zabranska, H., Pichova, I., Thompson, J., Popovic, Z., Jaskolski, M., & Baker, D. (2011). Crystal structure of a monomeric retroviral protease solved by protein folding game players. *Nature Structural & Molecular Biology, 18*, 1175–1177.

Kirtiklis, K. (2017). Manuel Castells' theory of information society as media theory. *Lingua Posnaniensis, 59*(1), 65–77. https://sciendo.com/article/10.1515/linpo-2017-0006

Leininger, M. (1992). Current issues, problems, and trends to advance qualitative paradigmatic research methods for the future. *Qualitative Health Research, 2*(4), 392–415. https://doi.org/10.1177/104973239200200403

Lopez-Perez, M. V., Perez-Lopez, M., Rodriguez-Ariza, L., & Argente-Linares, E. (2013). The influence of the use of technology on student outcomes in a blended learning context. *Educational Technology Research and Development Journal, 61*, 625–638.

Luckin, R. (2008). The learner centric ecology of resources: A framework for using technology to scaffold learning. *Computers & Education, 50*(2), 449–462.

MacDougall, M. (2012). Research-teaching linkages: Beyond the divide in undergraduate medicine. *International Journal for the Scholarship of Teaching and Learning, 6*(2). https://digitalcommons.georgiasouthern.edu/ij-sotl/vol6/iss2/21/

Mandernach, B. J. (2006). Thinking critically about critical thinking: Integrating online tools to promote critical thinking. *Insight: A Collection of Faculty Scholarship, 1*, 41–50.

Martin, J. (2007). *The 17 great challenges of the twenty-first century*. Elon University. https://www.elon.edu/u/imagining/wp-content/uploads/sites/964/2019/07/17_Great_Challenges.pdf

Montebon, D. R. T. (2018). Pre-service teachers' concept of sustainable development and its integration in science lessons. *Jurnal Pendidikan Humaniora, 6*(1), 1–8. https://files.eric.ed.gov/fulltext/ED586264.pdf

Moore, M. (2011). Teaching physicians to make informed decisions in the face of uncertainty: Librarians and informaticians on the health care team. *Academic Medicine, 86*(11), 1345.

Mossman, A. P. (2018). Retrofitting the ivory tower: Engaging global sustainability challenges through interdisciplinary problem-oriented education, research, and partnerships in U.S. higher education. *Journal of Higher Education Outreach and Engagement, 22*(1), 35–60.

Okogbaa, V. (2017). Preparing the teacher to meet the challenges of a changing world. *Journal of Education and Practice, 8*(5), 81–86.

Oman Vision 2040. (2019). *Vision Document – ISFU*. https://isfu.gov.om/2040/Vision_Documents_En.pdf

Pratiwi, D., Arief, M., & Churiyah, M. (2018). The development of performance-based model of authentic assessment on archival subject. *KnE Social Sciences, 3*(3), 150–166. https://doi.org/10.18502/kss.v3i3.1881

Ramdiah, S., Abidinsyah, B. P., Royani, M., & Husamah, H. (2019). Understanding, planning, and implementation of HOTS by senior high school biology teachers in Banjarmasin-Indonesia. *International Journal of Instruction, 12*(1), 425–440. https://files.eric.ed.gov/fulltext/EJ1201152.pdf

Repko, A. F., Szoztak, R., & Buchberger, M. P. (2017). *Introduction to interdisciplinary studies* (2nd ed.). Sage Publications.

Romer P., (2007). Economic growth. In *The concise encyclopedia of economics*. Library of Economics and Liberty. https://www.econlib.org/library/Enc1/EconomicGrowth.html

Spring, J. (2006). Pedagogies of globalization. *Pedagogies: An International Journal, 1*(2), 105–122.

Tarrant, S. P., & Thiele, L. P. (2016). Practice makes pedagogy – John Dewey and skills-based sustainability education. *International Journal of Sustainability in Higher Education, 17*(1), 54–67. https://doi.org/10.1108/IJSHE-09-2014-0127

UNESCO. (2010). *Education for sustainable development lens: A policy and practice review tool* (No. 2). http://unesdoc.unesco.org/images/0019/001908/190898e.pdf

UNESCO. (2018). *Education for sustainable development*. https://en.unesco.org/themes/education-sustainable-development

Vision 2030 Kingdom of Saudi Arabia. (2019). *Saudi Vision 2030*. https://www.vision2030.gov.sa/v2030/overview/

Wagner, T. (2011). *The global achievement gap*. Basic Books – First Trade Paper Edition.

Wiseman, A. W., & Anderson, E. (2012). ICT-integrated education and national innovation systems in the Gulf Cooperation Council (GCC) countries. *Computers & Education, 59*, 607–618.

CHAPTER 4

How Students Were Engaged during the Second Wave of COVID-19 by EFL, Linguistics and Translation Instructors in Distance Learning

Reima Al-Jarf

Abstract

This study reports 15 types of activities that EFL, linguistics and translation instructors at a sample of Saudi universities used in distance learning during the COVID-19 pandemic. Examples include (1) searching for linguistic and translation key terms and concepts, (2) problem-solving questions, (3) online debates, (4) summarizing a research paper, (5) attending a thesis defense, (6) inviting guest speakers, (7) project-based assignments, (8) connecting writing and speaking topics with the Kingdom of Saudi Arabia's Vision 2030, (9) collecting and analyzing translation errors, (10) translating Wikipedia articles, (11) interpreting contests, (12) linguistic analyses of family speech and videos, (13) student-created podcasts and digital stories, (14) dynamic online speaking activities, and (15) integrating technology such as Slido and Padlet. The participating students found those activities beneficial, enjoyable, and helpful. Their skills improved as a result of reading, preparing and synthesizing information and the feedback received.

Keywords

COVID-19 – online activities – distance learning – Saudi Arabia – language and translation

1 Introduction

As in many countries around the world, there was a sudden transition from face-to-face to distance learning (DL) at Saudi universities starting in March 2020 due to the outbreak of COVID-19 pandemic. Since then, all college courses have been delivered online using a variety of platforms such as Blackboard,

Zoom, Microsoft Teams, WebEx, Google Classroom and others. A study by Al-Jarf (2020b), conducted end of Spring Semester 2020, showed that more than half (55%) of the students and instructors at language and translation colleges in Saudi Arabia were not happy with DL, found it ineffective and frustrating and preferred face-to-face instruction. In addition, 59% of the students had difficulty understanding online lectures. Instructors used the same class material that they were using before the pandemic. No supplementary digital material or multimedia resources were made available for the students. To 58% of the students, online learning was a lot of hard work. 69% of the students indicated that they had difficulty communicating with their instructors and classmates. It was not possible for some students to follow the online lectures, thus preferred lecture recordings.

Similarly, 64% of the instructors surveyed by Al-Jarf (2020b) reported that many students were not interested in doing assignments for their online courses, refused to give oral presentations, did not ask questions as they used to when they were studying face-to-face before the pandemic. The students did not participate in online class discussions and did not do homework or assignments. They were not enthusiastic, were disappointed and demotivated. There was little interaction between the students and the instructor and among the students themselves in the DL environment. More than two-thirds of them (74%) indicated that the online course attendance was not high as in face-to-face classes. Most students preferred lecture recordings, which they could play without having to attend the live online lectures. The university administrations canceled the marks allocated to attendance and classwork during the lockdown. In online translation classes, the students did not revise, nor corrected their own translations, and did not participate in the online discussion of their translations, nor other classmates' translations. They did not post anything relevant on Blackboard. They were not willing to consult additional online dictionaries or translation sources.

The most common concern for the large majority (91%) of the students was course grades and passing their final exams with high marks. Furthermore, 69% of the instructors indicated that online exams during the lockdown in spring 2020 were ineffective. To avoid students' complaints about grades and to alleviate the negative effects of the COVID-19 lockdown on students' morale, university administrators in Saudi Arabia mandated that instructors be lenient in grading exams, give easy and straightforward questions on final exams, rather than higher-level thinking questions, and give the students extra exam time. Only 20% of the total course mark was allocated to final exams rather than the usual 50% stipulated before the pandemic. The students were given several options: to drop the course, to have the course marks included in their GPAs, to choose between a letter grade or a pass/fail result for their courses. As a result, all the students passed their final exams and did not feel that they had to work hard to earn their grades.

Moreover, 57% of the instructors reported that they had no prior experience with DL, and they could not adjust to DL as a new mode of teaching and learning. They did not know how to use the different tools of the DL platform, and how to adapt the course material to the new online teaching environment.

Furthermore, during the lockdown in spring 2020, some students did not have devices and internet to access their online courses. A big majority (83%) of the participants reported that the internet was slow, and they had difficulty logging into the platform. No technical support was available to the instructors and students during online classes and the technical support staff did not respond to their needs and solve Blackboard and connection problems quickly. The instructors received no academic support to help them prepare online teaching material, activities, and assignments (Al-Jarf, 2021d).

In the summer and fall of 2020, Saudi universities had taken numerous actions towards offering online pedagogical training workshops and support for the instructors, helping students, who had devices or no devices, to gain internet access, solving platform problems, and improving internet connection. In appreciation of such efforts, Umm Al-Qura[1] University won the Blackboard Catalyst Award 2021 for training and professional development at the world level (Al-Jarf, 2021d).

Since language, linguistics and translation courses require intensive practice, the present study aims to explore the changes that have taken place in the delivery of these courses, and the types of online activities that a sample of language and translation instructors at some Saudi universities were using during the second wave of the COVID-19 pandemic, i.e., in the fall 2020 and spring 2021. It aims to find out how language, linguistics and translation instructors engage students online in the absence of face-to-face activities and interaction and to report students' views on those activities.

Findings of the present study are significant for EFL, linguistics, and translation instructors at Saudi university because there is a need to deliver good online courses during the COVID-19 pandemic. The findings will raise instructors' awareness of the new types of online language, linguistics and translation activities that can be practiced during the pandemic and how students engaged in them. It will give instructors an opportunity to share and exchange their online teaching experiences in the areas of EFL, linguistics and translation teaching and learning.

2 Literature Review

In education, *student engagement*[2] refers to the degree of attention, interest, curiosity, optimism, and passion that students show when they are learning or being taught. Learning improves when students are interested, inquisitive, or inspired. On the contrary, learning tends to suffer when the students are bored, disaffected, dispassionate, or disengaged. Stronger and improved student engagement are common instructional objectives expressed by educators. Student engagement can be intellectual (cognitive), emotional, physical, social, and/or cultural. It has many benefits:[3] higher grade point averages, learning life skills, developing leadership skills, learning inclusive practices, interpersonal skills, learning with peers, having fun and others. Student engagement can be achieved through:[4] educational technology and blended learning, classroom management strategies, active learning, quick writes, reciprocal teaching, class participation strategies, culturally responsive teaching, cooperative learning, personalized learning, service learning, inquiry-based learning, project-based learning, gamification, and interdisciplinary teaching. In brief, student engagement can be achieved through effective learning activities and strategies.

In the foreign language, linguistics and translation teaching and learning context, a review of the literature has shown numerous studies that utilized a variety of activities for promoting students' engagement in DL before the outbreak of the pandemic. In a Spanish language course for beginners at the Open University (UK), Fernando Rosell-Aguilar (2005) designed a full set of online tutorial materials for distance language learners utilizing an online audiographic conferencing virtual learning environment (VLE) for synchronous oral interaction.

In Australia, a class of sixteen French-speaking students enrolled in an M.A. course created multimedia resources for a group of students with no prior knowledge of French. Graduate students worked in pairs in creating multimedia activities for real students in a different location based on their culture. The students communicated with each other during weekly classes and via a group-exchange technology (Develotte et al., 2005).

At Universidade Aberta (Open University) in Portugal, Nobre (2018) employed curricular paths, which included online oral and written communicative practices. They followed a student-centered, task-oriented approach, with some examples of training activities in French, German, and English, focusing on oral practice, and based on digital resources consisting of multimedia materials, either produced by the instructor or students, in addition to other materials available on web 2.0. The researcher concluded that the multimedia resources were suitable for the online teaching and learning of foreign languages, especially for professionally engaged adult students, providing them with real-life situations that foster foreign language teaching and learning in virtual settings.

A second group of studies integrated social media in DL courses such as Ucar and Goksel (2020) who found that use of supplementary activities on Facebook contributed significantly to EFL students' motivation, interest, volition, and academic performance in an online distance course. Similarly, Moghadam and Shamsi (2021) found that Facebook could serve as a motivating and effective tool for engaging students in combination with the online platforms used during the global lockdown.

In Kunka's study (2020), Twitter increased students' engagement in the college classroom. Students who were hesitant to speak up in class were able to participate in class discussions held on Twitter. Twitter helped the students overcome their feelings of isolation due to a lack of communication intimacy and immediacy. It provided another communication channel, a space to share assignments, and a medium where students can actively engage with each other, the course content, and the instructor.

Likewise, Instagram was used as an interactive communication channel to engage first-year students during an introductory course. An open Instagram account was created where students' questions were gathered and answered by creating educational images and videos. Results showed that Instagram could serve as a useful pedagogical tool to complement existing distance learning platforms, even beyond the COVID-19 pandemic (Ye et al., 2020).

Moreover, at the Italian Language Program at Indiana University Bloomington, Ardeni et al. (2021) extensively used social media, such as Instagram and Facebook and a Karaoke Project that involved a series of video portraits, as community-building activities during and after the transition from face to face to online instruction.

A third group of studies focused on the strategies and activities that proved to be effective in enhancing engagement in DL courses during the COVID-19 pandemic. Examples include the following: using a learner-centered approach that offers rich learning choices to the students (Zayabalaradjane, 2020); promoting active learning in learners by providing opportunities to read, write, discuss, think, ask questions, solve problems, analyze and create new things depending on the learning content (Zayapragassarazan, 2020); involving cognitive engagement, metacognitive language learning strategies, self-regulated learning, English language learning motivation, critical thinking as a manifestation of students' cognitive engagement, and connecting teaching materials to the students' daily life (Yundayani et al., 2021); conducting interaction-based classes (Krause & Goering, 2021); doing small group activities and projects (Orlov et al., 2020); using asynchronous videos instead of synchronous, live meetings (Lowenthal et al., 2020); giving formative assessment (Chen et al., 2021); (8) building student-instructor relationships (Gares et al., 2020); supporting students through the course community and students' personal community (Borup et al., 2020; Billings & Lagunoff, 2020); and developing a social presence in communities of language learners (Lomicka, 2020).

In addition, Abou-Khalil et al. (2021) found that the most effective teaching-learning strategies in DL are student-content engagement strategies (screen sharing, summaries, and class recordings), followed by student-teacher strategies (Q and A sessions and reminders) and the least effective are student-student strategies (group chat and collaborative work). They also found that the effectiveness of the engagement strategies depended on the students' gender and degree of access to technology.

The above literature review shows lack of studies that explore online activities that EFL, linguistics and translation instructors at Saudi universities are using in developing language and translation skills to help students apply and practice those skills in the DL environment during the COVID-19 pandemic in fall 2020 and spring 2021. Therefore, the current study aims to fill a gap in the EFL, linguistics and translation literature and shed some light on how instructors and students at a sample of Saudi language and translation departments are coping with the emergency DL environment.

3 Methodology

3.1 Subjects

Subjects of the current study consisted of 35 female college instructors teaching a variety of EFL, linguistics and translation courses at seven Saudi universities: King Saud University, Princess Noura University, Prince Sultan University, King Abdul-Aziz University, Umm Al-Qura University, King Khalid University, and the Saudi Electronic University. *Almost half* (45%) of the instructors have a Ph.D. and 55% have an M.A. degree in TESOL, linguistics or English Literature. In addition, 75 female students enrolled in a variety of EFL, linguistics and translation courses at the sample institutions were selected. One fifth of the sample (20%) of them were M.A. students and 80% were undergraduate students in different college levels.

3.2 Data Collection

The instructor survey consisted of several open-ended questions that asked the instructors about the following: (1) the kind of online EFL, linguistics and/or translation activities they have been using in the Fall Semester 2020 and Spring Semester 2021, (2) benefits and shortcomings of teaching EFL, linguistics and/or translation via DL, (3) how instructors engage, encourage and support students in online EFL, linguistics and/or translation courses, (4) course material and teaching techniques used in online EFL, linguistics and/or translation instruction, (5) attendance, homework, participation, self-efficacy and level of perseverance in online EFL, linguistics and/or translation courses, (6) interaction and communication between the students and instructors in online EFL, linguistics and translation courses, and (7) how feedback is given by instructors and classmates.

Similarly, the questionnaire-survey for the students consisted of open-ended questions that asked the students about their experience practicing EFL, linguistics and/or translation skills online, and their reaction to online EFL, linguistics and/or translation activities, and whether they prefer to continue to practice EFL, linguistics or translation online after the pandemic is over and why.

One limitation of this study is that it was not possible to get students' marks in face-to-face EFL, linguistics and/or translation courses before the pandemic and students' marks enrolled in the online EFL, linguistics and/or translation courses offered during the spring 2020 and fall 2021. Therefore, comparisons of the face-to-face speaking and online speaking activities and the effect of online EFL, linguistics and/or translation activities on students' EFL, linguistics and/or translation skills development are based on students and instructors' responses to surveys sent to them via WhatsApp. Assessing the degree of engagement in each activity mentioned by the subjects was beyond the scope of the current study.

3.3 Data Analysis

Responses to the instructor and student surveys were analyzed qualitatively as it is more important to report and describe the kinds of EFL, linguistics and/or translation activities used by the sample of instructors rather than reporting percentages or frequencies of instructors and students giving the same response. The activities will not be classified according to subject area, because some of the activities can be used in any subject area such as attending thesis defenses, debates, searching for concepts and specialized terminology, project-based and problem-solving questions, student-created videos or student-created podcasts.

4 Results

4.1 Types of Activities Used by the Sample

Results of the survey in fall 2020 and spring 2021 showed that EFL, linguistics and/or translation instructors in the sample went beyond using a PowerPoint in DL as it was the case in fall 2020. They started to use online activities for increasing students' engagement in EFL, linguistics and/or translation. Students usually learn through activities that are meaningful and relevant to them, driven by their interests and self-initiated with guidance from teachers. The types of activities that EFL, linguistics and/or translation instructors reported are as follows:

1. *Searching for linguistic and translation key terms and concepts* given by the instructor, finding definitions, and giving examples about them. This is a very common activity in almost all linguistics courses such as pragmatics, semantics, contrastive analysis, text linguistics courses and others. Some translation instructors use this activity when they teach introduction to translation or problems of translation courses. Examples of translation terminology given are foreignization, domestication, modulation, calque, eponym, transliteration, polysemy, ambiguity and others.

2. *Answering problem-solving questions.* This is the second most popular activity. It is similar to the oral presentations described above. The difference is only in the EFL, linguistics and translation topics selected. Here, the students may propose solutions to first and second language acquisition, listening, speaking, reading, writing, grammar, vocabulary, specific translation problems and/or linguistic issues with or without prior preparation at home. Further problem-solving questions given are:
   - Solving the digital gap during COVID-19
   - Creating new jobs for the COVID-19 era
   - Misunderstanding Islamic expressions by foreigners
   - High school students' low proficiency level in English
   - Combating spelling weaknesses

3. *Online debates about some issues.* This is the third most common activity. Here, the students are divided into two teams with contradictory points of view. Each team tries to convince the audience with their point of by giving examples and justifications. Some of the debate topics given are:
   - Should we teach English to children under the age of six?
   - Is the grammar-translation method effective in teaching English to beginners?
   - The best theory of second language acquisition
   - The best foreign language teaching methodology
   - Does educational reform start from the teacher or the curriculum?

4. *Summarizing a research paper* in first and second language acquisition, linguistic theory, discourse analysis, error analysis, translation studies, and translation errors in writing or giving an oral presentation about it

showing its strengths and weakness. This assignment is usually given to graduate students.

5. *Attending a thesis defense* in EFL, applied linguistics, theoretical linguistics and/or translation, and writing a report about it (strengths and weaknesses). This activity is more common with graduate than undergraduate students.

6. *Inviting specialized guest speakers.* This is a common activity among some instructors, and is suitable for any college level being easily adaptable to the students' proficiency level. A subject specialist is invited to join the online class session to talk about research methodology in language teaching, linguistics and/or translation, translation strategies, translation problems. Sometimes graduate students studying abroad are invited to talk about their experience studying abroad and some of the challenges that some female students, in particular, face, or any other topics. Before the online session, the students prepare questions to ask. During the session, they take turns to ask the questions one at a time. They listen to the answer and take notes. After the session, they write a report in which they summarize the guest's answers to the issues raised in the interview.

7. *Project-based assignments.* Since plants and flowers in the environment around the students have common and botanical names, an intriguing assignment given by a lecturer at King Saud University to undergraduate students enrolled in her translation and linguistics courses is about plant/flower names in English and Arabic. The instructor asks each student to choose a plant/flower, plant it, take a picture of it and write a post about it. In the post, the students are required to explain the metaphorical meaning of the plant or flower name in English and/or Arabic, explain why the metaphorical name was adopted, then translate the common and/or botanical names from English to Arabic and vice versa as in the examples in Table 4.1.

8. *Connecting writing and speaking topics with the Kingdom's Vision 2030.* In writing assignments, few instructors choose topics based on the Kingdom's Vision 2030 such as improving life quality, humanizing cities, ecological balance and others. The students are asked to write an essay in which they relate such topics to Vision 2030.

9. *Collecting and analyzing translation errors.* Few instructors ask the students to collect English/Arabic and Arabic/English translation errors from subtitled TV movies, news broadcasts, canned food labels, candy wrappers, street signs, billboards and ads. They are asked to correct the errors.

TABLE 4.1   Some flower names in English and Arabic

English (common) name	Latin (botanical) name	Arabic name
Frangipani, red paucipan, red-jasmine, red frangipani, common frangipani, temple tree	plumeria	الفتنة - الياسمين الهندي
Snap dragon, great snapdragon, lion's mouth, rabbit's mouth, bonny rabbits, calf snout, toad's mouth, bulldogs, lion's snap	antirrhinum majus	فم السمكة - حنك السبع
Flaming Glorybower	clerodendrum splendens, verbenaceae	طربوش الملك - اكليز
Elephant bush, dwarf jade plant, porkbush, spekboom	portulacaria afra	دمعة الطفل - العقيق - غذاء الفيل - نبات الفيل
Rose moss, eleven o'clock, Mexican rose, moss rose, sun rose, rock rose, moss-rose purslane	portulaca grandiflora	صباح الخير - زهرة الصباح - رجلة الزهور
Paper flower, Santa Rita, Napoleón	bougainvillea bugambilia, veranera, trinitaria, papelillo	الجهنمية - المجنونة - البوغَنْفيلِيَة - البوغَنْفيليا

10. *Translating Wikipedia articles* from English to Arabic. Students enrolled in translation courses select some Wikipedia articles that they would like to translate. The translated articles are posted online for the instructor and classmates to make comments on the translation quality and accuracy. However, students enrolled in the same course are not usually critical of their classmates' translated articles. They mainly give compliments and positive rather than negative feedback and judgments of the translation quality.
11. *Interpreting contest.* Sometimes, interpreting contests are held online where the instructor can play parts of an audio of a lecture or conference talk, which the students listen to, and engage in interpreting each part. Contests are held for both consecutive and simultaneous interpreting.
12. *Analyzing family speech.* Few instructors give some assignments that require the students to listen to family members in spontaneous speech

at home and focus on particular linguistic issues that the students study in linguistics (pragmatics, semantics, stylistics, etc.) classes such as:
- analyzing errors in daily speech (قاعدة أمشي)
- collecting examples of collocations and idiom (طار من الفرح، نجوم السماء) (اقرب له محلك سر، هلا وغلا، كفيت ووفيت، اصل وفصل
- collecting examples of slips of the tongue (فاهمة علي، سامعتني، ماشي، تمام)
- collecting examples of mannerisms
- observing and collecting phrases or forms that small children use such as overgeneralizing the sound feminine plural (هديات)

13. *Linguistic analysis of a video*. Few instructors who teach undergraduate students enrolled in pragmatics, semantics, and linguistics courses ask the students to select a stand-up comedy, an Oprah Winfrey Talk Show or a speech video and analyze it in terms of (1) the formal, lexical, conceptual semantic theories, (2) the speech acts contained in it, (3) interaction, and (4) pragmatic relations and other linguistic issues. The students give examples and discuss them in writing or orally.

14. *Student-created digital stories*. Few instructors ask the students to create a video that is 3–4 minutes long in which they tell a digital story using some semantic notions. For example, a student created an ethnolinguistic profile of herself, which can be found at https://www.youtube.com/watch?v=WuxPs2Vc87o&ab_channel=MadaAlk

15. *Student-created podcasts*. A lecturer at the English Department at King Saud University created a Speaking Center on Twitter where volunteer students enrolled in her online courses create their own podcasts on topics of their choice. The students record, stream and/or upload their podcasts using the SoundCloud App. During the pandemic, the students have created a total of 17 podcasts. The following are examples of student-created podcasts:
- Acacia Iteaphylla, https://soundcloud.com/user-902447197/acacia-iteaphylla
- Foreign Language in a Nutshell, https://soundcloud.com/user-902447197/foreign-language-in-a-nutshell
- Are We Evil? https://soundcloud.com/user-902447197/are-we-evil
- Self-sufficiency, https://soundcloud.com/user-902447197/are-you-being-your-best-self
- What Shaped Our 90's, https://soundcloud.com/user-902447197/what-shaped-our-90s
- Flat Earth Theory, https://soundcloud.com/user-902447197/
- Code-switching: With or against, and why? https://soundcloud.com/user-902447197/code-switching-with-or-against

- What could possibly happen in our sleep? https://soundcloud.com/user-902447197/what-could-possibly-happen-in
- Being Mindfully Present, https://soundcloud.com/user-902447197/being-mindfully-present

16. *Integrating Technology*
    - *Slido:* Some instructors ask questions about an issue and the students use Slido to answer the questions. The answers appear on a PPT slide. The students vote for the best answer and give reasons for their choice. They can also write a one-page reflection on an issue that was discussed.
    - *Padlet:* Some instructors in the sample use Padlet, an app that is similar to paper for the screen. The instructor starts with an empty page and then puts whatever she likes on it. The instructor or students can upload a video, record an interview, or snap a picture. Students write their own text posts, upload some documents, and watch their Padlet come to life. Once other students add to it, the page will update in real time. Students write comments on each other's views and expectations.
    - *ConnectionYard:* Instructors at the Saudi Electronic University use ConnectionYard, a social engagement platform that can be integrated with Google Classroom, Zoom, Microsoft Teams, Edmodo, Moodle, Canvas, Blackboard. It has different types of messaging (text, social media, or email) to reach everyone using their current devices on their preferred messaging channels. It allows interaction with learning content, improving measures of performance and attendance. It has an analytics capability that allows measuring and tracking high performing classrooms, teachers, and students.

4.2   *Student-Instructor Communication*

The students reported that during the DL English, linguistics and/or translation classes, they communicate with their instructors and sometimes make comments and/or ask questions via the platforms' hand raising tool and chat. Before and after classes, they mostly communicate with their instructors via WhatsApp. Some instructors form a WhatsApp group for students enrolled in a particular section or course. A student may communicate with her instructor privately if she does not wish to ask questions or seek help in public. Other social media such as Facebook, Twitter, Telegram, or Instagram are not used for student-instructor communication.

4.3   *Motivating the Students*

Most of the online EFL, linguistics and/or translation activities used to develop the students' English, linguistic and translation skills in the DL environment are student-centered, project-based, and require problem-solving. Students search for and prepare the assigned topics at home, read about the topic, summarize and/or synthesize information from different sources. They usually prepare an online oral presentation or a written response. Students take their activities seriously and work hard because they are given marks for each assignment. Unlike DL during the lockdown when marks allocated to attendance and semester work were canceled and only 20% of the course mark was allocated to final exams; in fall 2020 and spring 2021, the instructors used formative assessment in the online EFL, linguistics and translation courses as the university administration emphasized the allocation of marks to attendance and classwork. The instructors gave marks for participating in the online activities, class attendance, and completing written or oral assignments. Some instructors used an assessment rubric such as creativity 2 marks, originality 1 mark, grammar 1 mark, accuracy 2 marks, division of work 1 mark, presentation of examples 1 mark, and clarity 1 mark. The components of the assessment rubrics and marks allocated to them differed from one type of activity to another, from course to course, and instructor to instructor.

4.4 Students' Views

Analysis of the students' responses to the survey showed that the online EFL, linguistics and translation activities were beneficial, enjoyable, and helpful. Their English language, linguistic analysis and/or translation skills improved a lot as a result of reading, preparing and synthesizing information from different resources and the feedback given to them from their instructors during the online class sessions. Although at the beginning of the semester, many students were shy, nervous and were hesitant to participate, but at the end of the semester they gained self-confidence due to weekly practice and instructors' encouragement, and support. The online sessions reduced their stress especially because they could turn off their video and just focus on listening to the content presented. Some students wrote:

- *Samia*: The activities are valuable. My translation skills have improved as a result of weekly assignments, preparation and online discussion.
- *Hana*: the teacher was kind, patient, and she paid attention to each student.
- *Sara*: the teacher provided valuable feedback. I learned a lot from the commented on my translation, grammatical and stylistic errors.
- *Madawi*: the online practice we received in the pragmatics course was beneficial. I learned how to apply pragmatic theory to real-life situations.
- *Dalia*: practicing English writing on the DL platform helped me focus better on generating ideas and connecting them with the Kingdom's Vision 2030.
- *Lara*: The online class is quiet with no distractions. I go online in the comfort of my home. I can turn my webcam off. Thus, I concentrate better.

The students found the hand-raising tool useful because they could use it to ask questions. During the online EFL, linguistics and/or translation practice, the students chose to turn off their video and use the audio only.

Other advantages of online EFL, linguistics and translation courses reported by the students were that they could join the platform through their laptop or smart phone. They did not have to commute to college and waste time in the traffic jam. They could replay the recording of the class session, especially if they miss a live EFL, linguistics and/or translation session.

Conversely, some students indicated that online EFL, linguistics and translation activities are not like face-to-face activities in the sense of community they feel with their classmates in the classroom. In the real classroom, there is eye contact, gestures, and more rapport among classmates which are absent in DL. They can also engage in some collaborative, small-group activities and projects, which they could not engage in in DL as they cannot meet with some classmates in person due to the social distancing measures during the pandemic.

4.5 Instructors' Views

EFL, linguistics and translation instructors at the sample institutions in the current study indicated that DL in fall 2020 and spring 2021 has been more effective than DL in spring 2020. In the Fall Semester 2020 and the Spring Semester 2021, the students became more attentive, interactive, and interested in learning, participating, and doing assignments and working on projects. Most instructors in the current study had a positive attitude toward the online EFL, linguistics and translation classes. There was more engagement in the activities, interaction and communication among the students and instructors. Back in spring 2020, various issues occurred–the university dismissed the marks allocated to classwork and attendance, the students were not proficient enough to use the DL platform and its tools, they had no previous DL experience, and they had problems operating DL platforms and getting internet connectivity. As instructors, they gained more experience in handling the different tools in Zoom, WebEx, Microsoft Teams and/or Blackboard. They had a chance to practice and explore and thus became more familiar with the platform. They also learned from colleagues who are more competent in using the DL platforms and digital material.

By contrast, in teaching EFL, linguistics and translation courses via Zoom, WebEx, Microsoft Teams, and similar applications, the instructors and students could only hear each other's voices but not see each other's faces on the screen as both instructors and students turned off their platform video.

Another challenge that the instructors have is reading the questions in the chat while listening and paying attention to students' online oral presentations,

debates and discussions in addition to responding to students' queries on WhatsApp. As the students stated in their responses, some face-to-face EFL, linguistics and translation activities cannot be performed in small groups via the platform as the students could not get together to work on their projects. Some instructors wrote:
- *Lana*: I am enjoying my online classes because the students are hardworking, and they submit intriguing responses to their projects and assignments.
- *Abeer*: I am pleased because the students are making progress and respond positively to feedback.
- *Muneera*: DL has given me a chance to explore new teaching strategies that I did not try face-to-face in the classroom.
- *Dana*: DL gives me an opportunity to exchange knowledge and expertise about online activities and digital material related to the courses that I teach.
- *Salwa*: Students in my courses do not sufficiently interact with each other probably because they do not know each other, especially in lower college levels.

5 Discussion

Findings of the present study showed that EFL, linguistics and translation activities utilized by instructors at the sample universities mainly focus on searching for linguistic and translation key terms and concepts, online debates about some issues, summarizing a research paper, attending a thesis defense and writing a report about it, translating Wikipedia articles from English to Arabic, interpreting contests, answering problem-solving questions, project-based assignments, inviting specialized guest speakers, linguistic analysis of a video, student-created digital stories, analyzing family-speech, relating writing and speaking topics to Vision 2030, collecting and analyzing translation errors, student-created podcasts, and using technologies such as Slido, Padlet and ConnectYard in combination with the platform. However, none of the instructors in the present study integrated social media such as Facebook, Twitter and Instagram for interaction, communication and learning purposes as in prior studies by Ucar and Goksel (2020), Moghadam and Shamsi (2021), Kunka (2020), Ye et al. (2020), and Ardeni et al. (2021). Similarly, none of the instructors in the current study used audiographic conferencing VLE, multimedia resources, asynchronous video, the Karaoke Project, or small group activities and projects as in prior studies by Rosell-Aguilar (2005), Develotte et al. (2005), Nobre (2018), and Lowenthal et al. (2020).

As in Abou-Khalil et al.'s study (2021), the activities applied by instructors in the current study seem to be effective in promoting students' engagement with the content and with the instructor but not as much with the students themselves. The students were able to engage with the content using screen sharing, summaries, and class recordings. They were able to interact with the instructor through question-and-answer sessions and reminders. There was little interaction-based learning among the students. The students did not show much interaction with each other through the group chat and collaborative work as most of the activities were conducted individually and the students made few comments on each other's performance.

Furthermore, the types of activities applied in the current study are consistent with the teaching approaches and strategies recommended by Yundayani et al. (2021), Krause and Goering (2021), Orlov et al. (2020), Zayabalaradjane (2020), Zayapragassarazan (2020), Lowenthal et al. (2020), Chen et al. (2021), Gares et al. (2020), Borup et al. (2020), Billings and Lagunoff (2020), and Lomicka (2020). Activities in the current study are learner-centered. They promote active learning, cognitive engagement, metacognitive language learning strategies, self-regulated learning, motivate students to learn, encourage critical thinking, and connect the subject matter to the students' daily life. They also use formative assessment. In addition, they focus on student-instructor relationships, and a learning environment that supports students through the course community.

6   Recommendations and Conclusion

Although most of the activities used by EFL, linguistics and translation instructors at the sample universities in the current study are intriguing and innovative in nature, they are not all-inclusive. More engaging, interactive, and interesting EFL, linguistics and translation activities can be utilized in the DL environment during the COVID-19 pandemic as in the following examples:
– Integrating mobile apps to help students use TOEFL, IELTS, prefixes, suffixes, monolingual and bilingual dictionaries, literature, history of the English language and additional linguistics resources (Al-Jarf, 2020c, 2021f).
– Integrating mobile audiobooks only. Mobile audiobooks are those that combine reading and speaking activities and/or are those that combine listening and speaking activities which students can use on their own at home, and then perform some activities during the online class session such as summarizing the content, answering auditory comprehension questions, or reflecting on the story orally or in writing (Al-Jarf, 2021e).

- Using a variety of online speaking activities such as preparing a topic at home and giving an online oral presentation about it; using online debates; answering problem-solving questions; student-created podcasts; combining listening and speaking activities; using some apps (Al-Jarf, 2021b).
- Using TED Talks as a listening resource in EFL instruction (Al-Jarf, 2021h).
- Using a class blog to write about COVID-19 and current global events (Al-Jarf, 2022a, 2022b).
- Enriching students' vocabulary with online vocabulary tasks, mobile apps and mobile flashcards (Al-Jarf, 2021f, 2022c, 2022d).
- Struggling EFL college students may collaborate in mobile ebook reading (Al-Jarf, 2021a).
- Students enrolled in online EFL courses may read multicultural children's stories at home and give a summary, answer questions, or reflect on the story orally or in writing during the online class session (Al-Jarf, 2015).
- Inspirational quotes can be used as online activities for practicing reading comprehension, vocabulary skills, literary appreciation and linguistic analysis (Al-Jarf, 2021a).
- Integrating linguistic landscapes in reading and linguistics activities. Linguistic landscapes cover street signs, direction, warning signs, names of places and tourist attractions and ads displayed in public spaces. They are concise, and make use of authentic language, and specific grammatical structures, idioms and imagery. They can be used to practice vocabulary skills, abbreviations and acronyms, and British and American varieties of English. They can also be used to practice on grammatical structures (negative structures, commands, passive, ellipsis, reduced clauses, and emphatic structures). Moreover, they are useful for building reading comprehension skills, working out inferring meaning of difficult words and the purpose of a sign, drawing students' attention to differences in font types and sizes in the signs, resolving anaphora, analyzing imagery, and making pragmatic and discoursal analysis (Al-Jarf, 2021d).
- Students can engage in synchronous or asynchronous collaborative Arabization and translation practice on Twitter or an online discussion forum (Al-Jarf, 2017, 2019, 2020d).
- Social media such as Twitter, Facebook, Telegram, and Instagram can be used for oral and written communication between students and instructors and among the students themselves (Al-Jarf, 2020a).

Finally, this study recommends that future studies investigate levels of engagement in each type of activity and assess the impact of each activity on EFL, linguistics, translation, and interpreting skill development. Since the students are going to be studying face-to-face starting from the Fall Semester 2021, research studies that explore whether instructors and students prefer to continue to practice EFL, linguistics and translation online in combination with face-to-face EFL, linguistics and translation classes is open for further investigation by researchers in the future.

Notes

1. twitter.com/uqu_edu/status/1419736748595290116?s=08
2. https://www.edglossary.org/student-engagement/#:~:text=In%20education%2C%20student%20engagement%20refers,and%20progress%20in%20their%20education
3. https://www.csusb.edu/student-engagement/benefits-engagement
4. https://www.prodigygame.com/main-en/blog/student-engagement-strategies/

References

Abou-Khalil, V., Helou, S., Khalifé, E., Chen, M., Majumdar, R. & Ogata, H. (2021). Emergency online learning in low-resource settings: Effective student engagement strategies. *Education Sciences, 11*, art. 24.

Al-Jarf, R. (2015, April 23–24). *Enhancing reading and speaking skills in EFL through multicultural children's short stories* [Paper]. 7th International Conference Building Cultural Bridges (ICBCB), Integrating languages, linguistics, literature, translation, and journalism into education. Suleyman Demire lUniversity, Almaty, Kazakhstan. https://doi.org/10.2139/ssrn.3848464

Al-Jarf, R. (2017). Exploring online collaborative translator training in an online discussion forum. *Journal of Applied Linguistics and Language Research (JALLR), 4*(4), 147–160. https://files.eric.ed.gov/fulltext/ED613072.pdf

Al-Jarf, R. (2019). Effects of electronic homework-assignments on Arabization skill development in student-translators. *Journal for Research Scholars and Professionals of English Language Teaching, 16*(3), 1–14. https://files.eric.ed.gov/fulltext/ED613087.pdf

Al-Jarf, R. (2020a). Communication among instructors and students via Twitter. In I. Vassileva, M. Chankova, E. Breuer, & K. P. Schneider (Eds.), *The digital scholar: Academic communication in multimedia environment* (pp. 265–280). Frank & Timme GmbH.

Al-Jarf, R. (2020b). Distance learning and undergraduate Saudi students' agency during the Covid-19 pandemic. *Bulletin of the Transylvania University of Braşov Series IV: Philology and Cultural Studies, 13*(62), 37–54. https://doi.org/10.31926/but.pcs.2020.62.13.2.4

Al-Jarf, R. (2020c). Mobile apps in the EFL college classroom. *Journal for Research Scholars and Professionals of English Language Teaching*, 4(22), 1–5.

Al-Jarf, R. (2020d). Issues in interactive translation practice on Twitter. In *Proceedings of the 16th international scientific conference eLearning and software for education* (3, pp. 427–437). http://dx.doi.org/10.2139/ssrn.3842157

Al-Jarf, R. (2021a). Collaborative mobile ebook reading for struggling EFL college readers. *IOSR Journal of Research and Methods in Education*, 11(6), 32–42. https://www.iosrjournals.org/iosr-jrme/papers/Vol-11%20Issue-6/Ser-2/D1106023242.pdf

Al-Jarf, R. (2021b). EFL speaking practice in distance learning during the coronavirus pandemic 2020–2021. *International Journal of Research – GRANTHAALAYAH*, 9(7), 179–196. https://doi.org/10.29121/granthaalayah.v9.i7.2021.4094

Al-Jarf, R. (2021c). Enhancing EFL freshman students' reading skills with inspirational quotes. *Asian Research Journal of Arts & Social Sciences (ARJASS)*, 13(4), 1–11. https://doi.org/10.9734/arjass/2021/v13i430219

Al-Jarf, R, (2021d). Investigating equity in distance learning in Saudi Arabia during the COVID-19 pandemic. In *Proceedings of the 17th international scientific conference eLearning and software for education*, Bucharest, Romania (Vol. 1, pp. 13–21). doi:10.12753/2066-026X-21-001

Al-Jarf, R. (2021e). Mobile audiobooks, listening comprehension and EFL college students. *International Journal of Research – GRANTHAALAYAH*, 9(4), 410–423. https://doi.org/10.29121/granthaalayah.v9.i4.2021.3868

Al-Jarf, R. (2021f). Standardized test preparation with mobile flashcard apps. *United International Journal for Research & Technology*, 3(2), 33–40. https://uijrt.com/paper/standardized-test-preparation-with-mobile-flashcard-apps

Al-Jarf, R. (2021g). Teaching English with linguistic landscapes to Saudi students studying abroad. *Asian Journal of Language, literature, and Culture Studies (AJL2CS)*, 4(3), 1–12.

Al-Jarf, R. (2021h). TED talks as a listening resource in EFL college classrooms. *International Journal of Language and Literary Studies*, 2(3), 256–267. https://doi.org/10.36892/ijlls.v2i3.691

Al-Jarf, R. (2022a). Blogging about the COVID-19 pandemic in EFL writing practice. *Journal of Learning and Development Studies*, 2(1), 1–8. https://doi.org/10.32996/jlds.2022.2.1.1

Al-Jarf, R. (2022b). Blogging about current global events in the EFL writing classroom: Effects on skill improvement, global awareness and attitudes. *British Journal of Teacher Education and Pedagogy*, 1(1), 73–82. https://doi.org/10.32996/bjtep.2022.1.1.8

Al-Jarf, R. (2022c). Learning vocabulary in the app store by EFL college students. *International Journal of Social Science and Human Research*, 5(1), 216–225. doi:10.47191/ijsshr/v5-i1-30. http://ijsshr.in/v5i1/30.php

Al-Jarf, R. (2022d). Online vocabulary tasks for engaging and motivating EFL college students in distance learning during the pandemic and post-pandemic. *International Journal of English Language Studies, 4*(1), 14–24. doi:10.32996/ijels.2022.4.1.2

Ardeni, V., Dallavalle, S. & Serafin, K. (2021). Building student communities in spite of the COVID-19 pandemic. *Journal of Teaching and Learning with Technology, 10*, 88–102.

Billings, E., & Lagunoff, R. (2020). *Supporting English learners during school closures: Considerations for designing distance.* Crisis Response Resource. https://files.eric.ed.gov/fulltext/ED605945.pdf

Borup, J., Jensen, M., Archambault, L., Short, C., & Graham, C. (2020). Supporting students during COVID-19: Developing and leveraging academic communities of engagement in a time of crisis. *Journal of Technology and Teacher Education, 28*(2), 161–169.

Chen, Z., Jiao, J., & Hu, K. (2021). Formative assessment as an online instruction intervention: Student engagement, outcomes, and perceptions. *International Journal of Distance Education Technologies, 19*(1), art. 4, 50–65.

Develotte, C., Mangenot, F., & Zourou, K. (2005). Situated creation of multimedia activities for distance learners: Motivational and cultural issues. *ReCALL, 17*(2), 229–244.

Gares, S., Kariuki, J., & Rempel, B. (2020). Community matters: Student-instructor relationships foster student motivation and engagement in an emergency remote teaching environment. *Journal of Chemical Education, 97*(9), 3332–3335.

Krause, A., & Goering, E. (2021). Like peas in a pod: A strategy for creatively transposing interaction-based classes into an online learning environment. *Journal of Teaching and Learning with Technology, 10*, 279–293.

Kunka, B. (2020). Twitter in higher education: Increasing student engagement. *Educational Media International, 57*(4), 316–331.

Lomicka, L. (2020). Creating and sustaining virtual language communities. *Foreign Language Annals, 53*(2), 306–313.

Lowenthal, P., Borup, J., West, R., & Archambault, L. (2020). Thinking beyond Zoom: Using asynchronous video to maintain connection and engagement during the COVID-19 pandemic. *Journal of Technology and Teacher Education, 28*(2), 383–391.

Moghadam, M., & Shamsi, H. (2021). Exploring learners' attitude toward Facebook as a medium of learners' engagement during COVID-19 quarantine. *Open Praxis, 13*(1), 103–116.

Nobre, A. (2018). Multimedia technologies and online task-based foreign language teaching-learning. *Tuning Journal for Higher Education, 5*(2), 75–97.

Orlov, G., McKee, D., Berry, J., Boyle, A., DiCiccio, T., Ransom, T., Rees-Jones, A., & Stoye, J. (2020). *Learning during the COVID-19 pandemic: It is not who you teach, but how you teach.* NBER Working Paper 28022. National Bureau of Economic Research, Inc. https://ideas.repec.org/p/nbr/nberwo/28022.html

Rosell-Aguilar, F. (2005). Task design for audiographic conferencing: Promoting beginner oral interaction in distance language learning. *Computer Assisted Language Learning, 18*(5), 417–442.

Ucar, H., & Goksel, N. (2020). Enhancing online EFL learners' motivation and engagement through supplementary activities on Facebook. *Asian Journal of Distance Education, 15*(1), 154–168.

Ye, S., Hartmann, R., Söderström, M., Amin, M., Skillinghaug, B., Schembri, L., & Odell, L. (2020). Turning information dissipation into dissemination: Instagram as a communication enhancing tool during the COVID-19 pandemic and beyond. *Journal of Chemical Education, 97*(9), 3217–3222.

Yundayani, A., Abdullah, F., Tantan Tandiana, S., & Sutrisno, B. (2021). Students' cognitive engagement during emergency remote teaching: Evidence from the Indonesian EFL milieu. *Journal of Language and Linguistic Studies, 17*(1), 17–33.

Zayabalaradjane, Z. (2020). COVID-19: Strategies for online engagement of remote learners. *F1000Research, 9*(246), 1–11. https://doi.org/10.7490/f1000research.1117835.1

Zayapragassarazan, Z. (2020). COVID-19: Strategies for engaging remote learners in medical education. *F1000Research, 9*(273), 1–18. https://eric.ed.gov/?id=ED604479

CHAPTER 5

When Learning Was Disrupted in Saudi Arabia

Full-Scale Distance e-Learning as a Solution to Face COVID-*19*

Amani Khalaf Alghamdi and Wai Si El-Hassan

Abstract

This case study investigated the experiences of Saudi university students and faculty concerning a switch to e-learning from the traditional mode of lecturing in response to the national lockdown started in March 2020 due to the COVID-19 pandemic. By using purposive sampling of eight Twitter feeds (five Saudi universities, one faculty association and two from the Ministry of Education), this study thematically analyzed over 2,000 social media (Twitter) postings in Spring 2020 to investigate how Saudi students and faculty members met this crisis head on. Four major concerns over the use of emergency distance education to complete semester studies emerged: (1) information technology and technical issues, (2) understanding online learning materials, (3) student assessment issues, and (4) faculty compliance and student support. Findings showed there is a need to train faculty and students to engage with distance learning, embrace fair and balanced student assessment strategies, and implement course design intelligence.

Keywords

e-learning – technological solutions – higher education – social media (Twitter) – Saudi Arabia

1   Introduction

This paper was first written in August 2020 exploring how both university students and faculty responded to distance e-learning (DeL) in the form of emergency distance education in Saudi Arabia during an ongoing global health threat. When the world was hit by COVID-19, the coronavirus pandemic caused an enormous global upheaval. Learners of all ages, regardless of geographical location, education level or abilities, were facing learning disruptions. Although many students expected the 2020 spring term to be 'business-as-usual,' it all changed the minute their government announced their respective lockdowns.

In a vast country where local populations are sparsely spaced out, such as Saudi Arabia, university students make daily efforts in traveling to their universities, which often means journeying through deserts. Lockdowns imposed because of the pandemic have caused students to stay home and adopt distance e-learning via online platforms. However, this alternative approach has not necessarily provided comfort to them in learning, despite that physically traveling to university is no longer required.

Responding to the impact on Saudi higher education caused by the pandemic, various scholars collected research data in a timely manner. For example, Shawaqfeh et al. (2020) conducted a survey to investigate pharmacy students' perceptions whereas Alrefaie et al. (2020) drew up a portfolio to monitor online learning during the pandemic. Furthermore, Khalil et al. (2020) conducted a qualitative study using virtual focus group discussions to explore medical students' perspectives.

Khalil et al.'s (2020) study has a central focus on medical students; therefore, does not give a broad view of students from other disciplines across the country. As a result, Twitter, a popular online microblogging platform used among students and faculty in Saudi Arabia, was utilized to collect massive data to capture their experience of emergency distance education.

The guiding research question of this study is "what were the experiences of Saudi university students and faculty concerning a switch to e-learning from the traditional mode of lecturing in response to the national lockdown started in March 2020 due to the COVID-19 pandemic?"

This case study has examined the filtered data and from the findings, eight implications were made in the hope to strengthen the distance education in Saudi Arabia, where teacher-centered, traditional classroom approach was prized.

2   Literature Review

The nature of education is evolving and was spurred on by successive industrial revolutions, four in total. The concept of the industrial revolution pertains to technology being invented to help make people's lives easier (Pouspourika, 2019). The evolution in education within the last 300 to 400 years has been astonishing (Alhawaj, 2020). The Fourth Industrial Revolution (4IR), also known as the technological or digital revolution, started "in the dawn of the third millennium" when the internet became widely available (Pouspourika, 2019, para. 12).

While attending the Davos economic world summit in winter 2019, Schleicher (2019) identified several megatrends that are shaping education during the 4IR. Schools must deal with issues resulting from economic inequality; diverse student social and cultural backgrounds; economic insecurity; digitalization (that causes the world to become more complex, uncertain and unstable than ever before); and misuse of the internet (e.g., excessive personal screen time and cyberbullying). During this fourth industrial revolution, which is still unfolding unpredictably, it seems that "education must be prepared to change with technology" (Schleicher, 2019, para. 12). However, steps should be taken to ensure that technology does not drive education; it should augment it.

Adding to the trajectory of educational challenges brought about by technological advancement (Schleicher, 2019), the COVID-19 pandemic stopped human activities in their tracks. The whole world ground to a halt, almost overnight. Although daily lives were disrupted, universities and schools around the world found a 21st century technological solution to ensure that education and learning could persevere. Ways were being found to deliver curricula via technology while trying to ensure student academic success and meet their social, mental and emotional needs. Additional concerns of social distancing and safety for one's life have entered the fray, meaning educators must find ways to use technology to address social-emotional learning and trauma-induced consequences of struggles with learning and adapting to fear and uncertainty (Cheung et al., 2020).

Crises, such as pandemics, can be a catalyst for real and substantive educational change (Moran, 2012). To face the 2020 pandemic's disruption in education, DeL was adopted out of necessity on almost on a global scale. It seems that distance education will prevail, develop and be perfected alongside traditional classroom learning, which itself may require less frequent in-person attendance (Daniel, 2020; Zhao, 2020). As Zhao (2020) concluded in his paper titled, "COVID-19 as a Catalyst for Educational Change," education must be reconfigured in the wake of the pandemic, so it routinely includes DeL.

> I am hopeful that COVID-19, because of its disruptions to education, can inspire more schools to think of online education not as a lesser version of face-to-face education, but as a different way to organize education. (Zhao, 2020, p. 4)

This may be a wild hope, because there are many aspects of face-to-face learning that students usually miss when they move to DeL: robustness of in-class dialogue; dynamics and spontaneity in real-time classrooms; accuracy of assumptions about and perceptions of others; and the sense of being in a learning community (Stodel et al., 2006). That said, like Zhao (2020), we still view COVID-19 as a precursor to and catalyst for educational change.

3 Method

A social media platform (Twitter) was used to collect data from university students and teaching staff across Saudi Arabia to discern their insights and learning experiences during the 2020's COVID-19 global lockdown. The intent was to discover any pedagogical implications and make recommendations around the governmental/institutional support required for emergency distance education and DeL.

Launched in 2006, Twitter is a social networking service that is now a global phenomenon. Heading into 2020, there were 152 million monetizable daily active Twitter users worldwide (Clement, 2020). During the pandemic, "this platform was where Arabs were most actively conversing about coronavirus-related distance education" (Al Lily et al., 2020, p. 5). Registered users can post, like, comment, and retweet tweets, which were previously limited to 140 characters (but has now been expanded to 280 characters). Although usernames (usually fictitious) are visible, age, academic level and discipline are not easily identifiable thereby ensuring anonymity. The content of the tweets illuminates the different standpoints of both students and faculty. Twitter provides (1) readily accessible, extremely current data (Ahmed, 2019) and (2) participants can offer instant reactions, which can be deemed honest and truthful instead of being too polite to avoid causing offence or saying what someone wants to hear (e.g., courtesy bias). Also, it is deemed a useful way to immediately access emergent views on an unfolding situation.

Twitter data "represent a key source of information for anyone seeking to study 21st century society" (Ahmed, 2019, para. 2). Collecting research data using Twitter is a growing research design strategy (Ahmed, 2019). Panagiotopoulos et al. (2016) investigated using Twitter as a tool for emergency management and communicating with the public. Al-Ahdal et al. (2021) illustrated the pragmatic benefits of using tweets to communicate the spread of COVID-19 in Saudi Arabia. Arab scholars Al Lily et al. (2020) chose social media (specifically Twitter) to explore university students' reactions to crises distance education. They used the Twitter search bar to search for key words and specific #hashtags. This Saudi case study was conducted before their research was published.

3.1 *Sample Frame*

The study protocol employed purposeful sampling, which enables researchers to select the sample frame on purpose, because those people can best provide information to answer the research question (McGregor, 2018). The sample frame comprised eight Twitter feeds in total. To access university student and faculty member tweets, which are public knowledge, the researchers chose five large and accredited public Saudi universities and read their Twitter feeds to find comments pursuant to the shift to online distance e-learning during the COVID-19 pandemic.

The university Twitter accounts included King Saud University (@_KSU), Princess Nourah Bint Abdulrahman University (@_PNU_KSA), Imam Mohammad Bin Saud Islamic University (@IMSIU_edu_sa), King Abdulaziz University (@kauweb), and King Faisal University (@KFUniversity). There are close to 60 government-funded and private universities in Saudi Arabia (Allahmorad & Zreik, 2020) with these five institutions considered major Saudi universities (Quacquarelli Symonds, 2019). Plus, they are also located in Saudi Arabia's five main cities thereby better ensuring fair representation of educational offerings in the nation.

Another source was @saudi_dr for faculty members chosen because it reflects faculty and university issues. Finally, the sample frame included two Twitter feeds from the Ministry of Education (MoE) comprising university education (@mohe_sa) and general education (@moe_gov_sa). They were chosen, because they concern university- and education-related issues in Saudi Arabia, including delivery modes. Also, Saudi university students sometimes post their concerns at the MoE Twitter accounts.

3.2 Data Collection

Data were collected between March 18, 2020 and July 20, 2020 (a total of 4 months). One of the researchers and a research assistant (both Arabic-speaking) accessed Twitter feeds tendered from the early days of the 2020 spring semester after Saudi Arabia began its lockdown, and universities reverted exclusively to online learning platforms. The Arabic-language data were translated to English before both researchers coded and analyzed the collection. The data collection process used a code-in-use approach beginning with a preliminary start code list to which other terms were added as the coding unfolded (Miles & Huberman, 1994). The code list included such terms as COVID, coronavirus, pandemic, crisis, online learning, distance learning, distance education, exams, assessment, and assignments. Related tweets were identified through both hashtags and the tweet text. Per the latter, tweet texts were iteratively reread to discern emotions, sentiments, issues and concerns around the use of distance e-learning during the COVID-19 crisis. Also, researchers went to the section in each Twitter account called What's Trending.

The final N = 2,009 tweets found using this process comprised the final data set organized using two categories: students and university/MoE tweets. All Arabic-language tweets were translated to English before analysis. For clarification, we did not distinguish by specific institution in this paper. Also, comments from faculty and students were simply identified as such rather than assigning pseudonyms for individual people.

3.3 Data Analysis

The data set was then thematically analyzed to generate key messages embedded within. Ahmed (2019) identified thematic analysis as one of five popular research methods for analyzing Twitter feed data with others including content analysis, social network analysis, semantic analysis, and time-series analysis. Our process involved the researchers familiarizing themselves with the data set through iterative readings allowing patterns to emerge that they eventually defined, named and described using direct quotes from the tweets as evidence. That is, the researchers filtered the data and categorized the content into pervasive areas of concern as expressed by students and faculty members (Braun & Clarke, 2006). The main focus was qualitative data in the form of direct quotations; however, quantitative data emerged during data extraction and analysis. When relevant, these were reported as frequencies (Nicholson et al., 2016).

Coding occurred in a three-stage process. First, line-by-line coding of tweet text revealed pertinent data that were recorded word for word into the database. These entries reflected, as noted, emotions, sentiments, issues and concerns around the use of distance e-learning during the COVID-19 crisis. Second, iterative readings yielded groupings of codes based on similarities and differences. Third, these groupings were further refined and assigned a name representing the key message (Nicholson et al., 2016). To ensure the criterion of maximum variation sampling (Al Lily et al., 2020), a minimum of 20 tweets was collected as evidence for overall major concerns (key messages) emergent from the data (excluding "retweets" and spam). This amounted to 5% of the data set generated through the raw coding process. Ahmed (2019) confirmed that anywhere from 1% to 10% of the dataset is sufficient for thematic analysis.

To ensure trustworthy qualitative data, we ensured data saturation, and provided thick descriptions of the key messages using sufficient quotes to justify the theme claimed. We also strived for confirmability (i.e., made sure findings reflected respondents' themselves instead of any researchers' bias, credibility (i.e., analyzed data until a full answer was provided for the research questions) and dependability (i.e., provided sufficient method-related details so others can use the same research protocol in their context) (McGregor, 2018).

4 Findings and Discussion

The thematic analysis yielded four major concerns (key messages) expressed by Saudi university students and faculty members in their tweets about experiencing crisis distance education during the COVID-19 lockdown: (1) information technology and technical issues, (2) students' understanding of online

TABLE 5.1 Major emergency distance education concerns expressed by Saudi students and faculty members (N = 2,009 tweets from 8 Twitter feeds)

Theme	Percentage of total tweets
Technological and technical issues	34
Students' understanding of online learning materials	31
Assessment of students' learning	22
Faculty compliance with emergency distance education	9
Positive student feedback in the midst of pervasive negativity	4

learning materials, (3) student assessment issues, and (4) faculty compliance with emergency distance education and support for students. Also, there was positive student feedback in the midst of pervasive negativity (see Table 5.1). As an update, Al-Jarf's (2016; 2020a; 2020b; 2020c) recent survey results (September 17, 2020) revealed virtually the same thing with more than half (55%) of Saudi students registering deep dissatisfaction with many aspects of distance e-learning.

4.1 *Technological and Technical Issues*

Analysis revealed 20 overall student complaints about technical issues with DeL during the lockdown, which were further categorized into major areas: no laptops reflecting the digital divide, no or poor internet connection, and grade calculations in the Learning Management System (LMS) (see Figure 5.1). The possible solutions are tendered by the researchers not the sample frame.

Although Saudi Arabia is viewed as a rich country, a digital divide exists. Students basically have smartphones, but not everyone possessed a laptop or desktop computer with 15% of the tweets containing comments saying this situation made the mandatory distance e-learning inaccessible. And because of the lockdown, students said they could not readily purchase computers. The digital divide in Saudi Arabia was revealed patently. The government is urged to continue to resolve related issues through targeted budgeting and financing of IT and communications.

In some major cities, internet service is provided, but not every building where students lived had the infrastructure to support an internet connection. These affected students said their learning was badly impacted especially due to limited freedom of movement (i.e., the COVID social isolation imperative). Nearly three-quarters (70%) of the tweets reflected complaints about poor,

Technological issues		Possible solutions
1) No laptops/digital divide	➢	Provision of e-learning tools and devices, which will require government support
2) No internet connection	➢	Provision of 4G, which requires assistance from the private sector
3) Poor internet connection and its consequences	➢	See above. University collaboration in providing IT troubleshooting tips and relevant training
4) Grade calculations in the LMS	➢	To be discussed among the faculty members and university management

FIGURE 5.1 Technical issues with emergency distance education and possible solutions

sporadic and slow internet connection. This glitch caused a myriad of technical problems: the lecturers could not hear the students, the program or test failed to run, or the program or test froze and was unavailable. Many commented that the technical issue "could not be solved."

Some students strongly felt that their grades had suffered because of these technical issues with one student suggesting that the grade calculations in the LMS should be revised to reflect the grade that would have been earned had the technical issues not materialized. Our analysis revealed that both teaching staff and students were unprepared and lacked experience using LMS to conduct distance e-learning. They endured a steep learning curve. And technology-induced stress abounded, exemplified in this student's tweet about the online learning program freezing while taking an exam: "If all the course tests will be in this way, we will fail in all the courses."

To be fully prepared for the anticipated subsequent lockdowns, both the government and universities will need to (1) ensure a well-developed infrastructure for sustained internet connection and (2) make e-learning mandatory, so students can become accustomed to and comfortable with this alternative mode of learning. Furthermore, technical and administrative staff should compile a list of troubleshooting issues and train both teaching staff and students to handle these on their own (i.e., "self-help"). Otherwise, like students in our study, learners can feel as if they have been left in the lurch ("How the racial digital divide ...," 2020).

4.2 *Students' Understanding of Online Learning Materials*

Many Saudi university students rated their understanding of the online learning materials as "zero." They said they did not benefit from the online learning or achieve anything from it at all. One student tweeted: "The scientific benefits are 0.038%" (i.e., almost "zero")." In essence, students said their ability to comprehend what they were trying to learn online was affected by poor internet connections that caused the learning program to freeze. Some students expressly said they preferred traditional classroom teaching and learning, where they could interact with faculty and peers and ask for clarification in order to gain better understanding of the learning targets. Pilotti et al. (2019) remarked that Saudi Arabia has a tradition of verbatim learning, which is also teacher-centered.

Many students believed that any final assessment of their academic achievement would not do them justice. So, they recommended that final exams be scrapped. Data indicating ineffective DeL should matter to any conscientious educator. This feedback is alarming and must be investigated to discover hidden factors that are affecting student learning via DeL apart from the obviously stated ones: poor internet connections that disrupted viewing the teaching videos, taking online assessments or submitting assignments.

One student tweeted "There are 2 million YouTube viewers. Did they all benefit from watching YouTube videos? Did the channel freeze on them?" In reality, a video is just a storage unit of information. But learning is not just about obtaining information. A student may or may not have learned anything from viewing a video. Gaining knowledge involves internalizing the information and being able to apply and critique it, which necessitates understanding it. This same student tweeted that, in addition to the video, the lecturer gave "a boring explanation," which, despite "being at the elementary level, was not understandable."

Although not all students had issues with mental health (depression and anxiety) while engaging with crisis distance education, many were struggling. For some, their ability to learn under these circumstances seemed grim amongst all the uncertainty. One student lamented, "how can we focus and study?" Another tweeted, "we are now engaging in a psychological warfare." Another said, "we are all living in psychological anxiety." Two others said, "we are tired… exhausted." One student was waiting for a time when "conditions will be better, and we will be better." Another student tweeted that one of "the biggest injustices is… psychological stress." Others have reported that abrupt disruption in traditional modes of learning during COVID university shutdowns and loss of education time due to closures has caused students enormous stress and anxiety (Fegert et al., 2020; Maler, 2020).

Because this pandemic triggered mental health issues among some Saudi students, universities must provide a psychological safety net (e.g., counseling) to reassure students and bolster their academic performance, which can be deeply compromised due to mental health issues (Al Lily et al., 2020; Fegert et al., 2020; Fiorillo & Gorwood, 2020). Daniels (2020) concurred, asserting that "these are anxious times for students…. Uncertainties about when life will return to 'normal' compound the anxiety. Even as institutions make the changes required to teach in different ways, all should give the highest priority to reassuring students… with targeted communication" (Daniels, 2020, p. 3).

4.3 *Assessment of Students' Learning*

Regarding the final student assessment during the lockdown, some faculty members insisted on giving written final exams to assess whether a student could graduate or move on to the next level. In Saudi Arabia, summative written exams are traditionally regarded as the only reliable tool to determine a student's achievement despite, as one faculty member tweeted, evidence that a more valid and reliable assessment tool is formative "continuous course assessment." This takes the form of course projects, presentations, research projects, quizzes, coursework, diagnostic assessments, midterm assessments and so on.

Students tweeted about the issue of online final exams to be administered at the end of the spring semester 2020. Several pleaded that (1) the hot weather (averaging 88.5°F or 31°C) and (2) fasting during Ramadan (a religious obligation observed) were affecting their ability to cope with intensive coursework and prepare for final exams. One student tweeted that "the research and assignments increased by double (in two weeks, we have 10 research projects due), and the tests will be taken a week earlier in most universities, meaning today is the research submission day and tomorrow is the test, which means no time to review." Another student said there were suddenly "400 pages to review for one final exam." Other students expressed fatigue and said that the suffering they had endured was difficult to bear because of the sheer amount of coursework they were required to complete before final exams (see Al-Jarf, 2020c for similar Saudi results).

A few students pleaded for professors to postpone the final assessment, but half ($\approx$ 50%) of the tweets contained content related to specifically requested universities to abolish final exams, a sentiment expressed across the sample frame and prevalent in the literature (Al-Jarf, 2020a; 2020b; Daniels, 2020). About one third (30%) of the coded tweets from students who made these comments intimated that work done to date amounted to 80% of course requirements. They felt this work-to-date was a reliable indicator of their academic performance (e.g., assignments, projects, group discussions, short tests/

quizzes, research, case studies, class participation, etc.). One student tweeted dismay over the university's decision to determine students' success or failure by giving them a final exam that only lasted 20 minutes. As one student said, "If we could go to the university and be tested, we could obtain a better grade than the distance education grade." Veletsianos (2020) challenged this assumption saying that students learn well using both approaches, i.e., in-person mode is not decisively better than the mode of distance learning.

About one quarter of students' tweets reflected the strong feelings that faculty did not successfully deliver well-thought-out and fair online assessments. The notion of "Where is the justice" was prevalent. They said faculty lacked experience conducting continuous course assessment, which needed to be better spaced out. Instead, some faculty asked for all the coursework to be submitted at once. One student queried whether it is reasonable to request students to switch on their laptop camera, so they can be monitored when taking the test. These and other incidents reinforced the need for faculty members to receive guidelines or training on how to deliver online teaching and assessment (Cheung et al., 2020).

The authors feel that, with all points considered, the final assessment, although traditionally deemed important, should have been scrapped under these circumstances in these unprecedented times. As indicated earlier, hindsight is wonderful. In this study, there was a lack of administrative supervision of the delivery of remote teaching in terms of scheduling of online lectures and online assessments. One student tweeted:

> A faculty gave us two assessments in a row with little time allocated to us to answer the questions. So, were these assessments supposed to be a challenge or a fair evaluation of our learning? (paraphrased)

In the future, faculty need to set up their LMS course folders (e.g., diagnostic tests, formative assessment, summative assessment, coursework) prior to the start of the semester, and continuous assessment items should be scheduled tentatively with fine adjustments made subsequently (see also Daniel, 2020).

4.4 *Faculty Compliance with Transitional Distance Education*

As a case in point, tweets revealed that Blackboard (an LMS) was installed as a teaching and learning online platform in one of the public universities in the sample frame. However, it was not widely used by faculty (especially male professors) despite (senior) administrative efforts to encourage teaching staff to use it. At the university where one of the authors works, for example, the Preparatory Year program (English) had previously employed experienced faculty to set up Blackboard so that course materials, continuous assessment and so on were readily available online. However, other faculty at the university were not uniformly employing Blackboard for teaching purposes, so its mandatory adoption during the pandemic came as a sharp surprise.

The authors can attest that the Saudi government has been funding universities to install Blackboard for the last seven to eight years. However, Blackboard has often remained idol with university administration and faculty member taking it for granted until the pandemic hit. University communities suddenly realized that they were not fully prepared to offer DeL, and students lacked DeL experience and had no idea of how to benefit from it. Imposition instead of gradual introduction of DeL hampered teaching and learning (see also Al Lily et al., 2020).

Faculty members' tweets revealed that, in addition to issues with inexperience using Blackboard to deliver DeL, they were burdened with heavy workloads and inordinate pressure arising from both (1) responsibilities for students' learning and, in some cases, chances to graduate and (2) university management obligations in a time of acute health and educational crises. They needed to shift gears, so they could learn how to and then create course content, materials, lessons, and assessment tools to upload to Blackboard to comply with the imposition of emergency distance education protocols. Several faculty members commented that the practical part of learning Blackboard "was inefficient" and it "can be difficult to make a lab be like a normal lab." "It has been a trying and tiring week." On the other hand, some faculty members liked the technology with some expressing relief. "It was excellent, thank God." Another said, "I personally see it as a great experience, but only for theoretical lectures." These mixed faculty reactions were felt worldwide not just in Arab countries (Al Lily et al., 2020).

As faculty members adjusted to the pedagogical shift, Saudi university students suddenly received an incredible increase in course workload from instructors scrambling to meet university mandated Key Performance Indicators (KPIs) and learning outcome obligations while using an unfamiliar delivery mode. As one student tweeted, "every professor thinks we don't have anything to take other than his course, so he increases the number of assignments and research." Another student criticized faculty decisions, explaining that "each faculty member has a method without taking into account the student's different situation with the rest of the faculty."

This lack of inter-faculty coordination caused pervasive student anxiety, pressure and clashes of deadlines for attending online classes, submitting coursework and taking examinations while also using an unfamiliar learning mode. Students tweeted that these problems were not a subject for discussion with faculty members, exemplified in this tweet. "I hope that you hear our voice and read the comments...," "We hope you are monitoring faculty and encouraging them to consider our situation." One student pleaded thus: "I ask King Salman and the Crown Prince to alleviate our suffering." Another felt unduly punished saying, "We are all following the government's instructions."

Students also tweeted comments about faculty's lack of compliance with the provision of remote teaching in response to the pandemic lockdown. They voiced and shared concerns about this issue exemplified in one tweet wherein the student said their own "negative DeL was compounded with a myriad of technical issues, mental stress, difficult course materials and the faculty's lack of empathy and support." Regarding the latter, faculty members ironically believed that students loved the experience. One said, "the students' interaction and cooperation were distinctive." Another opined, "my lecture using Zoom application was perfect with good interaction from students." A third commented that "interaction of students with the use of Blackboard technology increased their enthusiasm."

Students on the other hand wished that faculty would provide good support and show some empathy toward them. For example, one late submission (due to technical issues) scored zero. Some faculty were unforgiving when students experienced technical issues causing the learning program to freeze. One quarter of the tweets reflected students' comments about unrealistic faculty demands to attend online lectures almost around the clock leading to timetable clashes or scheduling conflicts. As one student noted, they were expected to attend "lectures at 12 (midnight)!! Violation of student rights; we need the professor's cooperation."

4.5 *Positive Student Feedback*

Amidst the negativity that Saudi students espoused about emergency distance education, positive feedback was evident (see also Al-Jarf, 2020a, 2020b, 2020c; Al Lily et al., 2020; Flaherty, 2020). Many Saudi students tweeted that DeL during the lockdown was valuable, comfortable and successful. One student said, "I am proud to be a member of this wonderful educational system." Some students also found the LMS (Blackboard and *Tamkeen*), mobile/computer apps (e.g., Zoom, Google Hangouts, Microsoft Teams, etc.) and email useful and easy to use. Several students expressed their gratitude towards the MoE, which made distance e-learning possible to university students during the national lockdown. "All thanks and appreciation to the Minister and his team for their efforts to the students."

Some students enjoyed student interactions while engaging with distance e-learning with one student observing there was "full attendance" in class, intimating this was an anomaly. One student wished distance learning had been incorporated into education sooner. Several students were grateful for distance learning, because it enabled them to continue their university education during the pandemic (Al Lily et al., 2020). One realistically tweeted, "these circumstances dictate us. [With distance education,] we will continue the education process.

The following student tweet further illustrates this finding.

> For me, it is excellent. It helped me continue the learning process and discover new channels of communication. It was a valuable experience. I hope that e-learning will be activated in general education, even in normal situations, and that some courses will be taught electronically to facilitate the transition when needed.

Another student tweeted:

> In the light of the diseases and problems currently occurring in the world that have caused some to stop learning… distance learning is an important way to continue the learning process… and complete formal studies… without embarrassment.

Al Lily et al. (2020) also reported that Saudi Arabian students found a way to appreciate emergency distance education. And despite low faculty familiarity with online learning platforms, it seems that a cadre of students in our study did enjoy the experience. This result affirms Kane et al.'s (2016) assertion that student satisfaction with DeL is not linked to faculty members' familiarity with using the technology. Instead, its sheer availability, staving off losing the entire academic year seemed to play a large role in this emergency scenario.

Figure 5.2 shows the findings of this case study illustrating different elements of crisis distance education in the Saudi context. A crisis poses disruptions, threats and challenges, but it can also present opportunities.

5 Discussion and Recommendations

The 2020's COVID-19 pandemic lockdown revealed issues with DeL in Saudi Arabia – both good and bad. We conclude that change is the keyword – the Saudi distance education system can change for the better. Pandemics, although generally disruptive, can be blessings in disguise (Zhao, 2020). Arab scholars Al Lily et al. (2020) concurred, claiming that "widespread distance education may be a 'good' outcome of the 'wickedness' (i.e., coronavirus)"

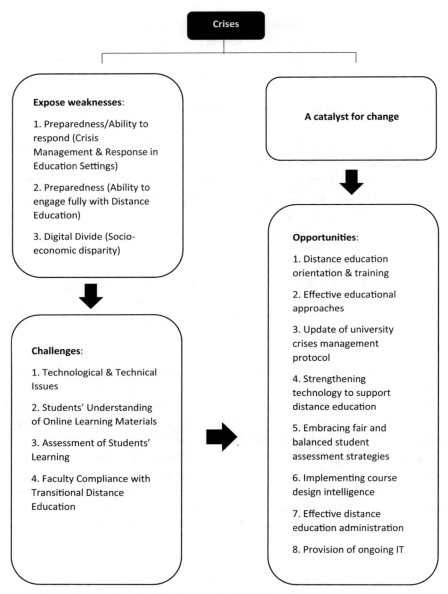

FIGURE 5.2   Crises as a catalyst for change in Saudi higher education

(Al Lily et al., 2020, p. 2). There are lessons to be learned from social media messages and tweets about emergency distance education. In that spirit, in addition to valuable insights from other scholars on this issue (Al Lily et al., 2020; Daniels, 2020; Flaherty, 2020), we tender eight recommendations arising from our findings, ideas that target government, higher education institutions, faculty professional development initiatives, and the private sector.

5.1   Distance Education Orientation and Training

Now that the barrier to using distance education has been breached in Saudi Arabia with mixed but promising degrees of success (see also Al Lily et al., 2020), the researchers recommend continued governmental support of DeL. We also urge higher education institutions to orient and train both students and faculty members to its use on an ongoing basis (Capone et al. 2019; Flaherty, 2020). Emergency distance education seems to be our best option in the current emergency (Llewellyn & Llewellyn, 2020).

5.2   Distance Educational Approaches

Research supports the companion recommendation to employ a blended learning approach (for instance, flipped classroom), which entails a calculated combination of asynchronous and synchronous (Flaherty, 2020) and to start to develop the second generation of blended learning for the post-pandemic era. Flaherty (2020) additionally predicted that students would ask for this blended approach once they gain familiarity with it and trust that it does not have to impede their learning. Findings seemed to affirm this assumption with a cadre of students enjoying DeL and wishing it had already been in place. Moreover, learning in the post-pandemic era may take place in a new learning environment where not only asynchronous and synchronous learning resources are used, but also the locations can be both fixed and various (Fawns, 2019).

5.3   Updating University Crises Management Protocol

It is imperative that Saudi higher education institutions formalize (if not already) and update their crises management protocol and policies pertaining to disruptions to educational offerings and related services (Al Lily et al., 2020; Reich, 2020). Emergency management skills need to be developed and new strategies and directions for achieving a successful provision of DeL are essential. Asking institutions to take on this planning exercise is not untoward, because education is continually evolving (Alhawaj, 2020; Pouspourika, 2019).

We also strongly believe that DeL should be transformed from being technology driven (i.e., education determined by what technology can do) to intelligence driven (i.e., education determined by what students can learn via technology) as Mansour (2020) asserted (see also Neyland, 2011). In principal, any policy and procedural changes must accommodate anticipated new features in online learning and teaching (see also Cheung et al., 2020).

5.4   Strengthening Technology to Support Distance Education

Financing the maintenance and upgrading of technology within university settings is expensive and ongoing. University personnel must constantly engage with emergency-management plans and operational procedures, which involves predicting and addressing future challenges (Gainey, 2009; Kharroub, 2020) including funding. Resounding student complaints about inadequate Saudi internet connections and technical problems with university-provided learning platforms prompted the recommendation that the private sector could become involved in supporting university LMS and Saudi Arabia's 4G infrastructure. In the meantime, the authors can attest that many Saudi universities are entering a new era of self-funding by turning to endowments to support university infrastructure. Such revenues could be a source of funding to support distance education and e-learning.

5.5 *Embracing Fair and Balanced Student Assessment Strategies*
Findings support the recommendation that Saudi university faculty members attend to their pedagogical inclinations and shift to a more balanced assessment style – one that contains both summative and formative strategies. Respectively, the ubiquitous final exam can be augmented with continuous assessment items that are administered as learning unfolds and knowledge forms (e.g., course projects, presentations, research projects, quizzes, etc.). The latter would be tentatively scheduled appreciating that adjustments to activities, weights and due dates may subsequently be required (Capone et al., 2019; Daniel, 2020).

5.6 *Implementing Course Design Intelligence*
Petrie et al. (2020) pointed out that, when effectively and creatively used, digital learning platforms can offer students an opportunity to "get a much wider view of pedagogical strategies" (p. 14). To supplement the previous recommendation of shifting pedagogies, we also recommend that university educators invest and devote their time and energy to improving the quality and content of their online courses by focusing on course design intelligence (CDI). Intelligent course design simply means using the intelligence built into online learning software to creatively design courses (Baines, 2015) that encompass three key features: (1) independent, self-directed learning; (2) remote learning; and (3) instructor as facilitator and guide instead of just a lecturer (Mansour, 2020). Students in our study lamented the lack of instructor support and facilitation and felt inadequate in the self-directed learning mode; instead, most were more comfortable with and preferred familiar, traditional classroom instruction.

5.7 *Distance Education Administration*
When Saudi universities forced to shut and swung into distance mode (sometimes within a matter of days), some faculty members' knee-jerk reaction was to overload students with pre-designed assignments, course work and

assessment tools instead of stopping to rethink if what had been planned could feasibly be completed. Findings revealed that students truly struggled with these unprecedented academic demands exacerbated by being forced to use unfamiliar and undependable learning platforms. We recommend that a purposely built computer software program be implemented university-wide that tabulates faculty course requirements and promotes faculty member collaboration and coordination. We have in mind more than timetabling course collections, envisioning as well collating specific course requirements with associated deadlines and due dates. This would mitigate faculty panic and student angst in the event of future crises. It would minimize scheduling conflicts, overlapping due dates and unmanageable course workload.

5.8 *Ongoing IT Support*

In agreement with Mansour (2020), we concur that DeL provides enhanced learning experiences only when the technology and its supportive infrastructure works. Findings herein support a strong recommendation that, as a general practice, Saudi universities must have in place reliable and competent IT support staff especially for distance education platforms. The students' tweets indicated pervasive IT issues when engaging with distance learning to that point that they could not attend the lessons, access posted learning resources, submit timely assignments or engage with faculty members.

Personal communication with two of the universities in the sample frame further revealed internal institutional struggles with the normal routine of IT troubleshooting, which was disrupted due to the lockdown and social distancing imperatives. Technicians could no longer physically inspect the hardware when health risks were posed, and there were too few of them to field the unwieldy, never-before-experienced scope of student IT access issues. Universities also experienced a shortage of laptops, because their suppliers were US- or China-based, and supplies had dried up due to trade stoppages. We recommend that plans and protocols be established that ensure adequate ongoing faculty and student IT support and timely IT trouble shooting on a regular basis with contingency plans for future crises exigencies (Lott, 2012; Reich, 2020).

6 Limitations

Future studies should return to the eight Twitter feeds to discern how sentiments change over time. And different Saudi universities could be studied perhaps ensuring each region is represented in addition to each major city. Future sample frames could include public and private universities as well as colleges and technical/vocational schools (Allahmorad & Zreik, 2020). Other researchers are encouraged to employ alternative research methods when drawing of social media platforms for data including content analysis, social network analysis, semantic analysis, and time-series analysis (Ahmed, 2019).

7 Conclusion

When embarking on this research journey, the authors (who personally experienced the lockdown and crisis-induced distance education imposition) were convinced that crises could be viewed as an opportunity for change. We were interested in understanding Saudi university students and faculty members' responses to such a profound, abrupt shift in educational delivery mode. Analyses of Twitter comments revealed that when technology worked and people had equitable access to it, students viewed DeL as a good thing. Distance e-learning was valuable and enjoyable, and they realized that technology provides an alternative mode of learning when traditional classroom learning is not an option. Conversely, when technology did not work or was not accessible, immense student angst and frustration emerged with attendant feelings of compromised academic success.

This global pandemic is not over yet, and a resurgence (second or even third wave) is expected if not happening already.[1] Society is trying to prepare for a new normal and that includes a new educational normal (Daniel, 2020). The authors admit that DeL cannot replace students' experience gained through traditional classroom, face-to-face teaching and learning but combined, they can afford valuable learning experiences. Students can learn from this blended approach (Chen et al., 2017), and crises can be a catalyst for change. That said, findings reinforced both the need to (1) respect resistance to enforced change and (2) scaffold student and faculty members' transition to changes in educational delivery and learning modes. Furthermore, in view of blended learning that will evolve in a new learning environment in the post-pandemic era, Saudi educators should start preparing for a new curriculum that allows both in-person instruction and DeL to intricately support each other in case of a sudden strike of an emergency.

If managed properly, pandemics such as COVID-19 can become junctures of opportunity and transformation. As discussed, on-campus learning and distance learning can co-exist and benefit students, provided that the technological delivery system is dependable and reliable, and students and faculty are oriented toward and trained in how to use it effectively. Even if DeL becomes more prominent (and most educational pundits think it will), real-time field trips, lab work, tutorials, workshops, practicums and conferences will still be needed. We are convinced that a blended mode of learning can be implemented and perfected in Saudi Arabia during the pandemic and in the post-pandemic era, and thus tendered recommendations to that effect. It can become the new educational normal.

Note

1 At the time this book is published, a new coronavirus variant "Omicron" has emerged and shown signs of waning off. Some countries, such as Spain, US, and China, have seen their third waves of COVID-19.

References

Ahmed, W. (2019, June 18). Using Twitter as a data source: An overview of social media research tools (2019). *LSE*. https://blogs.lse.ac.uk/impactofsocialsciences/2019/06/18/using-twitter-as-a-data-source-an-overview-of-social-media-research-tools-2019/

Al-Ahdal, A. A. M. H., Al-Ghamdi, N. A. S., & Alrefaee, Y. (2021). Coronavirus, critical discourse analysis, and Saudi tweets: Unravelling the dominant culture. *Sage Open* (in press).

Alhawaj, A. Y. (2020). *Virtual forum on education excellence sustainability – II*. Ahlia University. https://www.ahlia.edu.bh/cms4/wp-content/uploads/2020/06/Education-Excellence-Sustainability-Speakers.pdf

Al-Jarf, R. S. (2016). College administrator-student communication via Twitter. *Journal of Basic and Applied Research International, 14*(3), 176–184. https://www.ikprress.org/index.php/JOBARI/article/view/3825

Al-Jarf, R. S. (2020a). Distance learning and undergraduate Saudi students' agency during the Covid-19 pandemic. *Bulletin of the Transylvania University of Braşov Series IV: Philology and Cultural Studies, 13*(62), 37–54. https://doi.org/10.31926/but.pcs.2020.62.13.2.4

Al-Jarf, R. S. (2020b, April 23–24). Issues in interactive translation practice on Twitter. In *Proceedings of the 16th international scientific conference on eLearning and software for education*, Bucharest (Vol. 3, pp. 427–437). http://dx.doi.org/10.2139/ssrn.3842157

Al-Jarf, R. S. (2020c). Communication among instructors and students via Twitter. In I. Vassileva, M. Chankova, E. Breuer, & K. P. Schneider (Eds.), *The digital scholar: Academic communication in multimedia environment* (pp. 265–280). Frank & Timme GmbH.

Allahmorad, S., & Zreik, S. (2020, April 9). Education in Saudi Arabia. *World Education News and Reviews.* https://wenr.wes.org/2020/04/education-in-saudi-arabia

Al Lily, A. E., Ismail, A. F., Abunasser, F. M., & Alhajhoj Alqahtani, R. H. (2020). Distance education as a response to pandemics: Coronavirus and Arab culture. *Technology in Society.* https://doi.org/10.1016/j.techsoc.2020.101317

Alrefaie, Z., Hassanien, M., & Al-Hayani, A. (2020). Monitoring online learning during COVID-19 pandemic; Suggested online learning portfolio (COVID-19 OLP). *MedEdPublish.* https://doi.org/10.15694/mep.2020.000110.1

Baines, S. (2015, May 19). *Going big on training.* https://www.orange-business.com/en/blogs/connecting-technology/it-management/going-big-on-training

Braun, V., & Clarke, V. (2006). Using thematic analysis in psychology. *Qualitative Research in Psychology, 3,* 77–101. http://dx.doi.org/10.1191/1478088706qp063oa

Capone, R., Regno, F. D., & Tortoriello, F. S. (2019). E-teaching in mathematics education: The teacher's role in online discussion. *Je-LKS: Journal of E-learning and Knowledge Society, 14*(3). https://doi.org/10.20368/1971-8829/1538

Chen, F., Lui, A. M., & Martinelli, S. M. (2017). A systematic review of the effectiveness of flipped classrooms in medical education. *Medical Education, 51*(6), 585–597. https://doi.org/10.1111/medu.13272

Cheung, R., Francois, A., Hyler, M. E., Lit, I., Robinson, J., & Schultz, K. (2020, May 21). *A deeper dive into how educator preparation programs are adapting during COVID-19.* Learning Policy Institute. https://learningpolicyinstitute.org/event/webinar-deeper-dive-how-educator-preparation-programs-are-adapting-during-covid-19

Clement, J. (2020, February 20). *Twitter – Statistics & facts.* Statista.com. https://www.statista.com/topics/737/twitter/

Daniel, J. (2020). Education and the COVID-19 pandemic. *Prospects, 49,* 91–96. https://doi.org/10.1007/s11125-020-09464-3

Fawns, T. (2019). Postdigital education in design and practice. *Postdigital Science and Education, 1,* 132–145. https://doi.org/10.1007/s42438-018-0021-8

Fegert, J. M., Vitiello, B., Plener, P. L., & Clemens, V. (2020). Challenges and burden of the coronavirus 2019 (COVID-19) pandemic for child and adolescent mental health: A narrative review to highlight clinical and research needs in the acute phase and the long return to normality. *Child and Adolescent Psychiatry and Mental Health, 14*(1), art. 20. https://doi.org/10.1186/s13034-020-00329-3

Fiorillo, A., & Gorwood, P. (2020). The consequences of the COVID-19 pandemic on mental health and implications for clinical practice. *European Psychiatry, 63*(1), e32. https://doi.org/10.1192/j.eurpsy.2020.35

Flaherty, C. (2020, April 29). Zoom boom. *Inside Higher Education.* https://www.insidehighered.com/news/2020/04/29/synchronous-instruction-hot-right-now-it-sustainable

Gainey, B. S. (2009). Crisis management's new role in educational settings. *The Clearing House, 82*(6), 267–274.

How the racial digital divide impacts online education during the pandemic. (2020, May 25). *Journal of Blacks in Higher Education.* https://www.jbhe.com/2020/05/how-the-racial-digital-divide-impacts-online-education-during-the-pandemic/

Kane, R. T., Shaw, M., Pang, S., Salley, W., & Snider, J. B. (2016, June 22–29). Faculty professional development and student satisfaction in online higher education. In M. N. Clay & J. Stone (Eds.), *Proceedings of the distance learning administration conference*, Jekyll Island, GA (pp. 105–115).

Khalil, R., Mansour, A. E., Fadda, W. A., Almisnid, K., Aldamegh, M., Al-Nafeesah, A., Alkhalifah, A., & Al-Wutayd, O. (2020). The sudden transition to synchronized online learning during the COVID-19 pandemic in Saudi Arabia: A qualitative study exploring medical students' perspectives. *BMC Medical Education, 20*, 285. https://doi.org/10.1186/s12909-020-02208-z

Kharroub, T. (2020, March 25). Coronavirus exposes information crisis and digital inequality in Arab world. *The New Arab.* https://english.alaraby.co.uk/english/comment/2020/3/24/coronavirus-exposes-arab-worlds-information-crisis-and-digital-inequality

Llewellyn, K. R., & Llewellyn, J. (2020, May 14). Connection, not real-time teaching, is priority for crisis education. *The Star.* https://www.thestar.com/opinion/contributors/2020/05/14/connection-not-real-time-teaching-is-priority-for-crisis-education.html

Lott, M. K. (2012). *Crisis management plans in higher education: Commonalities, attributes, and perceived effectiveness* (UMI No. 3532192). ProQuest Dissertations and Theses database.

Maler A. (2020, June 9). *County-level coordination provides infrastructure, funding for community schools initiative.* https://learningpolicyinstitute.org/blog/covid-county-coordination-community-schools

Mansour, A. (2020, June 4). *Virtual forum on education excellence sustainability – II.* Ahlia University. https://www.ahlia.edu.bh/cms4/wp-content/uploads/2020/06/Education-Excellence-Sustainability-Speakers.pdf

McGregor, S. L. T. (2018). *Understanding and evaluating research.* Sage.

Miles, M. B., & Huberman, A. M. (1994). *Qualitative data analysis.* Sage.

Moran, A. (2012). Crises as catalysts for change: Re-energising teacher education in Northern Ireland. *Educational Research, 54*(2), 137–147. https://doi.org/10.1080/00131881.2012.680039

Neyland, E. (2011). Integrating online learning in NSW secondary schools: Three schools' perspectives on ICT adoption. *Australasian Journal of Educational Technology, 27*(1). https://doi.org/10.14742/ajet.989

Nicholson, E., Murphy, T., Larkin, P., Normand, C., & Guerin, S. (2016). Protocol for a thematic synthesis to identify key themes and messages from a palliative care research network. *BMC Research Notes, 9*(1). https://doi.org/10.1186/s13104-016-2282-1

Panagiotopoulos, P., Barnett, J., Bigdeli, A. Z., & Sams, S. (2016). Social media in emergency management: Twitter as a tool for communicating risks to the public. *Technological Forecasting and Social Change, 111*, 86–96. https://doi.org/10.1016/j.techfore.2016.06.010

Petrie, C., Aladin, K., Ranjan, P., Javangwe, P., Gilliland, D., Tuominen, S., & Lasse, L. (2020). *Spotlight on quality education for all during Covid-19 emergency.* HundrED.

Pilotti, M. A., El Alaoui, K., Mulhem, H., & Al Kuhayli, H. A. (2019). The illusion of knowing in college: A field study of students with a teacher-centered educational past. *Europe's Journal of Psychology, 15*(4), 789–807. https://doi.org/10.5964/ejop.v15i4.1921

Pouspourika, K. (2019, June 30). *The 4 industrial revolutions.* Institute of Entrepreneurship Development. https://ied.eu/project-updates/the-4-industrial-revolutions/

Quacquarelli Symonds. (2019). *QS Arab region university rankings 2019.* Top Universities. https://www.topuniversities.com/university-rankings/arab-region-university-rankings/2019

Reich, J. (2020, June 24). A crisis-management system for education leaders. *Education Week.* https://www.edweek.org/ew/articles/2020/04/24/a-crisis-management-system-for-education-leaders.html

Schleicher, A. (2019, January 22). What the fourth industrial revolution could mean for education and jobs. *OECD Education and Skills Today.* https://oecdedutoday.com/what-the-fourth-industrial-revolution-could-mean-for-education-and-jobs/

Shawaqfeh, M. S., Al Bekairy, A. M., & Al-Azayzih, A. (2020). Pharmacy students' perceptions of their distance online learning experience during the COVID-19 pandemic: A cross-sectional survey study. *Journal of Medical Education and Curricular Development, 7.* https://doi.org/10.1177/2382120520963039

Stodel, E., Thompson, T., & MacDonald, C. (2006). Learners' perspectives on what is missing from online learning: Interpretations through the community of inquiry framework. *International Review of Research in Open and Distributed Learning, 7*(3). https://www.learntechlib.org/p/49693/

Veletsianos, G. (2020, July 1). Learning from home? Here are some tips for finding a perfect online course. *Halifax Today* (Reprinted from The Conversation). https://www.halifaxtoday.ca/coronavirus-covid-19-local-news/learning-from-home-here-are-some-tips-for-finding-the-perfect-online-courses-2448731

Zhao, Y. (2020). COVID-19 as a catalyst for educational change. *Prospects.* https://doi.org/10.1007/s11125-020-09477-y

CHAPTER 6

Equity and Inclusion in Saudi Education during the Pandemic

Mohammed Alharbi

Abstract

The main purpose of this chapter is to explore the role of the Ministry of Education to ensure equity and inclusion in education, and how that role developed during COVID-19. Equity in education is the backbone for providing high-quality education for all students. For the purpose of this chapter, I used multiple strategies for data collection. As an educator who works at the Ministry of Education, I conducted an observation strategy to understand the aim of the process of school reopening during the years of the COVID-19 pandemic. I also reviewed official documents issued by the Ministry of Education and interviewed school principals and teachers from different schools in Makkah. The study found that centralization in decision-making was one of the key elements of a successful educational experience during the pandemic. The Ministry of Education was the only source for making the decision that helped to resume education and to initiate platforms for students to access high-quality education. The study also found that ensuring equity in distance education is very challenging. Although the Ministry of Education uses multiple education resources to ensure that all students have access to free learning materials, it requires collaboration with other aspects of society such as parents, community institutions, and public and private sectors.

Keywords

equity in education – COVID-19 – Saudi education – inclusive education

1   Introduction

In February 2020, the Saudi government updated an emergency plan to ensure the safety of its populations and to address challenges associated with the COVID-19 pandemic. By March of the same year, the Ministry of Education (MoE) started to prepare for the likelihood that the pandemic would affect school attendance. On March 8, a ministerial directive was issued to close schools. Within 24 hours, the MoE shifted to distance learning and activated educational TV channels that were operational years ago, but were not used effectively, to avoid any discontinuity of education (Ministry of Education, 2020). Within the next school year, the MoE developed multiple strategies to help students to access free educational resources such as the iEN and the Unified Education System, which represented the basis for the establishment of blended learning in Saudi Arabia. Therefore, the step to move from traditional to blended learning needs to be investigated from the perspective of educational equity.

This study has three main purposes. First, it provides an overview of the importance of equity and inclusion in education. Second, it examines the status of equity and inclusion in education in Saudi Arabia. Third, it explores the role of the MoE in developing an education system that ensures equity and inclusion for all students during the COVID-19 pandemic.

A qualitative research inquiry with a phenomenological design was conducted to explore the procedures and strategies implemented by the MoE during the COVID-19 pandemic. A phenomenological inquiry was used to analyze participants' perceptions and experiences of the phenomena under consideration (Flynn & Korcuska, 2018), which, for this study, was equity and inclusion in education in Saudi Arabia during the COVID-19 pandemic. Phenomenological study differs from other qualitative inquiry methods. It attempts to understand the essence of a phenomenon from the perspective of the people who experienced it (Eddles-Hirsch, 2015). Therefore, I observed schools and students, reviewed official documents, and interviewed school principals and teachers during the pandemic to understand the phenomenon from their various perspectives. The use of three different methods of data collection helped ensure the trustworthiness and credibility of the study (Creswell & Poth, 2018). Although all public schools in Saudi Arabia followed the same approaches for pupils and students to return to school, the sample for this study was limited to schools in the Holy City of Makkah.

2 Equity and Inclusion in Education

Equality in education is a fundamental issue at present, as it goes beyond the educational field to influence economic, social, and cultural factors. According to the Organization for Economic Co-operation and Development (OECD), "a fair and inclusive system that makes the advantages of education available to all is one of the most powerful levers to make society more equitable" (as cited in Zhang et al., 2014, p. 1). Equity in education requires developing an education system to ensure that every student has an equal opportunity to succeed and achieve his or her potential. This requires familiarity with students and their challenges and providing the needed support to overcome those challenges.

Field et al. (2007) identified two dimensions to the construct of equity in education:

> The first is fairness, which basically means making sure that personal and social circumstances – for example gender, socio-economic status, or ethnic origin – should not be an obstacle to achieving educational potential. The second is inclusion, in other words ensuring a basic minimum standard of education for all – for example, everyone should be able to read, write and do simple arithmetic. The two dimensions are closely intertwined: tackling school failure helps to overcome the effects of social deprivation, which often causes school failure. (Field et al., 2007, p. 11)

Zhang et al. (2014), in agreement, expanded on this by arguing that the first dimension of equity in education, fairness, refers to the issues of providing equal opportunities of education such as regional, urban-rural, social class, and gender and ethnic equities. Inclusion, which is the second dimension of equitable education, refers to the issues of equal rights of accessing educational resources.

Field et al. (2007) elaborated on the benefits of developing an education system that ensures educational equity for all students in three elements. First, education rights are required for every child to help them to be effective participants in developing their societies. Second, equity in education protects society from long-term financial difficulties and health issues by reducing failure through providing equitable education for all students. Third, equity in education is the key element in enhancing social cohesion and trust in a multicultural community.

Multiple theories and teaching philosophies in the field of education have sought to develop educational reform that ensure equity and inclusion in schools. Theories such as culturally responsive teaching (Gay, 2010) and culturally relevant pedagogy (Ladson-Billings, 2009) emphasize the role of race, ethnicity, and cultural background in enhancing equity in education. For example, Gay (2013) proposed a theory for "culturally responsive teaching," which seeks to use students' cultural backgrounds and prior experiences to empower them to achieve their future goals. Geneva Gay stated that "[culturally responsive teaching] is an equal educational opportunity initiative that accepts differences among ethnic groups, individuals, and cultures as normative to the human condition and value to societal and personal development" (2013, p. 50). Equity in education requires understanding students and their needs and using their cultural knowledge as bridges to achieve their goals.

Multicultural education is an educational philosophy that highlights the need for equity in education. According to Banks (2015), multicultural education aims to reform educational institutions to provide equitable education services for all students from different ethnic, racial, and cultural background groups. It provides students with the needed educational experiences that enable them to be an active part of developing their communities. Alharbi (2020), moreover, stated that multicultural education reform empowers the education system at a number of levels – the student, the school, and the community. Multicultural education emphasizes diversity among students and aims to ensure equity for all the different groups.

3 Equity in Education in Saudi Arabia

Seeking equity in education is an essential objective for many education systems. Saudi Arabia, as the other UN Member States, is involved in developing the Sustainable Development Goals (SDG s) and the Education 2030 Framework for Action that aims to "ensure inclusive and equitable quality education and promote lifelong learning opportunities for all" (UNESCO, 2018, p. 11). The Saudi government has implemented several major projects to ensure equal educational opportunities for all groups of populations (United Nations Sustainable Development Knowledge Platform, 2018).

Educators have different views on the responsibility of addressing equity in education. Levin (2003) stated two approaches to addressing equity in education. The first approach is equality of opportunity, which focuses on equality in accessing educational services. The second approach is equality of the educational results, which focuses on academic achievements, graduation, and access to employment. This section shows the status of equity in education in Saudi Arabia from three different angles: providing free and high-quality education to all students in cities and rural areas, educating students with special needs, and educating students from different cultural backgrounds.

4 Equity in Public Education

The Saudi government provides free high-quality education to all students in the nation. From the early days of the unification of the nation, it was the intent of the Saudi government to increase the number of new schools in all cities and villages, hiring teachers from Arab countries to keep up with the growing demand for formal education. The year 1925 is considered as the real beginning of formal education in Saudi Arabia with the founding of the Directorate of Education. The main objective of the Directorate of Education was to deliver free education – only for boys – by founding new schools and education offices across the kingdom (Mani & As-Sbit, 1981). However, women's formal education started years later with the establishment of the General Directorate of Girls' Education in 1956. This delay in funding women's education was a reflection of the social and political events during that time (Hamdan, 2005). In order to ensure equality in education between both genders, the General Directorate of Girls' Education was abolished, and the education of girls and boys was merged under the umbrella of the Ministry of Education.

December 1953 witnessed a great development in the history of education in Saudi Arabia when the Saudi government established the Ministry of Education (MoE) as a way of moving into the modern education era. Unlike the Directorate of Education, the MoE is responsible for funding schools, training teachers, and developing curriculums. The need for funding of this Ministry was to expand the number of schools around the country, which was a big challenge faced by the Directorate of Education (Mani & As-Sbit, 1981). The intention of increasing the number of schools at the birth of the nation implies the interest of the government in providing equal education opportunities for students in all parts of the country, where education moved from education for some to mandate for parents to enroll their children in elementary education.

5 Equity in Special Education

Educating students with special needs was the sole responsibility of their parents until 1958, when some blind students enrolled in education programs using Braille that was provided by non-profit organizations (Aldabas, 2015). Two years later, the Saudi government established Al-Noor Institute, which is considered as the main launch pad for special education in Saudi Arabia. Al-Noor Institute is officially known as a special education school for male students with poor vision and blindness that provides education from elementary through high school using the same curriculum for general public education with modifications to meet the need for students with visual impairments (Aldabas, 2015). In 1962, the MoE established the Department of Special Education that aimed to provide educational services for students with blindness, deafness, and mental retardation (Alquraini, 2010). The delay in paying attention to special education was due to the lack of educational capabilities and the absence of laws and regulations regarding the rights of education for this community.

Rights for people with disabilities in Saudi Arabia emerged after the passing of the Legislation of Disability by the government in 1987. The Legislation of Disability highlights the right to equitable services for people with disabilities and requires public agencies to deliver rehabilitation services and supporting programs that ensure independent living (Alquraini, 2010).

In the field of education, the MoE introduced the first regulations for students with disabilities in Saudi Arabia in 2001, known as the Regulations of Special Education Programs and Institutes (RSEPI). The RSEPI supports the right of equity and inclusion for students with disabilities to obtain free high-quality education in general education schools, taking into account their physical and mental differences (Alquraini, 2013). However, Binmahfooz (2019) criticizes the difference between RSEPI and the field application of inclusion of special education. She states that students with mild and moderate mental disabilities are offered the special education curriculum in a special classroom in public schools. Many students with disabilities cannot attend any further education after middle school, except at some vocational training centers that prepare them to learn employment skills to live independently. Moreover, Alquraini (2010) suggested that, for successful inclusion in special education, more educational research is needed to addresses elements such as modification of general curricula and collaborations between public sectors.

6 Multicultural Education

Educating students from various cultural backgrounds is the last category to investigate equity in education in Saudi Arabia. The number of diverse ethnic groups in Saudi Arabia has increased rapidly over the last few years. Statistics released by the General Authority for Statistics in Saudi Arabia show that the non-Saudi population was 31% in 2010, and this increased to 37.8% in 2019 (General Authority for Statistics, 2019). According to Alharbi (2020), this increase in the percentage of the non-Saudi population emphasizes the need for a multicultural education reform movement that provides students of different races, social classes, languages, and cultural backgrounds equal opportunity to achieve their educational potential.

Equity and inclusion in providing education for students from different cultural groups can be investigated by measuring their performances on standardized exams. International standardized tests such as TIMSS, PIRLS, and

PISA are used to examine the extent of equity in education based on the academic success of students in various countries (Alharbi, 2020). In the status of Saudi education, there is no distinction between students based on their nationalities. All students have the right to free education and equal access to all sources of learning in school. Immigrant students have the same quality of education as Saudi students. Unlike many OECD countries, the PISA 2018 results showed that immigrant students performed higher than other Saudi students in reading; Saudi students scored 400 in the mean average, whereas immigrant students scored 437 (OECD, 2019), which reflects the quality of education that non-Saudi students received.

Investigating social segregation across schools was another goal of PISA 2018, that measures which students are likely to communicate with classmates from diverse cultural backgrounds. According to PISA 2018, the higher the score, the more segregation between students across schools. The result showed that Saudi Arabia was below the average of OECD countries in social segregation (OECD, 2019). This finding from PISA indicates that the school system in Saudi Arabia is inclusive for students from various cultural backgrounds; they did not feel isolated in schools and were more likely to communicate with peers from different cultures.

7 Equity and Inclusion during Pandemic

The COVID-19 pandemic has created the largest disruption to education systems in history, affecting nearly 1.6 billion learners in more than 190 countries all over the world. The closures of schools and other educational institutions affected 94% of students in the world, and the percentage rose to 99% in low- and lower-middle-income countries (United Nations, 2020). Saudi Arabia, like many other countries, developed a strategy that helped to continue the provision of education and ensure health and safety for all students and their families. Centralization in decision-making was one of the most important aspects that helped to continue education for students during the pandemic. The role played by the MoE had the greatest impact on providing high-quality and equal education for all types of learners. The MoE launched several online platforms to ensure equitable education for all students. These technical solutions had multiple options for students from different learning styles (Ministry of Education, 2020).

In this section, I assess the procedures that had been done by the MoE to relaunch schools and how these procedures ensure equitable education for all students. The section is divided into three phases that have different characteristics of school reopening. The first phase is distance learning, where lessons are developed and broadcast by the MoE through multiple online platforms. The second phase is the launch of The Unified Education System (UES), which allows online connection between teachers and their students. The third phase is the blended learning stage, where students are required to attend schools and participate in the UES platform.

8 Ensuring Equity during the First Stage of School Reopening

Benefiting from online learning requires all students to have reliable access to the internet. During the first stage of school reopening, the MoE offered students a different learning mode to ensure students' equitable access to learning materials.

From the first day of the school closure, the MoE began broadcasting lessons via iEN Satellite TV educational channels to all students. The number of iEN channels reached 20, displaying scheduled lessons covering all subjects to students based on their grades. In order to ensure equity and reach out for the highest number of students, the MoE launched the iEN YouTube channel, which allowed students to have full access to educational materials using their favorite medium (Ministry of Education, 2020). Moreover, inclusion was another significant characteristic of iEN channels. Students were able to learn from several instructors who applied different learning strategies to fulfill their needs. Use of sign language was also included in over 450 lessons, catering to students with special needs (Ministry of Education, 2020). The iEN channels were the first step for distance education, as the MoE desired to build a strong base for distance education that can be used for the future and does not stop with the end of the COVID-19 pandemic. The MoE also wanted to reach the largest possible number of students at the lowest cost.

In Saudi Arabia, the majority of households have internet access. According to the General Authority of Statistics (2018), the percentage of households that have access to the internet reached 86.8% in 2017; this number increased to 92.77% in 2019. Although this percentage is very high, it might cause some students to fall behind, especially those from low-income families. To overcome this obstacle, and in an effort to keep all students connected to the internet during the pandemic, the MoE worked in conjunction with the Ministry of Communications and Information Technology to offer free access to educational sites, such as The National iEN Gate. Such site was hosting distance education platforms, and it provided listing of those domains under the free access listing (Ministry of Education, 2020).

Increasing the number of households who access the internet does not guarantee that equitable educational services will be provided to all students. Having a computer for each student at home is impossible for many families. The percentage of families who have at least one computer at home was 53.41%, compared with 99.27% of the families who have a smartphone (General Authority for Statistics, 2019). The lack of computers compared forced some students to use smartphones to access education materials; these students' equitable access to all educational sources was compromised. However, the MoE took a serious step to meet this challenge by working with non-profit organizations to provide students in need with electronic devices such as tablets, laptops, and desktop computers. Takaful Foundation, for example, supplied 20,000 students with new devices that they could use to access online education (Ministry of Education, 2020).

Communication is at the heart of cooperation between parents and schools. An equitable education system, in distance education, needs to develop a method of communication between parents and schools that helps to find support for technical issues. The MoE, as the only decision-maker during the first stage of the school reopening, set up a 24/7 communication line to contact parents, answer questions, and solve technical issues that students might face during the distance learning journey. However, the disadvantage of this stage is the absence of direct communication between teachers and their students, as the role of the teacher at this stage is limited to sharing pre-recorded videos by the iEN channels without significant intervention.

9   Ensuring Equity during the Second Stage of School Reopening

The second stage is the return of the interaction between teachers and their students. The educational process has shifted from a passive to an interactive learning process. Instead of passively watching recorded lessons, students were able to attend synchronized lessons with their teachers and classmates. At the beginning of the 2020 school year, the MoE launched the Unified Education System (UES), which aimed to start a new phase of distance education to achieve greater interaction between students and educational resources. In addition, teachers had a greater role compared to the first stage, in preparing and presenting lessons to students through direct communication using this platform. The UES has been linked to Microsoft Teams, and login details have been created for all educators and students in public schools across Saudi Arabia.

Students and parents were encouraged to enroll in the UES. The MoE sent text messages to students, parents, and educators to enroll in this platform and benefit from the educational resources (Ministry of Education, 2020). Attending the platform became a necessity, after the completion of the pilot phase in the first weeks of the school year, and attendance at synchronized classes became an alternative to physical attendance at schools. To ensure equitable access to the platform, the MoE provided technical support and encouraged school principals to follow up with students who faced challenges logging in to the platform. However, not all students were successful attendees at synchronized classes every day. The lack of technical skills among some parents was an obstacle that prevented students from taking full advantage of the platform.

Equity and inclusion in education during the second phase can be examined from three angles: free access to the internet, providing technical support to log in to the platform, and separation between elementary and upper grade-level classes during school hours.

Although 92.77% of the Saudi population is able to access the internet (the General Authority for Statistics, 2018), as in the first phase, the Ministry of Communications and Information Technology provided free access to educational resources in the UES. This free access to the internet enables students from different economic levels to have an equal opportunity to learn and attend distance schooling. However, some teachers and parents stated they were only able to get free access to the UES during the initial weeks, but then had to pay internet fees to be able to access the educational resources. Additionally, some teachers and students complained about the weak internet signals in their neighborhoods. The slow internet and frequent disconnections were obstacles that prevented some students and teachers from actively participating in the synchronized lessons.

The technical issue was another challenge faced by students and educators during the second phase. To ensure equitable access to the platform, the MoE provided 24-hour technical support and encouraged school administrators to follow up with students who had challenges logging into the platform. However, not all students were successful attending synchronized classes every day. Distance education requires a high amount of technical knowledge and skills that enables students to overcome some recurring technical problems and to make the most of the educational platform. The lack of technical skills among some students and their parents was an obstacle that prevented some students from taking full advantage of the UES.

The separation between elementary and upper grade-level classes in school hours was another strategy the MoE used to ensure equity and inclusion in accessing distance learning for all students. The MoE decided that students should be divided into two groups: upper elementary students accessing the UES in the morning, and elementary students accessing it in the evening. From this separation, the MoE aimed to provide equal opportunity to make the most of all available resources, such as the share of the computer by more than one child in the same family and protection of the UES from crashing due to high usage by large numbers of students at the same time.

10 Ensuring Equity during the Third Stage of School Reopening

This phase of school reopening is the process of moving from online to blended learning. As online learning relies heavily on the internet to deliver content and instruction, blended learning is a mode of learning in which students learn in some part through online learning, with some control over time and place, and through supervised learning in the other part (Horn & Staker, 2014).

By the start of the school year of 2021, the MoE announced its plan for a safe return to schools, which differs from what was in place in the year 2020. The most prominent feature of this plan was the return of the largest possible number of students to their classrooms. This return was conditional: students aged 12 and over who had obtained the COVID-19 vaccine were allowed to return to the classroom; younger students continued to study remotely. The second condition to ensure the safety of students was to implement social distancing by dividing students into groups, in order to reduce the number of students attending the school on the same day, so that each group is present at school one day and study online on other days. Social distancing is also applied with the cancellation of all sports, social, and cultural activities at school.

As in the second stage, the MoE relied heavily on the UES platform. Students must attend school for a few days, based on the number of students in the classroom, and participate in asynchronous and synchronous lessons with their teachers via the UES. Moreover, to ensure applying social distancing and reducing physical connection between all school parties, the MoE prohibits teachers from sharing any paperwork in the classrooms, and all homework, activities, and tests should be done online using the UES or other platforms such as Google Forms.

Equity in education in the third stage can be examined from two angles. The first one is equity in attending online lessons. All strategies mentioned in using the UES during the second stage, such as free internet access, technical support, and grouping students during school time were applied during the third stage. The second angle is equity in attending schools. School attendance is restricted to students over 12 years old who are vaccinated and do not suffer from any health problems. To encourage students to get the vaccine, the MoE cooperated with the Ministry of Health in allocating special vaccination centers for students at both public and university education levels to obtain the vaccine for free and without the need for prior reservation. In contrast, students who are 12 years of age or older but refuse to take the vaccine and do not have any health problems, have been transferred to remote education – only attending the school for the final exam – until the end of the school year of 2021.

11 Conclusion

Many countries in the world seek to reach the highest level of societal justice, and this requires equal educational opportunities for all segments of society. Equity in education is not just offering free education to all students. It also depends on the type of educational services provided to each category of students. Levin (2003) stated that the aim of government policy "cannot and should not be equality in the sense that everyone is the same or achieves the same outcomes" (Levin, 2003, p. 5). Rather, a commitment to equity infers that the difference in students' outcomes should not be attributable to diversity in social-economic status and cultural backgrounds.

The MoE developed several streams to ensure education equity for all populations. For example, the MoE started a program that focuses on adult education and the eradication of illiteracy. It launched summer campaign programs in remote areas to provide support in many aspects such as education, health, and agriculture. Moreover, the MoE established several centers for special needs that offer education and health support. These programs, and others not mentioned, exemplify the enhanced goals of the MoE to develop an equal educational system that includes the entire population. Although the MoE took serious steps toward equitable education, General Directorates of Education in some cities developed an educational reform that aimed to improve school environments by closing all appropriate school buildings, which caused segregating students based on their nationalities (Alharbi, 2020). This educational reform plan suggested that dividing students into two sets of school times, where Saudi students study in the morning and non-Saudi students study in the evening. Although all Saudi and non-Saudi students study the same school curriculum at the same school building but at different times, this segregation can negatively affect the community and create a generation that does not accept multiculturalism.

Centralization in decision-making is the key element for positive educational experience during the COVID-19 pandemic in Saudi Arabia. The MoE was the only authority for issuing decisions, which resulted in education continuing with minimal disruption during the pandemic. The MoE established educational channels and the UES facilitated access to them for the largest possible number of students by providing free internet and computers to students in need. This educational experience cannot be successful without the coordination and efforts made among all the communities. The private sector, for instance, had no significant impact on supporting education during the pandemic, as there was no collaboration mentioned by the MoE with any private institution in providing school supplies and computers for students in need. On the other hand, the most prominent cooperation was from the nonprofit sector.

Equity in distance learning has more special characteristics than traditional education. In addition to offering electronic devices for all students and free access to the internet, it requires cooperation between home and school to provide an appropriate learning environment for all family members. Therefore, having a private place to study and attend online sessions for each child is important, and this may be difficult for many middle- and low-income families. Although the MoE divided students into two sets of school times, this did not fully solve the problem. Several students are sharing rooms with a family member and attending class at the same time, which causes the students to be distracted and preoccupied during the lessons.

Parents are sometimes an obstacle to the success of distance education. Teachers mentioned that, during the first and second stages of the school reopening, some students were not held responsible for their homework and exams; parents were taking those responsibilities instead. Some parents are enthusiastic for their children to obtain high grades in exams and assignments, which led them to take the tests instead of, or with, their children, and did not give the children an opportunity to learn from their mistakes. Such behavior widened the gap in learning loss and put a big question mark on the success of distance education at a time when cooperation between home and school was much needed.

References

Aldabas, R. A. (2015). Special education in Saudi Arabia: History and areas for reform. *Creative Education, 6*(11), 1158–1167. https://doi.org/10.4236/ce.2015.611114

Alharbi, M. (2020). *Understanding multiculturalism in Saudi Education: A case study of two schools in Mecca* [Ph.D. thesis]. Andrews University. http://search.proquest.com/docview/2447564026/abstract/6ED51F69FCBB4BAEPQ/1

Alquraini, T. (2010). Special education in Saudi Arabia: Challenges, perspectives, future possibilities. *International Journal of Special Education, 25*(3), 9.

Alquraini, T. (2013). Legislative rules for students with disabilities in the United States and Saudi Arabia: A comparative study. *International Interdisciplinary Journal of Education, 2*(6), 601–614. https://doi.org/10.12816/0002942

Banks, J. (2015). *Cultural diversity and education: Foundations, curriculum, and teaching.* Routledge. https://doi.org/10.4324/9781315622255

Binmahfooz, S. (2019). *Saudi special education preservice teachers' perspective towards inclusion* [Ed.D. dissertation]. Digital Commons, University of South Florida. https://digitalcommons.usf.edu/etd/7746/

Creswell, J. W., & Poth, C. N. (2018). *Qualitative inquiry & research design: Choosing among five approaches* (4th ed.). Sage.

Eddles-Hirsch, K. (2015). Phenomenology and educational research. *International Journal of Advanced Research, 3*(8), 12.

Field, S., Kuczera, M., & Pont, B. (2007). *No more failures: Ten steps to equity in education.* OECD. https://doi.org/10.1787/9789264032606-en

Flynn, S. V., & Korcuska, J. S. (2018). Credible phenomenological research: A mixed-methods study. *Counselor Education and Supervision, 57*(1), 34–50. https://doi.org/10.1002/ceas.12092

Gay, G. (2010). *Culturally responsive teaching: Theory, research, and practice.* Teachers College Press.

Gay, G. (2013). Teaching to and through cultural diversity. *Curriculum Inquiry, 43*(1), 48–70. https://doi.org/10.1111/curi.12002

General Authority for Statistics. (2018, May 13). *GASTAT: 83.83% of individuals (12 to 65 years) use internet, and 92% use cell phone.* General Authority for Statistics, Kingdom of Saudi Arabia. https://www.stats.gov.sa/en/news/254

General Authority for Statistics. (2019). *Population statistics.* General Authority for Statistics, Kingdom of Saudi Arabia. https://www.stats.gov.sa/en/43

Hamdan, A. (2005). Women and education in Saudi Arabia: Challenges and achievements. *International Education Journal, 6*(1), 42–64. https://files.eric.ed.gov/fulltext/EJ854954.pdf

Horn, M. B., & Staker, H. (2014). *Blended: Using disruptive innovation to improve schools* (1st ed.). Jossey-Bass.

Ladson-Billings, G. (2009). *The dreamkeepers: Successful teachers of African American children* (2nd ed.). Jossey-Bass.

Levin, B. (2003). *Approaches to equity in policy for lifelong learning.* OECD. https://www.oecd.org/education/school/38692676.pdf

Mani, M. A., & As-Sbit, A.-R. S. (1981). *Cultural policy in the Kingdom of Saudi Arabia.* UNESDOC Digital Library, UNESCO. https://unesdoc.unesco.org/ark:/48223/pf0000046809

Ministry of Education. (2020). *The Saudi MOE: Leading efforts to combat coronavirus pandemic (COVID-19)*. https://iite.unesco.org/wp-content/uploads/2020/10/The-Saudi-MOE-Leading-Efforts-to-Combat-Coronavirus-Pandemic-COVID-19.pdf

OECD. (2019). *PISA 2018 results (Volume II)*. https://www.oecd-ilibrary.org/content/publication/b5fd1b8f-en

UNESCO. (2018). *Handbook on measuring equity in education*. UNESCO. http://uis.unesco.org/sites/default/files/documents/handbook-measuring-equity-education-2018-en.pdf

United Nations. (2020). *Policy brief: Education during COVID-19 and beyond* (p. 26). https://unsdg.un.org/sites/default/files/2020-08/sg_policy_brief_covid-19_and_education_august_2020.pdf

United Nations Sustainable Development Knowledge Platform. (2018). *Towards Saudi Arabia's sustainable tomorrow.* First voluntary national review, 2018 – 1439. https://sustainabledevelopment.un.org/content/documents/20230SDGs_English_Report972018_FINAL.pdf

Zhang, H., Chan, P. W. K., & Boyle, C. (2014). *Equality in education: Fairness and inclusion*. Springer.

CHAPTER 7

Comparative Study of Alternative Teaching and Learning Tools

Google Meet, Microsoft Teams, and Zoom during COVID-19

Kamran Ahmed Siddiqui and Shabir Ahmad

Abstract

The purpose of this chapter is to compare three giant video conferencing platforms, i.e., Google Meet, Microsoft Teams, and Zoom, as alternative teaching and learning tools during COVID-19. Analyses were made for three main issues: systems requirements, teaching and learning features, and security features. Firstly, Zoom has relatively low hardware requirements for video conferencing. Secondly, five teaching and learning features make Zoom the preferred choice for educators. These five features include LMS integration with Zoom, breakout rooms in Zoom meetings, polling, recordings, and in-conference chat. Finally, Zoom users are more vulnerable to security issues as compared to other video conferencing participants. Based on overall assessment, Zoom has been considered a better choice for educational purposes.

Keywords

Google Meet – Microsoft Teams – Zoom – video conferencing platforms – alternative learning tools – COVID-19 – education – teaching – learning

1   Introduction

Thanks to COVID-19, the world has experienced the hidden potential of video conferencing tools on a mass scale. In addition, the pandemic has made people think about avoiding public gatherings but still staying connected and communicating with each other. As a result, many business meeting and video conferencing software tools emerged throughout the world. In addition, the teaching-learning process at all education levels, including universities, has also changed due to the COVID-19 pandemic (Wiyono et al., 2021). Throughout the globe, traditional classroom-based education was suddenly shifted to the use of online platforms (Ismail et al., 2021). As a result, online teaching methods were different from traditional lecture formats (Toney et al., 2021). While some institutes were ready for the sudden transition, others had no other option except using general video conferencing platforms as an alternative to teaching (Ismail et al., 2021). Every educational institution had its protocol for providing student instruction during the pandemic (Zigelman, 2020). However, the survey shows that teachers were dissatisfied with technological support from their educational institutions and felt unprepared for this transition (Zigelman, 2020). Video conferencing platforms have gained worldwide popularity due to the pandemic. Individuals from all walks of life have utilized these platforms to do their jobs and communicate with their colleagues (Gauthier & Husain, 2020). This article has attempted to compare the three most popular video conferencing tools: Google Meet, Microsoft Teams, and Zoom.

Google Meet (formerly known as Hangouts Meet; commonly known as Meet) is a video-communication platform developed by Google LLC. Google is the largest search engine and provide internet-based services advertising (Google LLC, 2021). Google is ranked 4th in Interbrand's Top 100 Global Brands (2020), with massive brand equity of USD 165 billion (Interbrand, 2022).

Microsoft Teams is a video conferencing tool developed by world's largest software giant. The company produces computer software, consumer electronics and related services (Microsoft Corporation, 2022). Microsoft is ranked 3rd in Interbrand's (2022) Top 100 Global Brands, with massive brand equity of USD 166 billion.

Zoom Meetings (commonly known as Zoom) is a proprietary video teleconferencing software developed by Zoom Video Communications. It provides videotelephony and online chat services through a cloud-based peer-to-peer software platform. During COVID-19 this platform became the backbone of education, and social relations (Zoom Video Communications, 2022).

2 Systems Requirements

Video conferencing comprises a central cloud-based platform connecting calls between personal device clients and centralized cloud-based meeting room device endpoints. The quality of video conferencing services depends on the hardware and software employed in this service, irrespective of the video conferencing platform. Video conferencing system combines capable equipment, a robust network, and the software used to integrate it all together. However, three essential ingredients for any video conferencing system include (1) computer should have faster processing, (2) sufficient network bandwidth is needed, and (3) high-resolution webcams with microphones. Table 7.1 provides

TABLE 7.1   Comparative account of Meet, Teams, and Zoom for systems requirements

	Criteria	Google Meet	Microsoft Teams	Zoom
Hardware requirements	Processor – Minimum	Dual-Core processor	Dual-Core 1.1 GHz or higher	Single-Core 1.0 GHz or higher
	Processor – Recommended	Quad-Core processor	Quad-Core processor	Dual-Core 2.0 GHz or higher
	RAM – Minimum	2.0 GB dedicated	4.0 GB dedicated	1.0 GB
	RAM – Recommended	8.0 GB	8.0 GB	4.0 GB
Bandwidth	Minimum bandwidth	3.2 mbps	1.2 mbps	2.0 mbps
Operating systems supported	Apple Mac OS	Yes	Yes	Yes
	Google Chrome OS	Yes	No	No
	Linux	Yes	Yes	Yes
	Microsoft Windows	Yes	Yes	Yes
Mobile operating systems	Android	Yes	Yes	Yes
	Apple iOS 12.0	Yes	Yes	Yes
Browsers supported	Apple Mac: Safari	Yes	Partially supported	Yes
	Google Chrome	Yes	Yes	Yes
	Microsoft Edge	Yes	Yes	Yes
	Microsoft Internet Explorer	Yes	Yes	Yes
	Mozilla Firefox	Yes	No	Yes
Source		Google Meet Help (2021)	Microsoft (2021)	Zoom Support (2022c)

a comparative account of systems requirements for the three most popular video conferencing platforms, including Google Meet, Microsoft Teams, and Zoom.

Two observations can be made here. Firstly, all mainstream operating systems, including Apple Mac, Microsoft Windows, and Linux, were all supported by those three video conferencing platforms. Similarly, three video conferencing giants support two major mobile operating systems, including Android and Apple iOS. In addition, all mainstream browsers, including Google Chrome, Microsoft Edge, Microsoft Internet Explorer, Apple Mac: Safari, are all supported (fully or partially) by all three major players in the video conferencing industry. A second observation is related to hardware and internet bandwidth requirements. It appears that Zoom has relatively low hardware requirements for video conferencing. However, Microsoft Teams claims to be having minimal requirements for internet bandwidth usage as well.

3 Teaching and Learning Issues

Due to the outbreak of the COVID-19 pandemic, the teaching-learning process has undergone a significant revamping and moved from physical classrooms to virtual classrooms (Wiyono et al., 2021). Throughout the world, the lecturing process was conducted online. Many video conferencing tools were utilized for the lecturing processes, including Zoom Meetings, Microsoft Teams, and Google Meet. The use of video conferencing tools brings excellent benefits. On the other hand, it also causes students to face various problems. Therefore, this study aimed to compare the features of these video conferencing tools, the problems they posed, and strategies for solving them in the lecturing process.

Many teaching and learning features are standard among all three platforms, including inviting external participants, screen sharing, recording, virtual backgrounds, joining from the browser, native mobile apps, flexible layouts, student engagement tracking, accessibility, whiteboarding, classroom-oriented chat, specialized hybrid learning, in-conference text chat, event hosting with participant roles. However, five teaching and learning features make Zoom the preferred choice for educators. These five features include Learning Management System (LMS) integration with Zoom, breakout rooms in Zoom meetings, polling, recordings, and in-conference chat.

Zoom integrates more than 150 learning management systems, almost with all mainstream players, including Blackboard and SAP Litmos. LMS-Zoom integration enables the teachers to bypass the laborious step of manually enrolling each student in the session. LMS-Zoom integration can automatically notify enrolled students and record all data in a single system, providing easy setup procedures (Zoom Developer Support, 2021).

Zoom Breakout rooms allow the teacher to split the Zoom classroom meeting into up to 50 separate sessions and allocate participants to different breakout rooms. Alternatively, participants may also choose enter breakout sessions

TABLE 7.2 Comparative account of Meet, Teams, and Zoom for teaching and learning features

Assessment variable	Google Meet	Microsoft Teams	Zoom
Preferred for...	Online work meetings	Online work meetings	Online teaching & work meetings
Meeting length	300 hours	24 hours	30 hours
Meeting Participants	150	300	100
Unlimited number of meetings	Yes	Yes	Yes
Invite external participants	Yes	Yes	Yes
Screen sharing	Yes	Yes	Yes
Cloud Recording	Yes	Yes	Yes
Virtual background	Yes	Yes	Yes
Join from browser	Yes	Yes	Yes
Native mobile apps	Yes	Yes	Yes
Adjustable layouts	Yes	Yes	Yes
Student engagement tracking	Yes	Yes	Yes
Accessibility	Yes	Yes	Yes
White-boarding	Yes	Yes	Yes
Classroom oriented chat	Yes	Yes	Yes
Specialized hybrid learning	Yes	Yes	Yes
In-conference text chat	Yes	Yes	Yes
Event hosting with participant roles	Yes	Yes	Yes
LMS integration	No	Yes	Yes
In-conference private chat	No	No	Yes
Polling	No	No	Yes
Local recordings	No	No	Yes
Breakout rooms	No	No	Yes

SOURCE: RAMIREZ (2021), DATALINKNETWORKS[1]

as they please. In addition, the host can join any breakout room at any time (Zoom Support, 2022a).

Zoom's polling feature allows the teacher to create true/false or multiple-choice polling questions for students. The teacher will be able to launch the poll during the online session and gather the responses from students. If the poll is a graded item, LMS will automatically update all students' grades (Zoom Support, 2021).

Zoom recording feature also allows participants to record their meetings to cloud-based drive or on a local computer. This feature is not available with other two giants (Zoom Support, 2022d).

The in-conference private chat feature allows participants to send private messages to other participants while in a meeting. Private messages between participants are not viewable by the host. Disabling private chat prevents participants from privately messaging other participants but still allows participants and the host to send private messages to each other. Hosts can also disable chat for everyone in the meeting (Zoom Support, 2022b).

4 Security Issues

Zoom, Google Meet, and Microsoft Teams are the most popular video conferencing platforms, and they are examined for their security issues (Gauthier & Husain, 2020). They have made five observations for security concerns. First, none of those video conferencing platforms mentioned above have open-source code. Second, each video conferencing platform has documented their security settings and provided their security policies. Third, these platforms utilized state-of-the-art encryption methods. Fourth, Zoom seems to leave many options for users to customize in terms of security, and some users may overlook these features, which could leave them vulnerable. This could pose more of a problem than it seems. Fifth, Zoom does not encrypt data, if stored locally while the other two platforms, do encrypt all data at rest by default. Finally, Zoom does not require users to sign in by default when joining a meeting. Meet and Teams both require users to sign in by default and add that extra layer of security to ensure that contacts' identities are verifiable. It is easy to conclude that Zoom users are more vulnerable to security issues than the other two platforms: Google Meet and Microsoft Teams (Gauthier & Husain, 2020).

Zoom and its users have recently experienced a security crisis named *Zoombombing* (Young, 2021). The phenomenon has emerged in which aggressors join online meetings to disrupt and harass their participants ((Elmer, Neville, Burton, & Ward-Kimola, 2021; Walsh, Unertl, & Ebert, 2021). The idea was

TABLE 7.3 Comparative account of Meet, Teams, and Zoom for security features

Security features	Google Meet	Microsoft Teams	Zoom
Encrypted in transit	Yes	Yes	Yes
Encrypted at rest	Yes	Yes	–
Encryption Feature available	Yes	Yes	Yes
Contacts identities verifiable	Yes	Yes	–
Required sign in before joining by default	Yes	Yes	–
Option to require to sign in before joining	Yes	Yes	Yes
Security design properly documented	Yes	Yes	Yes
Code open source	No	No	No
Encrypted so the provider cannot read	No	No	No

SOURCE: GAUTHIER AND HUSAIN (2020)

started as 'online classroom pranks' and swiftly moved to organized disruption efforts, sometimes also used as a tool for racial harassment and hate speech (Nakamura, Stiverson, & Lindsey, 2021), which the law enforcement agencies have threatened to punish as serious offense (Secara, 2020).

From an information security point of view, many lessons were learned from this crisis. Firstly, it is becoming increasingly important for companies to incorporate privacy by design (Young, 2021), and this observation is not restricted to only video conferencing tools. Secondly, the only effective defense against Zoombombing is to create unique join links for each participant (Walsh, Unertl, & Ebert, 2021). Thirdly, Zoom has underestimated the privacy expectations of its exponentially growing customer base, and they must make details about their privacy practices to the general public, who has a growing interest in, and dissatisfaction with, corporate privacy practices (Young, 2021). Fourth, most Zoombombing attempts were made by insiders who had legitimate access to the Zoom meetings, particularly students in high school and college classes. Teachers can handle this issue in a class by using Zoom features like enabling the waiting room, restricting access to screen share or physical reporting, and imposing ultimate institutional punishments for Zoombombing attackers and their insider supporters. Fifth, this case has given a lesson for end-users as they need to prepare for the challenges and approaches adopted before, during, and after the Zoom meetings (Lan et al., 2021). Finally, this situation has taught another lesson of balancing the focus between the default settings for levels of customization versus the level of privacy (Secara, 2020).

5   Conclusion

This paper aims to provide a comparative account of three video conferencing platforms, i.e., Google Meet, Microsoft Teams, and Zoom, as alternative teaching and learning tools during COVID-19. Many lessons were learned during this exercise.

Firstly, all major operating systems (Apple Mac, Microsoft Windows, and Linux), major mobile operating systems (Android and Apple iOS), and all mainstream browsers (Google Chrome, Microsoft Edge, Microsoft Internet Explorer, Apple Mac: Safari) were all supported by those three video conferencing platforms, i.e., Google Meet, Microsoft Teams, and Zoom.

Secondly, many teaching and learning features (including inviting external participants, screen sharing, recording, virtual backgrounds, joining from the browser, native mobile apps, flexible layouts, student engagement tracking, accessibility, whiteboarding, classroom-oriented chat, specialized hybrid learning, in-conference text chat, event hosting with participant roles are standard among all three platforms.

Thirdly, many security features (protection against open-source code, well-documented security design, explicitly cover their compliance policies, threat protection, transparency policies, privacy policies, security features, and utilized state-of-the-art encryption methods) are shared among all three video conferencing platforms.

Finally, Zoom has relatively low hardware requirements for video conferencing and teaching features, make Zoom the preferred choice for educators. These teaching features include LMS integration with Zoom, breakout rooms in Zoom meetings, polling, recordings, and in-conference chat. However, Zoom users are more vulnerable to security issues than the other two platforms, i.e., Google Meet and Microsoft Teams. Overall. Zoom is the highest reviewed conferencing software for educational purposes and an excellent option for a stand-alone video conferencing solution.

Note

1   DatalinkNetworks is a US based premier IT Solutions provider; specialized in business, non-profits, K-12, higher education and government.

References

Elmer, G., Neville, S. J., Burton, A., & Ward-Kimola, S. (2021). Zoombombing during a global pandemic. *Social Media and Society, 7*(3). https://doi.org/10.1177/20563051211035356

Gauthier, N. H., & Husain, M. I. (2020, December 17–19). Dynamic security analysis of Zoom, Google Meet and Microsoft Teams. In Y. Park, D. Jadav, & T. Austin (Eds.). *Silicon Valley cybersecurity conference: First conference, SVCC 2020* (pp. 3–24). Springer.

Google LLC. (2022, February 23). In *Wikipedia*. https://en.wikipedia.org/wiki/Google

Google Meet help. (2021). *Requirements for using Google Meet.* https://support.google.com/meet/answer/7317473?hl=en

Interbrand. (2022). *Best global brands 2020*. Ranking the Brands. https://www.rankingthebrands.com/The-Brand-Rankings.aspx?rankingID=37&year=1342

Ismail, H., Khafaji, H., Fasla, H., Younis, A. R., & Harous, S., (2021). A cognitive style-based usability evaluation of Zoom and Teams for online lecturing activities. In *2021 IEEE Global Engineering Education Conference (EDUCON)* (pp. 1565–1570). IEEE. https://doi.org/10.1109/EDUCON46332.2021.9454100

Lan, Y., Gupta, K. C., Huang, T., Chelliah, S., & Spector, J. M., (2021). Organizing and hosting virtual PPTELL 2020 during the COVID-19 pandemic. *Educational Technology and Society, 24*(1), 64–74. https://eric.ed.gov/?id=EJ1292911

Microsoft. (2021). *Hardware requirements for Microsoft Teams.* https://docs.microsoft.com/en-us/microsoftteams/hardware-requirements-for-the-teams-app

Microsoft Corporation. (2022, February 21). In *Wikipedia*. https://en.wikipedia.org/wiki/Microsoft

Nakamura, L., Stiverson, H., & Lindsey, K. (2021). *Racist Zoombombing* (1st ed., pp. 1–64). Routledge. https://doi.org/10.4324/9781003157328

Ramirez, H. (2021, January 11). *Microsoft Teams vs. Google Meet for education.* datalinknetworks. https://www.datalinknetworks.net/dln_blog/microsoft-teams-vs.-zoom-vs-google-meet-for-education

Secara, I.-A. (2020). Zoombombing – the end-to-end fallacy. *Network Security, 2020*(8), 13–17. https://doi.org/10.1016/S1353-4858(20)30094-5

Toney, S., Light, J., & Urbaczewski, A. (2021). Fighting Zoom fatigue: Keeping the zoombies at bay. *Communications of the Association for Information Systems, 48*(1), 10. https://doi.org/10.17705/1CAIS.04806

Walsh, C. G., Unertl, K. M., & Ebert, J. S. (2021). Rapid supportive response to a traumatic "Zoombombing" during the COVID-19 pandemic. *Academic Medicine, 96*(1), e6–e7. https://doi.org/10.1097/ACM.0000000000003739

Wiyono, B. B., Indreswari, H., & Putra, A. P. (2021, August). The utilization of "Google Meet" and "Zoom Meetings" to support the lecturing process during the pandemic of COVID-19. In *Proceedings of 2021 International Conference on Computing, Electronics & Communications Engineering (iCCECE)* (pp. 25–29). IEEE. https://doi.org/10.1109/iCCECE52344.2021.9534847

Young, S. (2021). Zoombombing your toddler: User experience and the communication of Zoom's privacy crisis. *Journal of Business and Technical Communication, 35*(1), 147–153. https://doi.org/10.1177/1050651920959201

Zigelman I. (2020). Global pandemic contorts traditional classroom teaching for private school. In *Proceedings of 14th International Multi-conference on Society, Cybernetics and Informatics (IMSCI 2020)* (pp. 187–190). International Institute of Informatics and Systemics. https://www.iiis.org/CDs2020/CD2020Summer/PapersH1.htm

Zoom Developer Support. (2021). *How to integrate Zoom into a Learning Management System (LMS)/education website*. Zoom. https://devsupport.zoom.us/hc/en-us/articles/360060333271-How-to-integrate-Zoom-into-a-learning-management-system-LMS-education-website

Zoom Support. (2021, December 22). *Polling for meetings*. Zoom. https://support.zoom.us/hc/en-us/articles/213756303-Polling-for-meetings

Zoom Support. (2022a, January 25). *Enabling breakout rooms*. Zoom. https://support.zoom.us/hc/en-us/articles/206476093-Enabling-breakout-rooms

Zoom Support. (2022b, February 2). *Disable private chat*. Zoom. https://support.zoom.us/hc/en-us/articles/360060835932-Enabling-and-disabling-private-chat

Zoom Support. (2022c, February 7). *Zoom system requirements: Windows, macOS, Linux*. Zoom. https://support.zoom.us/hc/en-us/articles/201362023-System-requirements-for-Windows-macOS-and-Linux

Zoom Support. (2022d, February 24). *Enabling and starting local recordings*. Zoom. https://support.zoom.us/hc/en-us/articles/201362473-Local-recording

Zoom Video Communications (2022, February 8). In *Wikipedia*. https://en.wikipedia.org/wiki/Zoom_Video_Communications

CHAPTER 8

Reorientation of Teaching/Teachers about Education and Pandemic

Sami Ghazzai Alsulami

Abstract

This chapter is chiefly concerned with presenting an integrated worldview of teaching to deliver positive and effective teaching solutions during times of crisis. In particular, the chapter emphasizes the role of educational leadership and management and stresses the value of performance management, performance appraisal, emotional intelligence, and continuous education during the concurrent COVID-19 pandemic. Toward this end, the chapter addresses issues pertaining to anxiety management and cultivating task-oriented learning communities that are modern, inclusive, and reinvigorating. The objective is to produce a pedagogically useful document when reorienting contemporary teaching practice and teaching staff in Saudi Arabia.

Keywords

educational leadership – educational management – performance management – pandemic anxiety

1   Introduction

The current COVID-19 pandemic has a global and persistent impact on critical areas of human life, including health, education, and future planning. In specific terms, the crisis has made global education systems primarily contingent while accentuating the value of emergency management and contingency planning. Indeed, in the current global pandemic, successful educational solutions turn out to be those reiterating a bundle of innovative and service-driven dimensions. Still, deliberate answers and plans to resume traditional and face-to-face education remain primarily at the top of the Saudi education agenda. Indeed, the state of contingency and unpredictability posed by the global crisis raises significant concerns about the possibilities to deliver education solutions in Saudi Arabia to accommodate both positive and effective teaching narratives across all disciplines. This directs Saudi education toward a learner-focused and service delivery orientation. In this regard, it is shown empirically that reorienting the teaching institution and culture via the use of innovative educational solutions, e.g., distance education is a well-pronounced characteristic of the future delivery of education in Saudi Arabia.

In this view, this chapter explores both the aspects and implications of reorienting Saudi teaching and teachers into a culture of learner-focused and service delivery education.

The objective throughout this chapter is to offer clear guidelines via which Saudi education can be made cross-functional, integrated, and multidisciplined to ultimately satisfy the labor market requirements and promote the value of responsible citizenship.

2   Presentation and Organization

The chapter is organized and presented according to the major themes of presenting an integrated worldview of teaching and delivering positive and effective teaching solutions by emphasizing transformational educational leadership and management during times of crisis and stressing the value of teachers' continuous value-added education and skill development. Toward this end, the chapter further addresses issues pertaining to anxiety management and emotional intelligence to establish the pillars of educational environments that are modern, inclusive, and reinvigorating.

3   Integrated Worldview of Teaching

Presenting an integrated worldview of teaching to deliver positive and effective teaching solutions in Saudi Arabia demands a multitude of prerequisites. In fact, during the current COVID-19 pandemic, formulating and delivering effective teaching solutions can hardly be conceived without committing to sound educational leadership, meaningful teaching performance management and appraisal, emotional management, and continuous value-added education and task-oriented training for teachers and administrative assistants.

4 Transformational Educational Leadership

This section locates the transformational style of educational leadership within the context of formulating and delivering effective teaching solutions during the current age of global crisis. Most contemporary characterization of the term 'leadership' centers on the notion of the influential leader and the related extent to which the followers of that leader tend to respond and behave. The leadership-follower characterization of influence and response can be typically observed in a modern and teaching-oriented school world, and so may be helpful when understanding the features and attributes of schools and teaching institutions that are likely to survive the pandemic and continue to succeed in the future (Allison-Napolitano, 2013).

As opposed to traditional leadership styles, including transactional models and non-transactional laissez-faire approaches, transformational leadership theory is mainly interested in explaining the behavioral mechanism via which educational leaders succeed to create stimulated teacher followers. It causes teacher followers to perform according to the collective and strategic interest of the school, based on the dynamics of psychological and emotional attachment to their teaching institutions (Bass & Avolio, 1994).

Burns (1978) pioneered the specification of transformation leadership as a moral theory of the attachment, autonomy, and problem-solving skills of followers in response to the behavioral choices made by leaders (Bass & Steidlmeier, 1999). In exact terms, the pivot column of transformational leadership in an educational context explains and predicts the processes via which educational leaders directly stimulate and reassuringly motivate teacher followers to continuously surpass average requirements and overdo their sorted out or already understood potential and capabilities (Tu & Lu, 2016).

In such fashion, in an educational context, transformational leadership specifies educational leaders in terms of the multi-dimensional performance of charismatic leadership (also referred to as idealized influence), inspirational motivation, individualized consideration, and intellectual stimulation (Bass, 1990).

The dimension of charismatic leadership or, interchangeably, idealized influence, specifies that transformational educational leaders captivatingly act as role models to be looked up to and have their footsteps followed by the teacher followers for their dedication, willpower, self-actualization, and social (and moral) conduct (Yukl, 2012).

The dimension of inspirational motivation stipulates those transformational educational leaders address their teacher followers with clear and instructive vision in a fervent, consequential, and energized fashion that is easily and aptly comprehendible (Stone et al., 2004). The dimension of individualized consideration provides transformational educational leaders to deduce and recognize the higher-level needs of their teacher followers by audibly transmitting that they are authentically and rightfully recognizing the empowerment, self-development, affirmation, advancement, and endorsement of such teacher followers (Padilla et al., 2007). The dimension of intellectual stimulation prescribes that transformational educational leaders summon their teacher followers to continuously interrogate things, probe into the status quo, cross-examine established assumptions, analyze potentials, and oppose paradigm paralysis vial that may accommodate innate and fundamental know-how and problem-solving (Garcia-Morales et al., 2008). This further implies that, through the adjustment and improvement of the underlying belief systems of their teacher followers, transformational leadership theory predicts that educational leaders exhibiting the attributes of transformational leadership may tap into paving the communal and socioeconomic maps of their schools and teaching institutions (Bowen, 2005). In this concern, the historical development of transformational leadership theory stems from the traditional line of thought of visionary leadership (Conger & Kanungo, 1994). The theory is also related to neocharismatic theories of leadership to the extent to which individual traits and behavioral choice variables tend to explain observed attributes of leadership (Conger & Kanungo, 1994). However, in addition to individual traits and behavioral choice variables, the theory of transformational leadership allows for the emotional or psychological attachment that may be harbored by followers toward their leaders only to be transpired through zeal, devotion, and sincerity (Steinmann et al., 2018). Toward this end, teacher followers emotionally attached to school leadership have many presumptions for the success of the school or teaching institution as a whole as well as the determinants of the quality of work-life of teacher followers, including self-performance, organizational performance, job satisfaction level, and career growth (Avolio et al., 2004).

Guided by the behavioral traits of educational leaders and the psychological attachment developed as a result by teacher followers, transformational leadership theory predicts that the school or teaching institution as a whole may mirror an embodied and personalized vision of the educational leader in a style that varies positively with improved and mutually bolstered levels of the performance of both the educational leader and the teacher followers (Avolio et al., 2009).

In this vein, whilst appealing to the positive moral values of teacher followers, transformational educational leadership is far more than merely satisfying the somewhat transactional basic needs of teacher followers in terms of pay and compensational benefits (Aryee et al., 2012).

4.1 Criticism of Transformational Leadership Theory

Leaders exhibiting the four dimensions of transformational leadership theory are observed to succeed in follower dedication and motivation (see Bass & Riggio, 2006). In addition, success in terms of specific economic measures of performance such as the ratio of input-output efficiency (see Liang et al., 2011) and transformational educational leadership is predicted to be observed through specific individual traits and behavior choice variables that can barely be imitated, shared, or replicated in the cross-section. This makes transformational educational leadership a materialization of innate nature rather than qualifications (see Kovjanic et al., 2012). Undeniably, the emphasis of transformational leadership theory on exceptional individual peculiarities may nurture an instinctive habitat for the exercise of oligarchy, totalitarianism, and autocracy by transformational educational leaders (Kaiser et al., 2008). This places aspects of tremendous ethical conduct and excellent moral standards at the very heart of the realized and continued positive effects of transformational educational leadership.

Moreover, characterizing educational leadership in accordance with transformational leadership theory may also suffer from the lack of persistent measurement due to the mutual engagement of the overlapping conceptual dimensions of charismatic leadership, inspirational motivation, individualized consideration, and intellectual stimulation. For instance, charismatic leadership learned via the conceptual dimension of idealized influence is particularly troublesome for measurement purposes since the term 'charisma' is in and by itself obscure, enigmatic, and largely inconclusive (see Burns, 1978). Furthermore, when measuring the extent to which transformational educational leadership applies to a particular leader, it might be difficult to classify observed educational leadership behaviors according to the four transformational components given the complexity and evolving nature of the teaching and school world during times of crisis. This eventually may result in reporting transformational educational leadership scores that suffer from biases and that are not decision-useful due to lack of factor or component independence. In this view, given the fact that documented evidence on the objective and non-emotional impact of transformational leadership is scant (see Van Knippenberg et al., 2007), the need for formulating fitting and objective economic efficiency measurements of transformational educational leadership can hardly be overstated in Saudi Arabia during the current COVID-19 pandemic.

5 Teaching Performance Management and Appraisal

In the light of the above presentation of the transformational style of educational leadership, this section introduces teaching performance management and appraisal as another pivot for formulating and delivering effective teaching solutions in Saudi Arabia during times of global crises.

Performance management and performance appraisal are broad terms that may assume a latitude of meanings and implications. In particular, the definitions of performance management and performance appraisal vary across contexts, disciplines, and perspectives, notwithstanding teaching and education.

5.1 Teaching Performance Management

However, the ultimate goal of teaching performance management is improving the performance of teachers and faculty members via the ordinary and time-honored management activities of planning, organizing, and control. In this regard, the HRM (human resources management) perspective of performance management, where a conceptual association is established between educational HRM practices and the performance of teachers and faculty members, is particularly well-pronounced in the literature (Hutchinson, 2013). Under the HRM perspective of teaching performance management, educational management undertakes the activities of (1) setting goals and quantifying expected outcomes (i.e., performance planning), (2) measuring, monitoring, evaluating, and reviewing performance (i.e., performance measurement and performance variance analysis), and (3) developing performance improvement scenarios and enhancement strategies (i.e., performance improvement). The HRM perspective of performance management exhausts a well-developed area of the strategic performance management literature where the philosophy and activities of management are emphasized and underscored as an essential mechanism both inspiring and accelerating the pace of performance improvement (see Boselie, 2014; Appelbaum et al., 2000).

This notion of HRM performance management is paramount for the performance of Saudi teachers and faculty members during times of crisis where expectations and standards are both blurred.

In this concern, the fundamental premise of the literature on HRM and performance is to describe and analyze the effect of observed HRM interventions on performance improvement. The typical literature on the relationship between HRM and performance can be broadly categorized into three conceptual schools of performance: (1) best practice, (2) best fit, and (3) resource-based view (RBV) of the firm. The conjecture primarily maintained in any conceptual framework of performance in an educational setting is that HRM intervention strategies will eventually contribute to enhancing the performance of teachers and faculty members through the alteration of their personal tendencies. The three traditional performance schools of thought are very specific on the direction of the relationship and so were often subjected to the criticism of narrow causality. This ultimately led to the development of other conceptual frameworks, including the HR (human resources) causal chain and the AMO (ability-motivation-opportunity) performance theory. In relevance to Saudi efforts to reorient the teaching process and the teaching staff, the following subsections present the key conceptual developments of teaching performance management in four sections: best practice, best fit, RBV, and causal chain (and AMO).

5.1.1 Best Practice

The conceptual performance school of thought of best practice, also known as the performance universality model, is often described in the literature as high-performance management, high involvement work systems, and high commitment management (see Wood & de Menezes, 1998; Lawler, 1986; Appelbaum et al., 2000). In an educational environment, the best practice maintains and predicts that, due to supplementing and synergistically coefficient influences, a prevalent and comprehensive association is struck between performance and a consistent, reasoned, goal-congruent, and unified set of HRM intervention strategies regardless of the context and irrespective of the school size or location (see Combs et al., 2006). Furthermore, the best practice performance school of thought accommodates the negative effect that incoherent or meaningless combinations of HR interventions may have on the performance of teachers and faculty members, thus underlining the role of teamwork and performance mechanism designs. In an educational setting, schools and teaching institutions following the best practice conceptual framework apply universally successful and already identified HR interventions in their teaching settings. On this subject, the best practice approach, however, may be criticized for incoherency and inherent lack of universal agreement or consensus with respect to identifying generally accepted practices.

Although clear and straightforward to appreciate and apply, the best practice conceptual framework crucially suffers from internal inconsistency and inadequacy for situation analysis (see Boxall & Purcell, 2011). Moreover, the best practice school of thought can be further criticized in the educational management context for assuming that the set of intended HR practices and interventions will be the same experienced by teachers and faculty members without any loss or misinterpretation (see Purcell, 1999).

5.1.2 Best Fit

The best fit conceptual framework of performance is often referred to in the literature as the contingency model.

Unlike best practice, the best fit is context-driven. Best fit employs contemporary contingency theory and probability analysis to maintain that the effectiveness of HRM practices in managing and enhancing performance depends on the extent to which such practices tend to reflect the particular environmental influences relevant to the school or teaching institution.

In such fashion, the best fit is an outside-in conceptual framework that is vertically integrated to allow for incorporating the specifics and variations of the school or teaching institution, including strategy, size, risk aversion, life cycle, operations, management, and leadership (see Boxall & Purcell, 2011). Due to the outright orientation on context and situation analysis, the best fit conceptual framework of performance can be criticized along the lines of the measurement difficulties and contextual complexities faced by both research and practice when uncovering the appropriate and context-relevant set of HRM interventions given the demanding and fluid nature of teaching environments and educational systems amid the current COVID-19 pandemic.

5.1.3 A Resource-Based View of the Firm (RBV)

Unlike best fit, the performance conceptual framework of the resource-based view of the firm is an inside-out school of thought that recognizes teachers and faculty members as an asset resource differentiated by contribution, potential, imitability, scarcity, and background (Barney, 1991). RBV, above all, stresses the role of school culture, management, leadership, ethical standards, and social values while relatively marginalizing the role of the external environment. RBV is often criticized for being far less structured as opposed to both best practice and best fit.

5.1.4 HR Causal Chain and AMO

The HR causal chain specifies and predicts teaching performance in HRM via the mediating influences of effective HRM practices and their manifestation across the spectrum of intended and perceived value-added teaching practices and documented attitudinal and performance outcomes. The AMO theoretical framework of performance reiterates the causal chain HR and entails predictions concerning the impact of HRM on teaching performance vial, the mediating variables of potential contribution, dedication, and opportunity (see Appelbaum et al., 2000).

5.2 *Teaching Performance Appraisal*

This chapter recommends multi-source teaching performance appraisal when reorienting Saudi teaching practice and teaching staff.

Also referred to as 360-degree appraisal, multi-source teaching performance appraisal is a comprehensive and all-inclusive philosophy to teaching performance appraisal. It emphasizes all-encompassing feedback retrieved from all stakeholders, including students, peers, teaching assistants, self, and administrative assistants. The 360-degree teaching performance appraisal, primarily distinguishable from traditional performance appraisal methods, is now becoming strongly associated with successful organizations worldwide (see Dai et al., 2011).

The 360-degree appraisers are often anonymous, encouraging honesty, confidentiality, impersonality, autonomy, and involvement. The 360-degree appraisals are typically filled out electronically via an online questionnaire that includes categorized and well-presented assessment questions and relevant statements while often allowing for the possibility of text comments.

Once completed, 360-appraisals are analyzed and evaluated to produce a set of scientifically corrected and objectively measured performance ratings that are factored into and represented as an overall score. In this fashion, 360-degree appraisals are considered valid, reliable, acceptable, and procedurally fair. Moreover, the 360-degree approach allows for greater self-awareness via self-appraisal through challenging teachers' self-perception of their performance. Though its benefits are overwhelming, the 360-degree approach is often challenged for being costly, demanding, and time-consuming. The approach is also associated with subjectivity and due complexities of data analysis owing to the multiple perspectives considered.

Moreover, given the impersonality involved in collecting appraisals, analyzing ratings, and delivering scores, the importance of feedback as a critical motivational device has been questioned.

In this view, the teaching performance management and control systems can be enhanced by allowing the full benefits of the 360-degree appraisals to power into effect in terms of accuracy, comprehension, validity, multidimensionality, reliability, decision usefulness, mutual acceptability, and procedural flow fairness. Such benefits can typically be materialized with instructive, meaningful, and appealing teaching performance measurement ratings that can be functionally summed up into an overall score comparable in the cross-section of teachers and faculty members. This demands schools and teaching institutions to ensure that sufficient time, analytical computer programs, and resources are used with discretion for the rather cumbersome performance appraisal to be meaningfully entertained. Moreover, schools and teaching institutions may opt to associate the results of the appraisal assessment with motivating compensation and bonus packages as part of an educational management culture that appreciates and recognizes favorable performance. Furthermore, it is highly encouraged that the 360-degree performance appraisal system at schools and teaching institutions be mandatory and carried out regularly to emphasize the significance that the school places on developing the performance of the teaching staff. The school's

360-degree performance appraisal system is also suggested to stress the value of and acceptable procedures for self-appraisal, which is essential for a school culture of self-awareness where teachers' self-perception of their performance is continuously questioned and improved. Ultimately, the school's teaching performance management system is enhanced to the degree where the school's culture and organizational climate support a community of meaningful performance appraisal, instructive continuous education and training, teacher involvement and commitment, and recognizing both individual and group achievement while rewarding favorable and praiseworthy teaching performance.

6   Continuous Education and Training Needs Analysis for Saudi School Teachers and Faculty Members

Besides transformational educational leadership and teaching performance management and appraisal, this section advances continuous education of Saudi schoolteachers and faculty members as a crucial factor when planning and delivering teaching solutions in Saudi Arabia during these challenging times of the global pandemic. The presentation starts with laying out the foundation for continuous education and training needs analysis. This is followed by a concrete hypothetical example where the important issues of learning theory and program design and delivery are underscored.

The objective of the continuous education and training needs analysis (TNA) is to determine the distance between available (or current) teaching capabilities and anticipated (or required) teaching skills of Saudi school teachers and faculty members for meeting dynamic and demanding teaching requirements during times of crises (Anderson, 1994). The determined distance is articulated in terms of gaps that are then employed as building blocks for continuous education and training needs to formalize and tailor effective continuing education programs for schoolteachers and faculty members (Brigid, 2013). The recommended continuous education needs analysis may follow the three levels of the TNA model initially introduced by McGehee and Thayer (1961). The three levels of TNA analysis covered by McGehee and Thayer's model are the organizational school or teaching institution level, the operational teaching process level, and the individual teacher level (Arraya & Porifirio, 2017). The following presents an example of continuous education TNA analysis on each of the three levels in an educational context while employing qualitative data collection and analysis. This is followed by presenting a hypothetical delivery of a teacher continuous education program while underscoring the roles of learning theory and program evaluation.

In this vein, this document strongly advocates the continuous education of teachers and faculty members as the principal mechanism when reorienting Saudi teaching practice and teaching staff during times of crisis.

6.1 *Continuous Education Needs Analysis at the Organizational Level*

The ultimate goal of the continuous education TNA analysis at the institutional school level is to decide whether and where exactly continuous education is needed.

The analysis singles out the most relevant continuous education or training program that matches with the overall mission and goals of a particular school or teaching institution (Holden et al., 2015). The institutional school level analysis is thus carried out via analyzing the specific objectives of the school or teaching institution along with reports at the strategic level with respect to the organization-wide mission (and priorities) of the school and the current levels of the capabilities and potential of its teaching staff (see Holton et al., 2015). Along this line, the organizational level analysis may show that though the school emphasizes rigorous education among its top organizational priorities, the number of dissatisfied students has risen alarmingly and consistently throughout the concurrent COVID-19 pandemic. In particular, the relatively long hours spent by teachers to demonstrate quantitatively demanding purely theoretical proofs may have turned out to be the common factor theme that intercepts among the cross-section of dissatisfied student feedbacks during the pandemic. This knowledge may direct the TNA analysis of the continuous education program on the teaching staff at the school or teaching institution. It may also be that the teaching department at the particular school is relatively large, with many teaching hours undertaken daily.

In this regard, the large volume of daily teaching hours coupled with the dissatisfied feedback from students identifies that training is needed for the school's teaching staff with respect to the particular issue of the long hours spent on purely theoretical illustrations. It follows that a training program targeted at the teaching staff is proposed to offer a solution to the school organizational problem of dissatisfied student feedbacks since such training may directly result in a measurable decrease in teaching hours directed toward theoretical matters and an increase in teaching hours directed at pragmatic, yet quantitative matters as per the strategic mission of the school (Boydell & Leary, 1996). In this fashion, the continuous education training proposed may be congruent with the school's strategic priority of improving the student experience and achieving competitively high levels of quantitatively-oriented and rigorously-trained graduates (Holden et al., 2015).

6.2 *Continuous Education Needs Analysis at the Teaching Process Level*

Instructed by continuous education needs analysis at the organizational level, the objective of the TNA at the operational teaching process level is to identify the specific style of task or job level continuous education that is deemed relevant for the teaching staff at the school or teaching institution. The analysis at this level assumes the micro-objective of achieving enhanced efficiency levels when teaching rigorous and quantitatively-demanding subjects (Kodwani, 2017). An imperative premise to the operational teaching process level TNA is to specify and decide on the teaching staff knowledge base and capabilities set that is considered crucial for the efficient teaching of quantitatively demanding courses (see McGehee & Thayer, 1961). In this concern, the operational teaching process level TNA analysis may rely on analysing the school's teaching staff's nature, specifications, and general job descriptions (Denby, 2010). The analysis may consult with the work performance standards of teaching staff in Saudi Arabia with respect to primary, middle, and secondary schools. The analysis will include teaching requirements, teaching bylaws and typical procedures, formal means to communication within the school and with peers, integrity standards and codes of ethical conduct, and key performance indicators (see Honey & Mumford, 1986). The analysis in this fashion may reveal that hours spent teaching quantitatively demanding courses were undertaken with strict and somewhat blind reference to the school manuals and bylaws issued by top management.

Although the teaching staff are primarily service-oriented, too much emphasis on strict procedures and policies hinders their proactivity, autonomy, and problem-solving when addressing the students' particular and evolving educational needs. Moreover, the formal and relatively rigid communication culture that the school's teaching staff has to endure may be responsible for less empathy and slow attention when addressing the students' concerns and issues. In this context, in order to meet the expected performance standard of the customer service employee in terms of prompt attention to the educational needs and concerns of the students, the task of the teaching staff at the school may be recommended to be carried out more autonomously and proactively (as opposed to reactively). This is where the educational needs of the students are anticipated, and pre-emptive solutions are advised (see Kirkpatrick & Kirkpatrick, 2006). Toward this end, the teaching staff's knowledge base and skill set required to provide the performance standard of prompt attention to the educational needs placed by the students could be identified as personalized attentiveness, emotional intelligence, effective communication, effective persuasion, and resourcefulness and time management.

6.3 Continuous Education Needs Analysis at the Teacher Level

On the individual teacher level, the ultimate objective of the continuous education TNA is to single out particular attitude, intellectual, and teaching know-how gaps (Shree, 2017). For purposes of undertaking a competency-based assessment where intellectual and know-how gaps are to be decided upon, the teaching job performance evaluations of the school teachers reported by immediate and senior management is sought out and analyzed using the qualitative data analysis tool of uncovering themes and identifying patterns in contexts (see Blaikie, 2010; Creswell, 2013). The recurring theme may be that the teaching staff are not meeting the school management expectations in issues like subject teaching planning, problem-solving, and school policy interpretation. In this regard, over the course of reviewing performance evaluations of the teaching staff, school management may have raised issues about the depth of understanding of the school organizational procedures and policies that may apply in different circumstances. The school management also may have brought to surface concerns about contingent problem solving and performance under pressure. Indeed, the inputs from management performance evaluation reports define the keys to this continuing education training program's problem solving and know-how aspects throughout its planning, introduction, and conclusion (Leigh et al., 2000). Moreover, to identify attitude gaps, reviewing the performance reports by school management may be further supplemented with structured interviews of a random sample of the school teaching staff to undertake a behavioral competency analysis where the attitudes and creativity levels are examined (see Roulston, 2010; Beevers & Rea, 2016). The structured interviews may, in this regard, reveal behavioral question marks with work and interpersonal attitude issues with the teaching staff, including logical persuasion, empathetic teaching, ability to think out of the box, and capacity to perform well under pressure.

On this subject and to further validate the problem solving, know-how, and attitude gaps already uncovered, the TNA analysis may employ the Skill Will Matrix (see Hersey & Blanchard, 1984).

In this regard and based on a validated Skill Will questionnaire, the average teaching staff member may exhibit low will and high skill, which suggests a continuous education program and school management style that are engaging and exciting (Landsberg, 2015). The results of the Skill Will Matrix may, nonetheless, stand in great contrast with reviewed school management reports on the subject of skills and operational proficiency of the teaching staff. This possibility, however, can still be explained in terms of three possible reasons.

First, the Skill Will Matrix is a relatively simple model with only two dimensions and four outcomes (Obolensky, 2017).

Therefore, a fair possibility is that the school's teaching staff may not necessarily be of the high skill but rather somewhere between the low and high skill categories depicted by the matrix. Second, according to the Dunning-Kruger effect, school teaching staff members of the lower skill type are likely on average to portray and declare themselves that they are of the high skill type (see Helzer & Dunning, 2012).

Third, the teaching staff members may have fallen victims to rigid and inflexible management evaluations given the strict top-down organizational structure of the school that regard following detailed policies and micro regulations as the gold standard for teaching performance.

A note here is to emphasize that the three-level continuous education TNA example above is conducted based on qualitative data collection and analysis. To this end, qualitative data collection is often criticized for being biased and anecdotal (Creswell & Miller, 2000). Furthermore, qualitative data analysis is also inductive and subject to a great deal of generalization and the production of stereotypical results and conclusions (Ritchie & Lewis, 2003).

7   Learning Theory, Design, and Delivery

In light of the three-stage continuous education needs analysis example, the objective of the continuous education program is to bring the level of observed (or employed) capabilities of the teaching staff during dissatisfactory or difficult times up to the level of anticipated (or required) capabilities. The learning outcomes of this continuous education program are categorized into (1) problem solving and know-how, and (2) disposition and conduct.

The program's problem solving and know-how outcomes are: improved demonstration of concrete examples, better anticipating the needs of the students, improved written and oral communication, improved persuasion, and enhanced knowledge of the assortment of quantitative subjects taught and advisory services offered by the teaching staff. The disposition and conduct outcomes of the continuous education program are enhanced emotional regulation, improved capacity to perform under pressure, heightened intelligence for a cheerful and boosting disposition that is always reassuring and empathetic for the students. Toward this end, the following section applies *Kolb's learning theory* to the continuous education program.

7.1   Kolb's (1984) *Learning Theory*

Taking the problem solving and attitude learning outcomes identified via the three-stage continuous education needs analysis, the continuous education program may be planned and introduced to satisfy those learning outcomes following Kolb's (1984) experiential learning theory cycle and learning styles. The experiential learning theory cycle defines four levels where teacher-learners begin the cycle with concrete stimuli. At this level, a new experience is introduced, and an existing experience is examined. The second level involves reflective observation, where inconsistencies between introduced and examined experiences are mitigated. At the abstract conceptualization level, stimuli experience learning is concluded. As for the active experimentation level, teacher-learners apply their marginally acquired experiences to solve problems and answer particular situations (Kolb et al., 1984). Kolb's experiential learning theory also addresses the learning styles most suited for each learning cycle level. Along these lines, the learning cycle levels of concrete experience and reflective observation are suited to diverging learning where teacher-learners tend to harbor vivid emotions, deep feelings, and eloquent imagination. The learning cycle levels of abstract conceptualization and active experimentation are suited to the learning style of assimilation where teacher-learners tend to favor inquiring systems and analytic deduction. The learning cycle levels of abstract conceptualization and active experimentation are suited to the learning style of converging, where teacher-learners tend to learn from experiments, observed patterns, and documented data. Finally, the learning cycle levels of concrete experience and active experimentation are suited to the accommodating learning style, where teacher-learners have preferences for intuition and comprehensive problem-solving. To such a degree, Kolb's learning theory has great relevance for the continuous education training program for Saudi teachers and faculty members, given the learning culture of learners from Saudi Arabia and the Gulf region. Toward this end, it is empirically supported that learners from different cultures are associated with a heterogeneous set of learning modes and preferences (Gündüz & Özcan, 2010). For instance, Saudi learners are documented to be of the emotional and imaginative learning type, where active (as opposed to reflective) learning through the senses is observed (Al-Otaibi, 1996). The empirically observed regularity of Saudi learners taken jointly with Kolb's learning theory cycle and learning styles may strongly underscore the planning and introduction of the continuous education tailored training program for Saudi teachers and faculty members. Toward this end, according to Kolb's learning theory, Saudi teachers and faculty members are mostly diverging with learning characteristics relevant to the concrete experience and reflective observation. However, Kolb's theory can be criticized for identifying learnings styles that are mutually exclusive (Sims, 1980). In this regard, Saudi teachers and faculty members can exhibit more than one learning style in any particular setting (Beevers & Rea, 2016).

In this concern, consulting the learning styles of interactive learners, reflectors learners, conceptual learners, and practical learners identified by Honey and Mumford (1992) taken jointly with the stylized fact that Saudi learners are of the active learning type, Saudi teachers and faculty members could be documented to show preferences toward imaginative and emotional learning through the senses.

An important implication Kolb's (1984) theory has for planning, continuous teacher education and training programs in Saudi Arabia is the position assumed by the trainer (Atherton, 2013). In this regard, it is relevant to revisit Saudi schoolteachers who hold undergraduate degrees with faculty members holding postgraduate degrees. Besides having proper academic training, Saudi schoolteachers and faculty members also have extensive work experience. Given this profile of Saudi schoolteachers and faculty members, the trainer needs to deliver tailored continuous education and teacher training programs in Saudi Arabia. Thus, it is highly recommended that the trainer to be a seasoned educational leader with wholesome experience, who conducts effective planning and gives inspiring program orientation. Throughout, it is suggested that the trainer adheres to a philosophy of facilitation and not instruction. Given the specific nature of Saudi school and college teaching, continuous education and teacher training programs in Saudi Arabia, it is suggested the coach facilitating style of delivery to be adopted. It should convincingly emphasize on the development of teachers' specific skills and attitudes as per the know-how and attitude learning outcomes identified above. The coach facilitating style of delivering the continuous education program may follow Fleming and Taylor's (2004) practice model where the focus is placed on analyzing the initial state, the program intervention, the ultimate state, and the concluding evaluation. Furthermore, in contrast to didactic approaches, suggested continuous education and teacher training programs in Saudi Arabia, taken in conjunction with Kolb's (1984) learning style of diverging learners, may adopt the inquisitive method that encourages continuous know-how learning and persistent attitude enhancement for teachers and faculty members (see Armstrong & Tsokova, 2019).

Another important consideration to the recommended continuous education and teacher training programs is the cost structure (Chiu et al., 1999). This consideration is particularly well-pronounced in the contemporary Saudi agenda amid Vision 2030 of the kingdom that pivots on economic efficiency and optimal allocation of scarce resources. In this concern, all costs of continuous education and teacher training programs, including opportunity costs in terms of teacher learners' time and availability, may be categorized into direct costs and indirect overhead costs concerning the particular program as a cost object.

8 Evaluation of Teacher Continuous Program

Continuous education and teacher training programs in Saudi Arabia may apply the Kirkpatrick and Kirkpatrick's (2006) model of measuring and evaluating the effectiveness of training programs in terms of the four dimensions of reaction, learning, behavior, and results (Kirkpatrick & Kirkpatrick, 2006).

Toward this end, the tailored training program for Saudi teachers and faculty members may ask learners to complete a validated and anonymous questionnaire at the end of the program. The questionnaire may follow the Likert scale model and be classified into the four sections covering Kirkpatrick and Kirkpatrick's model: (1) How did teachers and faculty members react to continuous education training? (2) What is the extent to which teachers and faculty members have improved their technical knowledge, skills, and attitudes? (3) Was the behavior and attitude of teachers and faculty members changed toward the particular school as an organization? And (4) What are the potential benefits that may accrue back to the school as an organization because of the continuous education and training program.

9 The Role of Teacher Emotional Management during Times of Crisis

In addition to transformational educational leadership, teaching performance management, teaching performance appraisal, and teachers' continuous education, this section continues to explore the elements necessary for effective delivery of teaching interventions during the times of crises in Saudi Arabia by proposing the role of teacher emotional management.

From a psychology perspective, emotion regulation can be broadly defined as a process of individual difference characteristics underlying a set of regulatory acts and strategies that accommodate a daily behavior consistent with established social rules (Dore et al., 2016). A process both voluntary and conscious, by definition, emotion regulation is accentuated in rewarding, stressful situations. Based on the type of emotion and the timing of experiencing that emotion, emotional regulation typically occurs with relative time and situation stability on two distinct process levels: (1) the cognitive process underlying the way the emotion is experienced, and (2) the response-focused process underlying the way the emotion is expressed (Aldao, 2013; Kuppens & Verduyn, 2015). These two process levels or strategies are referred to as cognitive reappraisal and expression suppression, respectively (Brockman et al., 2016). In this regard, whereas cognitive reappraisal is concerned with the antecedent interpretation of the emotional impact through construction and evaluation, expression suppression is concerned with controlling the response to an already occurring experience (Gross, 2008). Both cognitive reappraisal and expression suppression apply to rewarding and stressful situations (Kooji et al., 2013). For instance, when a rewarding situation is involved, cognitive reappraisal may imply a behavioral change that entails augmenting the positivity of the already positive emotion, and expression suppression may imply managing the positive expression (Gross, 2015). By the same token, when a stressful situation is involved, cognitive reappraisal may imply a behavioral change that entails curbing the already negative emotions, and expression suppression may imply hindering or obstructing the expression of the already negative emotion (Hofer et al., 2015). It thus follows that; emotion regulation is a non-trivial individual characteristic for teachers and faculty members to possess for professional success, especially when daily professional teaching activities involve exposure to uncertain situational outcomes that reflect direct and regular communications with students and others within the system of the school or teaching institution (Kalokerinos et al., 2015). Toward this end, there may exist a strong reason to believe that the level of emotion regulation of Saudi schoolteachers and faculty members, conceptualized in terms of the two process level strategies of cognitive reappraisal and expression suppression, may have a pronounced impact on their respective performance levels. The display of positive or at least neutral emotions by Saudi schoolteachers and faculty members is particularly encouraged given Vision 2030 of the kingdom that embraces a higher education policy of creativity, encouragement, motivation, and inspiration.

Furthermore, emotional intelligence, a closely related construct to emotional regulation, is paramount in building healthy relations with students and others within an educational context. Emotional intelligence entertains many defining elements, including self-management, self-awareness, social awareness, and the ability to control hasty feelings. It allows teachers and faculty members to achieve professional and personal objectives without emotional redirection (Palmer et al., 2001).

Self-awareness is understanding own emotions and how these emotions affect the processes underlying reflections and actions. Such understanding allows teachers and faculty members to control their emotions as well as their actions. The defining element of social awareness enables Saudi teachers and faculty members to understand the emotions of students and others within the school system. Controlling hasty feelings and having sound relationship management benefits students, peers, and others while resolving and understanding differences and perceptions (Palmer et al., 2001).

Here, teachers and faculty members can hardly implement emotional intelligence without considering cultural intelligence where the school organizational culture is in harmony with the objectives of the emotional intelligence exercised on the individual teacher level (Early & Mosakowski, 2004).

It is highly recommended that Saudi education to take into account the importance and value of teacher emotion regulation and emotional intelligence training. Such recommendation is made based on the above discussion, and in light of the hypothesized well-pronounced impact of the emotion regulation attributes of cognitive reappraisal and expression suppression on the performance level of teachers and faculty members in Saudi Arabia (especially during times of crisis).

Emotional intelligence plays a vital role in schools and teaching institutions, including universities and institutes of higher education (Palmer et al., 2001). Emotion regulation ensures that teachers and faculty members are aware of their emotions; hence, they can perform their teaching assignments objectively, unbiasedly, which does not suffer from the noise of emotions (Early & Mosakowski, 2004). Emotionally regulated teachers and faculty members can show resilience and not just go off the rails when something offensive happens during daily work hours. Emotional intelligence also improves mental health (Sanchez-Nunez et al., 2020). Interestingly, emotional intelligence helps teachers and faculty members deal with their emotions rather than suppressing them, which allows them to release stress (Morse et al., 2012). Toward this end, emotion regulation and emotional intelligence training can be viewed as a means for Saudi schools and teaching institutions to obtain a competitive advantage (Voola & Carlson, 2004). Here, Saudi schools and universities can incorporate programs of emotional intelligence training. One possibility via which such programs may be incorporated is organizing workshops across all levels of the school and university systems. The human resources departments and faculty deanships can manage training sessions where novice teachers and senior teachers can learn how empathy and social skills could help build a better relationship with students and peers.

Another possibility is organizing events and presentations on the value of emotional intelligence in education. HR and faculty deans can offer TED talks and videos to teachers and faculty members to help them better understand and express their emotions. While employing TED talks and videos, schools and teaching institutions, in general, can provide teachers and faculty members with emotional intelligence training materials.

Last but not least, inviting consultants with experience in emotional intelligence may be another avenue whereby Saudi schools and teaching institutions can incorporate emotion regulation and emotional intelligence training. On a final note, besides the important role of behavioral considerations, including emotion regulation, the value of personal, social, institutional, and contextual variables can barely be overestimated when explaining or improving performance.

References

Aldao, A. (2013). The future of emotion regulation research: Capturing context. *Perspectives on Psychological Science, 8*(2), 155–172. https://doi.org/10.1177/1745691612459518

Allison-Napolitano, E. (2013). *Transformational leadership coaching for sustainable change*. Corwin.

Al-Otaibi, A. (1996). The effect of demographic variables on achievement motivation among Kuwaiti students at Kuwaiti university. *Arab Journal of Administrative Sciences, 3*(2), 339–364.

Anderson, G. (1994). A proactive model for training needs analysis. *Journal of European Industrial Training, 18*(3), 23–28.

Appelbaum, E., Bailey, T., Berg, P., & Kalleberg, A. (2000). *Manufacturing advantage: Why high-performance work systems pay off*. Cornell University Press.

Armstrong, F., & Tsokova, D. (2019). *Action research for inclusive education: Participation and democracy in teaching and learning*. Routledge.

Arraya, M. A. M., & Porfírio, J. A. (2017). Training delivery methods as source of dynamic capabilities: The case of sports' organisations. *European Journal of Training and Development, 41*(4), 354–372. https://eric.ed.gov/?id=EJ1146039

Aryee, S., Walumbwa, F. O., Zhou, Q., & Hartnell, C. A. (2012). Transformational leadership, innovative behavior, and task performance: Test of mediation and moderation processes. *Human Performance, 25*(1), 1–25. https://doi.org/10.1080/08959285.2011.631648

Atherton, J. S. (2013). *Learning and teaching; Piaget's developmental theory.* http://acbart.com/learningandteaching/LearningAndTeaching/www.learningandteaching.info/learning/piaget.html

Avolio, B. J., Reichard, R. J., Hannah, S. T., Walumbwa, F. O., & Chan, A. (2009). A meta-analytic review of leadership impact research: Experimental and quasi-experimental studies. *The Leadership Quarterly, 20*(5), 764–784. https://doi.org/10.1016/j.leaqua.2009.06.006

Avolio, B. J., Zhu, W., Koh, W., & Bhatia, P. (2004). Transformational leadership and organisational commitment: Mediating role of psychological empowerment and moderating role of structural distance. *Journal of Organizational Behavior, 25*(8), 951–968. https://doi.org/10.1002/job.283

Barney, J. (1991). Firm resources and sustained competitive advantage. *Journal of Management, 17*, 99–120.

Bass, B. M. (1990). From transactional to transformational leadership: Learning to share the vision. *Organizational Dynamics, 18*(3), 19–31.

Bass, B. M., & Avolio, B. J. (1994). *Improving organizational effectiveness through transformational leadership.* Sage Publications.

Bass, B. M., & Riggio, R. E. (2006). *Transformational leadership* (2nd ed.). Lawrence Erlbaum.

Bass, B. M., & Steidlmeier, P. (1999). Ethics, character and authentic transformational leadership behaviour. *Leadership Quarterly, 10*(2), 181–217.

Beevers, K., & Rea, A. (2016). *Learning and development practice* (1st ed.). Chartered Institute of Personnel and Development.

Blaikie, N. (2010). *Designing social research* (2nd ed.). Polity Press.

Boselie, P. (2014). *Strategic human resource management: A balanced approach* (2nd ed.). McGraw Hill/Europe, Middle East & Africa.

Bowen, S. A. (2005). A practical model for ethical decision making in issues management and public relations. *Journal of Public Relations Research, 17*(3), 191–216.

Boxall, P., & Purcell, J. (2011). *Strategy and human resource management* (3rd ed.). Palgrave Macmillan.

Boydell, T., & Leary, M. (1996). *Identifying training needs.* Institute of Personnel and Development.

Brigid, D. (2013). Social work: A profession in flux. *Journal of Workplace Learning, 25*(6), 394–406.

Brockman, R., Ciarrochi, J., Parker, P., & Kashdan, T. (2016). Emotion regulation strategies in daily life: Mindfulness, cognitive reappraisal and emotion suppression. *Cognitive Behaviour Therapy, 46*(2), 91–113. https://doi.org/10.1080/16506073.2016.1218926

Burns, J. M. (1978). *Leadership.* Harper & Row.

Chiu, W., Thompson, D., Mak, W., & Lo, K. (1999). Rethinking training needs analysis: A proposed framework for literature review. *Personnel Review, 28*(1), 77–90.

Combs, J., Liu, Y., Hall, A., & Ketchen, D. (2006). How much do high-performance work practices matter? A meta-analysis of their effects on organizational performance. *Personnel Psychology, 59*(3), 501–528. https://doi.org/10.1111/j.1744-6570.2006.00045.x

Conger, J. A., & Kanungo, R. N. (1994). Charismatic leadership in organisations: Perceived behavioral attributes and their measurement. *Journal of Organisational behavior, 15*(5), 439–452.

Creswell, J., & Miller, D. (2000). Determining validity in qualitative inquiry. *Theory into Practice, 39*(3), 124–130. https://doi.org/10.1207/s15430421tip3903_2

Creswell, J. W., & Poth, C. N. (2013). *Qualitative inquiry and research design: Choosing among five approaches* (3rd ed.). Sage.

Dai, G., Tang, K., & De Meuse, K. P. (2011). Leadership competencies across organizational levels: A test of the pipeline model. *Journal of Management Development, 30*(4), 366–380.

Denby, S. (2010). The importance of training needs analysis. *Industrial and Commercial Training*, 42(3), 147–150.
Doré, B. P., Silvers, J. A., & Ochsner, K. N. (2016). Toward a personalised science of emotion regulation. *Social Personality Psychology Compass, 10*(4), 171–187. https://doi.org/10.1111/spc3.12240
Early, C., & Mosakowski, E. (2004). Cultural intelligence. *Harvard Business Review*, October, 139–146.
Fleming, I., & Taylor, A. (2004). *Coaching (The pocketbook)*. Management Pocketbooks Ltd.
García-Morales, V. J., Jiménez-Barrionuevo, M. M., & Gutiérrez-Gutiérrez, L. (2012). Transformational leadership influence on organizational performance through organizational learning and innovation. *Journal of Business Research, 65*(7), 1040–1050.
Gross, J. J. (2008). Emotion regulation: Personality processes and individual differences. In O. P. John, R. W. Robins, & L. A. Pervin (Eds.), *Handbook of personality: Theory and research* (pp. 701–722). Guilford.
Gross, J. J. (2015). Emotion regulation: current status and future prospects. *Psychological Inquiry, 26*(1), 1–26. https://doi.org/10.1080/1047840X.2014.940781
Gündüz, N., & Özcan, D. (2010), Learning styles of students from different cultures and studying in near east university. *Procedia Social and Behavioral Sciences, 9*(4), 5–10.
Helzer, E. G., & Dunning, D. (2012). Why and when peer prediction is superior to self-prediction: The weight given to future aspiration versus past achievement. *Journal of Personality and Social Psychology, 103*(1), 38–53.
Hersey, P., & Blanchard, P. (1984). The life cycle theory of leadership. *Training and Development Journal, 23*(5), 54–62.
Hofer, M., Burkhard, L., & Allemand, M. (2015). Age differences in emotion regulation during a distressing film scene. *Journal of Media Psychology: Theories, Methods, and Applications, 27*(2), 47–52. https://doi.org/10.1027/1864-1105/a000134
Holden, D., Saito, J., Komura, T., & Joyce, T. (2015). Learning motion manifolds with convolutional autoencoders. In *Proceedings SA '15 SIGGRAPH Asia 2015 technical briefs,* art. 18. ACM. https://doi.org/10.1145/2820903.2820918
Holton, E., Bates, R., & Naquin, S. (2000). Large-scale performance driven training needs assessment: A case study. *Public Personnel Management, 29*(2), 249–268.
Honey, P., & Mumford, A. (1986). *Using your learning styles* (2nd ed.). Peter Honey.
Hutchinson, S. (2013). *Performance management: Theory and practice*. CIPD Publications.
Kaiser, R. B., Hogan, R., & Craig, S. B. (2008). Leadership and the fate of organisations. *American Psychologist, 63*(2), 96–110. https://doi.org/10.1037/0003-066X.63.2.96
Kalokerinos, E. K., Greenaway, K. H., & Denson, T. F. (2015). Reappraisal but not suppression downregulates the experience of positive and negative emotion. *Emotion, 15*(3), 271–275. https://doi.org/10.1037/emo0000025

Kirkpatrick, D. L., & Kirkpatrick, J. D. (2006). *Evaluating training programs. The four levels* (3rd ed.). Berrett-Koehler Publishers.

Kolb, D. A. (1984). *Experiential learning: Experience as the source of learning and development* (Vol. 1). Prentice-Hall.

Kolb, D. A., Rubin, I. M., & McIntyre, J. M. (1984). *Organizational psychology: Readings on human behavior in organizations*. Prentice-Hall.

Kodwani, A. D. (2017). Decoding training effectiveness: The role of organisational factors. *Journal of Workplace Learning, 29*(3), 200–216.

Kooij, D. T. A. M., Guest, D. E., Clinton, M., Knight, T., Jansen, P. G. W., & Dikkers, J. S. E. (2013). How the impact of HR practices on employee well-being and performance changes with age. *Human Resource Management Journal, 23*(1), 18–35. https://doi.org/10.1111/1748-8583.12000

Kovjanic, S., Schuh, S. C., Jonas, K., Quaquebeke, N. V., & Van Dick, R. (2012). How do transformational leaders foster positive employee outcomes? A self-determination-based analysis of employees' needs as mediating links. *Journal of Organizational Behavior, 33*(8), 1031–1052. https://doi.org/10.1002/job.1771

Kuppens, P., & Verduyn, P. (2015). Looking at emotion regulation through the window of emotion dynamics. *Psychological Inquiry, 26*(1), 72–79. https://doi.org/10.1080/1047840X.2015.960505

Landsberg, M. (2015). *Mastering coaching: Practical insights for developing high performance*. Profile Books.

Lawler III, E. E. (1986). *High-involvement management: Participative strategies for improving organizational performance*. Jossey-Bass.

Leigh, D., Watkins, R., Platt, W. A., & Kaufman, R. (2000). Alternative models of needs assessment: Selecting the right one for your organization. *Human Resource Development Quarterly, 11*(1), 87–94.

Liang, T.-L., Chan, L., Lin, C.-W., & Huang, Y.-L. (2011). Relationship between leadership behaviors and task performance: The mediation role of job satisfaction and the moderation role of social distance. *African Journal of Business Management, 5*(14), 5920–5928.

McGehee, W., & Thayer, P. W. (1961). *Training in business and industry*. Wiley.

Morse, G., Salyers, M. P., Rollins, A. L., Monroe-DeVita, M., & Pfahler, C. (2012). Burnout in mental health services: A review of the problem and its remediation. *Administration and Policy in Mental Health and Mental Health Services Research, 39*(5), 341–352. https://doi.org/10.1007/s10488-011-0352-1

Obolensky, N. (2017). *Complex adaptive leadership: Embracing paradox and uncertainty*. Routledge.

Padilla, A., Hogan R., & Kaiser, R. B. (2007). The toxic triangle: Destructive leaders, susceptible followers and conducive environments. *The Leadership Quarterly, 18*(3), 176–194. https://doi.org/10.1016/j.leaqua.2007.03.001

Palmer, B., Walls, M., Burgess, Z., & Stough, C. (2001). Emotional intelligence and effective leadership. *Leadership and Organizational Development Journal, 22*(1), 5–10. https://doi.org/10.1108/01437730110380174

Purcell, J. (1999). Best practice or best fit: Chimera or cul-de-sac. *Human Resource Management Journal, 9*(3), 26–41.

Ritchie, J., & Lewis, J. (2003). *Qualitative research practice – A guide for social science students and researchers*. Sage Publications Ltd.

Roulston, K. (2010). Considering quality in qualitative interviewing. *Qualitative Research, 10*(2), 199–228.

Sánchez-Núñez, M. T., García-Rubio, N., Fernández-Berrocal, P., & Latorre, J. M. (2020). Emotional intelligence and mental health in the family: The influence of emotional intelligence perceived by parents and children. *International Journal of Environmental Research and Public Health, 17*(17), 1–21. https://doi.org/10.3390/ijerph17176255

Shree, S. (2017). Investigating training through the lens of dramatic possibilities. *Industrial and Commercial Training, 49*(4), 157–163.

Sims, H. P. (1980). Further thoughts on punishment in organizations. *Academy of Management Review, 5*(1), 133–138. https://doi.org/10.5465/amr.1980.4288941

Steinmann, B., Klug, H. J. P., & Maier, G. W. (2018). The path is the goal: How transformational leaders enhance followers' job attitudes and proactive behavior. *Frontiers in Psychology*. https://doi.org/10.3389/fpsyg.2018.02338

Stone, A. G., Russell, R. F., & Patterson, K. (2004). Transformational versus servant leadership – A difference in leader focus. *The Leadership and Organization Development Journal, 25*(4), 349–361. https://doi.org/10.1108/01437730410538671

Tu, Y., & Lu, X. (2016). Do ethical leaders give followers the confidence to go the extra mile? The moderating role of intrinsic motivation. *Journal of Business Ethics, 135*, 129–144. https://doi.org/10.1007/s10551-014-2463-6

Van Knippenberg, D., De Cremer, D., & van Knippenberg, B. (2007). Leadership and fairness: The state of the art. *European Journal of Work and Organizational Psychology, 16*(2), 113–140. https://doi.org/10.1080/13594320701275833

Voola, R., & Carlson, J. (2004). Emotional intelligence and competitive advantage: Examining the relationship from a resource-based view. *Strategic Change, 13*(2), 83–93.

Wood, S., & Menezes, L. D. (1998). High commitment management in the U.K.: Evidence from the workplace industrial relations survey, and employers' manpower and skills practices survey. *Human Relations, 51*, 485–515. https://doi.org/10.1023/A:1016941914876

Yukl, G. (2012). *Leadership in organisations* (8th ed.). Pearson.

CHAPTER 9

Students' Satisfaction with e-Learning in Saudi Higher Education during the COVID-19 Outbreak

Chaudhry Kashif Mahmood, Tayyiba Khalil, Aseel Fuad Ali Al-Karasneh and Talha Sarfaraz

Abstract

During the COVID-19 pandemic, e-learning has been used as an alternative teaching approach to cover the academic vacuum produced by the pandemic's new reality owing to countrywide school closures. The study aimed at investigating the students' satisfaction level toward e-learning implementation during the COVID-19 outbreak. A quantitative research design, where 345 university undergraduate students from the different clusters (Health, Science, and Management) were surveyed regarding their satisfaction with e-learning. A self-administered questionnaire was developed and sent to participants for data collection. The validity and reliability of the questionnaire were determined. SPSS was used to understand and interpret the results of the research. To analyze the data, multiple statistical analyses were performed, including mean, standard deviations, and ANOVA. The study's findings shows that students' satisfaction level with e-learning platforms is generally medium, but with varying degrees from one item to another. The findings revealed no statistically significant differences in the use of e-learning at the level ($\alpha = 0.05$) for gender. This study demonstrates that e-learning has grown in popularity among students all over the world, particularly during the COVID-19 pandemic lockdown period. However, there is a need of major reform of the curriculum in compliance with remote teaching and learning ideas. Faculty and student training toward the use of technology is also mandatory for continuous improvement for teaching best practices.

Keywords

higher education – e-learning – student's satisfaction level – COVID-19 outbreak

1   Introduction

The outbreak of the coronavirus pandemic in 2019 seems to have a wide-ranging impact on the education sector globally. It has an impact on almost every aspect of human activity across the world, including education, research, recreation, amusement, communication, transportation, interpersonal interactions, the economy, and business activities and institutions. Though the coronavirus pandemic is regarded as novel, but it already has noxious effects on mortality (Onyema, 2020). COVID-19 outbreak has created educational disruptions; consequently, institutions and teachers were forced to respond quickly to an unexpected and forced switch from face-to-face to remote teaching. Therefore, it was important to focus on altering teaching techniques to fulfill expectations while also ensuring the continuity of the educational process (ElFirdoussi, 2020). Learning that was previously carried out in face-to-face learning environments is now carried out in an environment dominated by computers and digital technologies. (Borba et al., 2018; Koller et al., 2013).

Online education is an emerging domain of learning that blends distance education with face-to-face instruction using computer-mediated communication. New technologies, such as the internet, video streaming, online meetings, and so on, have made higher education more accessible and inexpensive for many students, as well as others who would not have been able to pursue it in a conventional in-class environment due to a variety of factors. As a result, online learning has now become an essential component of the expanding curriculum of higher education institutions (Bianco & Carr-Chellman, 2007). In this learning environment, learners are looking for better educational quality programs and more opportunities to interact with their instructors than in traditional classrooms (Nejad & Nejad, 2011). Consequently, instructors suffer a heavy workload due to virtual learning environments, where education is carried out in a manner that is less constrained by time and space (Lakhal et al., 2017).

In times of crisis and hardship, people tend to look for ways to overcome problems and control damages. Education is one of the most critical domains that people need to consider. In order to become more productive and adaptable during this pandemic, higher education institutions are constantly looking for ways to improve their efficiency and develop new technologies to improve the curriculum and meet the varying needs of students (Bawaneh, 2021; Cain et al., 2016). In this regard, e-learning is an alternative that is used in times of hardship. Rather than being a mere extension of existing education systems, it is seen as a foundation of education systems (Triyason et al., 2020).

The rise of e-Learning has pushed traditional academics to consider the importance of these teaching and learning modes during the spread of the coronavirus. Educational systems in various countries have started implementing e-learning and online classes as part of their curricula. They thought about the various aspects of providing educational content and the various ways of assessing and evaluating students (Ramsey et al., 2016).

According to the MIT Technology Review (2020), more than 61 countries have closed their universities and schools to protect the safety of their students and teaching staff. It affected more than 420 million students globally leading to transference to digital and electronic education. Kingdom of Saudi Arabia closed its academic institutions throughout the country and made the switch to digitalized education in response to the national lockdown started in March 2020.

Students would have faced their own set of challenges, especially in the early stages of the pandemic when the global lockdown began (Barrot et al., 2021). During the COVID-19 outbreak, significant research was conducted (Pierce et al., 2020; Revilla-Cuesta et al., 2021), trying to demonstrate how it impacted the pattern of teaching and learning of various groups. Notwithstanding, little thought has been given to how this unusual period has affected student satisfaction levels while transitioning to an e-learning method. Hence, the purpose of this research paper is to determine the level of satisfaction of students from various clusters (Health, Science and Management) at Imam Abdulrahman Bin Faisal University (IAU), Kingdom of Saudi Arabia, with the induction of e-learning or online classes during the COVID-19 outbreak. The study's overall goal is to answer the following questions:

1. How satisfied are IAU students with the use of e-learning during the COVID-19 outbreak?
2. Do students' levels of satisfaction with the use of e-learning in their learning differ depending on their gender?

2 Objectives of the Study

1. Assessing IAU students' satisfaction with the induction of e-learning or online classes during the COVID-19 outbreak.
2. Demonstrating the presence of statistically significant variations for student satisfaction based on gender.

3 Literature Review

3.1 *The Practicality of e-Learning Systems and Student Satisfaction*
The digital transformation of education systems at all levels has enabled the integration of e-learning. It was not the first term used to describe the use of

computerized systems that facilitate learning. Web-based learning, e-learning, online learning, digital learning, virtual learning, distance education, and learning management systems are examples of computer-assisted learning concepts (Aparicio et al., 2019).

For decades, numerous studies have been conducted on various aspects of e-learning. Like, Rodrigues et al. (2019) asserted that e-learning is a web-based system associated with digital technologies, innovations, and other forms of educational resources, to provide students with a customized, learner-centered, interactive, interesting, and collaborative classroom environment that supports and enhances learning processes. Similarly, Sangrà et al. (2012) in their seminal work categorize e-learning into four different dimensions: (1) technology-driven (deliver learning and training programs with the help of technology), (2) delivery-system-oriented (electronic delivery of a learning, training, or educational intervention), (3) communication-oriented (learning that is aided through the use of digital technologies and information that is interactive in some way. Online engagement between the student and their instructor or classmates is an example), and (5) educational-paradigm-oriented. Information and communication technologies (ICTs) are indeed being employed to help students improve their learning.

The concept of e-learning is a pretty obvious revolution that has occurred in the education sector and constantly transforms the manner people learn in the classroom (Garrison, 2017). It is a technology-mediated learning method with great academic potential. It has become one of the main research lines of informational technology in recent decades (Valverde-Berrocoso, 2020). However, some educationalists repudiate e-learning based on evidence that its techniques are not as well-adjusted as those used in traditional education (Cain et al., 2016). Nonetheless, anyone who has followed e-learning path knows that as information and communication technologies tools develop, educational employment evolves to meet learning objectives (Zydney et al., 2019).

The three major exchanges in e-learning education are student-student engagement, student-instructor contact, and student-content interaction. These three exchanges are the essential interactions that contribute to the smooth operation of an e-learning environment (Luo et al., 2017). In contrast to a traditional classroom, the distance between students and an instructor is insignificant in e-learning (Gomez et al., 2016; Capece & Campisi, 2013). Consequently, the instructor can no longer monitor the tasks and activities of the students (Luo et al., 2017). Furthermore, student-instructor interaction confronts numerous problems as a result of the student's isolation within the learning environment (Kurucay & Inan, 2017).

Within the context of e-learning, trainers not only teach the course information but also serve as course designers, facilitators, motivators, and evaluators

(El Alfy et al., 2017). During the teaching process, the instructor motivates pupils and assigns them a range of assignments. This practice becomes more critical in an online setting since the learner and teacher do not engage in synchronous learning in an e-learning environment (Romi, 2017). This synchronized nature isolates the learner, and this isolation leads to dissatisfaction with the e-learning environment (Kurucay & Inan, 2017; Gomez et al., 2016; Shahabadi & Uplane, 2015).

The teacher in an e-learning setting uses a variety of techniques, including educational or pedagogical, social, technological, and administrative approaches (Alharbi & Sandhu, 2018). The pedagogical method imposes learning procedures and learning content delivery. The social method entails conveying course information using verbal cues and social context via virtual technologies. The instructor's technical approach allows him or her to provide the student with suitable technical tools, such as software, to achieve specific goals while also developing the student's skills and knowledge in using the technical tools. In this context, teacher interaction is an important contributor to user satisfaction in e-learning studies (Alharbi & Sandhu, 2018; Luo et al., 2017). Along with many other educational technology improvements that are rapidly emerging as a result of the expansion and fast pace of digital technology's distribution, many tools, applications, and approaches, such as motivational gamification, interactive video, and artificial intelligence may be utilized during virtual learning, which is expected to play an important role very soon (McSweeney, 2010; Raes et al., 2020).

Several studies have been conducted to investigate the impact of e-learning on student success and attitudes in various courses (Alakharas, 2018; Alsaedy & Tarkhanov, 2017; Raes et al., 2020; Glenda et al., 2019; Ozgur, 2015). Glenda et al. (2019) discovered that e-learning and virtual classrooms are helpful in raising students' achievement, ambition, and personality, as well as improving communication skills with colleagues and instructors. These studies also emphasized the value of virtual classes in improving students' knowledge of the material and their attitudes toward learning in general.

Alakharas (2018) has investigated the influence of e-learning on student success in mathematics when compared to the traditional technique. The data revealed that e-learning had a beneficial influence on student success, however, there were no differences based on the teacher's gender or specialty. Alsaedy & Tarkhanov (2017) investigated the impact of e-learning in education on achievement and student attitudes. The study's findings indicated that e-learning had a significant influence on students' success and attitudes about the course. Raes et al. (2020) recently investigated the impact of hybrid and virtual classrooms on students' integration and interaction, as well as their performance. Blended classes not only are promising helping students accomplish their goals, they also allow students the flexibility and freedom to select when and where they want to attend lectures. The findings, however, revealed that students' ambition and interaction with teammates were relatively low in digital classrooms. This might be because the generation today is digital native, and the initiative is always seeking contemporary, quick, innovative apps that are entertaining, beneficial, and improve the engagement of all parties involved in the teaching-learning process. According to the research, this is one of the problems confronting the educational process.

Similarly, Ozgur (2015) found in his seminal work that end-user satisfaction is the degree to which individuals believe the system satisfies their information requirements. However, because of their intricate interdependence, variables that contribute to contentment are sometimes difficult to identify and recognize. Despite this, we must continue to investigate teachers and their views about teaching, learning, and technology. The most recent e-learning research indicates that relatively little attention has been paid to students' satisfaction with e-learning. Thus, it is critical to focus attention on the e-learning content and its usability elements in order to increase e-learning interactions and student satisfaction. By focusing on the existing literature and by taking theoretical support, here, we take a first look at "How satisfied are IAU students with the use of e-learning during the COVID-19 outbreak? Is there a difference in students' levels of satisfaction with the usage of e-learning in their learning based on their gender?"

4   Research Methods

The researchers utilized a descriptive-analytical technique to achieve the study's objectives. The study's population consists of all students enrolled in all clusters at IAU for the academic year 2021–2022. The study sample was chosen using a stratified random technique. Stratified random sampling is a commonly used technique because it allows researchers to obtain a random selection that best represents the entire population being studied, ensuring that each subgroup of interest is represented and the results are depicted in Figure 9.1.

According to Figure 9.1, the study sample consisted of 345 students, 216 (63%) of whom were females and 129 (37%) were males. A total of 200 (58%) studying business, 30 (9%) pursuing medicine education, and 115 (33%) studying science subjects. They were distributed over the four years education level – Fourth Year: 165 (48%), Third Year: 82 (24%), Second Year: 60 (17%), and First Year: 38 (11%).

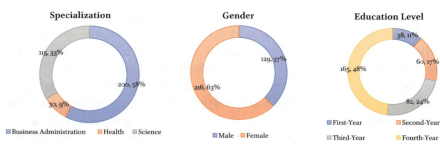

FIGURE 9.1   Demographics of students

A careful review of the literature (Bawaneh, 2021; Al-Rashidi, 2018) was conducted in order to find scales that had been developed and were being used in similar research initiatives. For this study, several questionnaires were found, modified, and adapted incorporating the Likert Scale with six levels (from 6 = strongly agree to 1 = strongly disagree). The first version of the study instrument consisted of 35 items, verified by six researchers who are related to the current study and members of the IAU faculty. Some items were eliminated, and the phrasing of others was changed. The developed version of the study instrument consists of a total of 27 items. After making final changes, a revised version was distributed among 35 students from the College of Business Administration to guarantee that the questionnaire is suitable as an instrument for collecting data in terms of the construct and its language (English), understanding of concepts, and questions in the instrument. The Cronbach Alpha coefficient was 0.80, which was deemed adequate for achieving the current study's goal (Hair et al., 2019). The following equation was adopted for parts classification (Bawaneh, 2021):

= (Scale's maximum bound − minimum bound)/number of required categories

= {(6 − 1)/3} = 1.67 (based on the equation, the categories as shown in Table 9.1 can be drawn).

TABLE 9.1   Categories for instrument items

Category	Range	Standard	Abbreviation
Category 1	1–2.67	Weak	W
Category 2	2.68–4.35	Medium	M
Category 3	4.36–6.0	Strong	S

5   Results

To answer the first question of this study: "how satisfied are IAU students with the use of e-learning during the COVID-19 outbreak?" As findings were plotted in Table 9.2, the mean and standard deviation of the instrument items developed for this purpose were computed by the researcher. The findings in Table 9.2 reveal that the overall Mean for IAU students' satisfaction level is (4.08), indicating that their degree of satisfaction with utilizing e-learning was medium. When we examine the category for all instrument objects, they can see that 10 items are strong, 16 items that are medium, and just one weak item. The study findings reveal that when the students were asked about e-learning usage during this pandemic, they responded that amid a pandemic, using e-learning is an appropriate solution (μ = 5.54, SD = 1.11, twenty-first item occupies the first rank), and they should be familiar with e-learning techniques and technological applications in learning (μ = 5.12, SD = 0.96, second item).

The findings of the study confirm that students' use of technology accelerates their learning and reduces the time required to master the knowledge and with less effort (μ = 4.96, SD = 1.70, second item). On the other hand, students confirm through their responses that the use of technology enhances students' responsibility toward their learning and increases self-reliance (μ = 4.75, SD = 1.16, item twenty-second), and this is what modern educational theories call for making the student the core of the teaching and learning process, and distance learning reduces psychological pressure. When the students were asked about the feasibility of the money that was paid in building the infrastructure to support distance learning (μ = 2.91, SD = 1.29), they answered that it was a wonderful and important investment. Also, they indicated that distance learning allows them to think more and more freely, with an open mind and a variety of ideas, according to the nineteenth item (μ = 3.01, SD = 1.22). The eleventh and twelfth items confirm that distance education is much better than traditional one and encourages creative and innovative thinking (μ = 3.02, 3.39; SD = 1.62, 1.72) respectively.

To answer the second question: "do students' levels of satisfaction with the use of e-learning in their learning differ depending on their gender?" Table 9.3 illustrates the mean and SD of students' overall satisfaction with e-learning based on gender. The results show a slight variation in the calculating Mean between the genders of the students (i.e., male and female). Where the computation Mean of female students is 4.089 and the standard deviation is 0.956, while the Mean for male students is 4.061, with a standard deviation of 1.05. The study's findings show that there are no discernible differences in the

TABLE 9.2 Means, standard deviation, and the category for all instrument items (N = 345)

No.	Item	Mean	SD	Category
1	Conventional methods of learning are more suitable than virtual classes.	4.41	1.66	S
2	e-learning classes save my time and effort.	4.96	1.7	S
3	e-learning does not account for the diversity of learners.	4.31	1.42	S
4	e-learning has helped me improve my research and exploration skills.	4.41	0.94	S
5	e-learning platforms also increase interaction between the student and the instructor.	3.82	1.72	M
6	e-learning supports me in improving my problem-solving abilities.	4.01	1.43	M
7	Every student, in my opinion, should be familiar with e-learning techniques.	5.12	0.96	S
8	I am concerned about and fearful of e-learning.	3.65	1.6	M
9	I am indeed a strong believer in the importance of e-learning.	4.31	1.5	M
10	I believe that e-learning has increased my self-confidence.	4.5	1.24	S
11	I believe that traditional teaching methods have better results than e-learning.	3.02	1.62	M
12	I believe that virtual classes encourage me to think creatively.	3.39	1.72	M
13	I do not feel happy, assigned to a task through an e-learning platform.	3.95	1.43	M
14	I don't believe in e-learning or online classes.	3.56	0.96	M
15	I enjoy learning through the computer and the internet.	4.28	1.16	M
16	I prefer online classes in normal circumstances.	4.21	1.43	M
17	I require training programs to assist me in making effective use of the e-learning platform.	3.55	1.55	M
18	I think that the money invested in e-learning or online classrooms seems to be a waste of resources.	2.19	1.29	W
19	I think virtual classes restrict students' freedom of thinking.	3.73	1.22	M

(cont.)

TABLE 9.2 Means, standard deviation, and the category for all instrument items (N = 345) (cont.)

No.	Item	Mean	SD	Category
20	I'm having a great time learning through virtual classes.	3.55	1.49	M
21	During a pandemic, using e-learning is an appropriate solution.	5.54	1.11	S
22	Online classes help with self-learning in my discipline.	4.75	1.16	S
23	Students bear a new burden as a result of the use of e-learning platforms.	4.01	1.49	M
24	Students' group incorporation suffers greatly as a result of e-learning usage.	4.62	1.43	S
25	The e-learning platform greatly helps me in learning fundamental concepts.	3.78	1.39	M
26	A large number of courses available through e-learning increased my stress, pressure, and panic about my results.	4.65	1.51	S
27	The use of e-learning empowers collaborative learning.	3.6	1.7	M
Overall mean		4.08	–	M

computation of Mean toward the satisfaction level of IAU students based on gender. The researcher used ANOVA to determine the validity of the differences, and the findings are shown in Table 9.3. Findings given in Table 9.3 demonstrate that there have been no statistically significant differences in satisfaction with e-learning and virtual classrooms based on gender with the statistical significance values at (α = 0.05, Sig. 0.672, F = 0.517).

6 Conclusion

The level of students' preference toward distance learning was generally medium. This outcome is deemed normal, since higher education institutions decided to use remote education during the COVID-19 outbreak, although students and teachers were not prepared mentally or competent for the abrupt, full shift in how they received/gave instruction in all classes at home. They

TABLE 9.3　Means, standard deviations, and ANOVA test of students' satisfaction level toward e-learning

Variable			Mean	SD
Gender	Male	129	4.061	1.05
	Female	218	4.089	0.956
	Total	345	4.08	1.01

Gender (male, female)	Sum of squares	df	Mean square	F	Sig.
Between groups	0.401	1	.143	0.617	0.715
Within groups	29.04	343	.261		
Total	29.441	344			

were not adequately prepared and lacked the necessary abilities to use distant learning systems. Students, on the other hand, believe that remote learning is the ultimate solution under exceptional circumstances and that the benefits outweigh the limits and obstacles. The findings of this study are congruent with the findings of many other studies throughout the world (Barrot et al., 2021; Bawaneh, 2021; Mulenga & Marbán, 2020; Onyema, 2020; Triyason et al., 2020; Valverde-Berrocoso et al., 2020). This demonstrates the significance of distance learning in light of the COVID-19 for the sustainability of student academic learning on the one hand, and the safety of all teaching and non-teaching personnel, students, parents, and society on the other. The data also revealed that there are no statistically significant variations in the degree of satisfaction of IAU students with e-learning based on gender (male and female).

7   Recommendations

Based on the study outcome, the authors make three recommendations: (1) a major curriculum reform to be made in compliance with remote teaching and learning ideas, (2) evaluation methodologies to be revised to match with the online teaching approaches, and (3) advanced automation to be sustained incorporating it into the teaching and learning process.

References

Al-Akharas, Y. (2018). The impact of the application of e-learning strategy on academic achievement in mathematics in basic grades in the capital governorate from the perspective of teachers of mathematics. *Dirasat: Educational Sciences, 45*(4), 70–80.

Alharbi, H., & Sandhu, K. (2018). Robust data findings of e-learning analytics recommender systems and their impact on system adoption for student experiences. *International Journal of Organizational and Collective Intelligence, 8*(3), 1–12. https://doi.org/10.4018/IJOCI.2018070101

Alsaedy, A., & Tarkhanov, N. (2017). A Hilbert boundary value problem for generalised Cauchy–Riemann equations. *Advances in Applied Clifford Algebras, 27*(2), 931–953. https://link.springer.com/journal/6/volumes-and-issues/27-2

Aparicio, M., Bacao, F., & Oliveira, T. (2019). An e-learning theoretical framework. *Journal of Educational Technology Systems, 19*(1), 292–307.

Barrot, J. S., Llenares, I. I., & del Rosario, L. S. (2021). Students' online learning challenges during the pandemic and how they cope with them: The case of the Philippines. *Education and Information Technologies, 26*, 7321–7338. https://doi.org/10.1007/s10639-021-10589-x

Bawaneh, A. K. (2021). The satisfaction level of undergraduate science students towards using e-learning and virtual classes in exceptional condition COVID-19 crisis. *Turkish Online Journal of Distance Education, 22*(1), 52–65. https://eric.ed.gov/?id=EJ1283700

Bianco, M. B., & Carr-Chellman, A. A. (2002). Exploring qualitative methodologies in online learning environments. *Quarterly Review of Distance Education, 3*(3), 251–260. https://eric.ed.gov/?id=EJ657869

Borba, M. C., de Souza Chiari, A. S., & de Almeida, H. R. F. L. (2018). Interactions in virtual learning environments: New roles for digital technology. *Educational Studies in Mathematics, 98*, 269–286. https://doi.org/10.1007/s10649-018-9812-9

Cain, W., Bell, J., & Cheng, C. (2016). Implementing robotic telepresence in a synchronous hybrid course. In *Proceedings – IEEE 16th International Conference on Advanced Learning Technologies (ICALT)* (pp. 171–175). IEEE.

Capece, G., & Campisi, D. (2013). User satisfaction affecting the acceptance of an e-learning platform as a mean for the development of the human capital. *Behavior and Information Technology, 32*, 335–343.

El Alfy, S., Gómez, J. M., & Ivanov, D. (2017). Exploring instructors' technology readiness, attitudes and behavioral intentions towards e-learning technologies in Egypt and United Arab Emirates. *Education and Information Technologies, 22*(5), 2605–2627.

Elfirdoussi, S., Lachgar, M., Kabaili, H., Rochdi, A., Goujdami, D., & El Firdoussi, L. (2020). Assessing distance learning in higher education during the COVID-19 pandemic. *Education Research International, 2020*. https://doi.org/10.1155/2020/8890633

Garrison, D. R. (2016). *E-learning in the 21st century: A community of inquiry framework for research and practice*. Routledge.

Glenda, K., Joslyn, H., & Mariel, P. (2019). Virtually connected. *International Teacher Magazine*. https://consiliumeducation.com/itm/2019/06/22/virtually-connected/

Gómez-Rey, P., Barbera, E., & Fernández-Navarro, F. (2016). Measuring teachers and learners' perceptions of the quality of their online learning experience. *Distance Education, 37*(2), 146–163.

Hair, J. F., Page, M., & Brunsveld, N. (2019). *Essentials of business research methods*. Routledge.

Koller, D., Ng, A., Do, C., & Chen, Z. (2013, June 3). Retention and intention in massive open online courses: In depth. *Educause Review*.

Kurucay, M., & Inan, F. A. (2017). Examining the effects of learner-learner interactions on satisfaction and learning in an online undergraduate course. *Computers and Education, 115*, 20–37.

Lakhal, S., Bateman, D., & Bedard, J. (2017). Blended synchronous delivery modes in graduate programs: A literature review and its implementation in the master teacher program. *Collected Essays on Learning and Teaching, 10*, 47–60.

Luo, N., Zhang, M., & Qi, D. (2017). Effects of different interactions on students' sense of community in an e-learning environment. *Computers and Education, 115*, 153–160.

McSweeney, D. (2010, October). *A framework for the comparison of virtual classroom systems* [Paper]. NAIRTL/LIN conference on flexible learning at the Royal College of Surgeons, Dublin, Ireland. https://arrow.tudublin.ie/itbinfocsecon/3/

MIT Technology Review. (2020). *Arab countries resort to distance education to face the repercussions of the Coronavirus*. https://technologyreview.ae/

Mulenga, E. M., & Marbán, J. M. (2020). Is COVID-19 the gateway for digital learning in mathematics education? *Contemporary Educational Technology, 12*(2), 269.

Nejad, M., & Nejad, E. B. (2011). Virtual education and its importance as a new method in the educational system. *International Journal of Computer Science and Information Security, 9*(9), 8.

Onyema, E., Eucheria, N., Obafemi, F., Sen, S., Atonye, F., Sharma, A., & Alsayed, A. (2020). Impact of Coronavirus pandemic on education. *Journal of Education and Practice, 11*(13), 108–121.

Ozgur, Y. (2015). The effects of "live virtual classroom" on students' achievement and students' opinions about "live virtual classroom" at distance education. *The Turkish Online Journal of Educational Technology, 14*(1), 108–115.

Pierce, M., Hope, H., Ford, T., Hatch, S., Hotopf, M., John, A., & Abel, K. (2020). Mental health before and during the COVID-19 pandemic: A longitudinal probability sample survey of the UK population. *The Lancet Psychiatry, 7*(10), 883–892.

Raes, A., Vanneste, P., Pieters, M., Windey, I., Van Den Noortgate, W., & Depaepe, F. (2020). Learning and instruction in the hybrid virtual classroom: An investigation of students' engagement and the effect of quizzes. *Computers & Education, 143*. https://doi.org/10.1016/j.compedu.2019.103682

Ramsey, D., Evans, J., & Levy, M. (2016). Preserving the seminar experience. *Journal of Political Science Education, 12*(3), 256–267.

Revilla-Cuesta, V., Skaf, M., Varona, J., & Ortega-López, V. (2021). The outbreak of the COVID-19 pandemic and its social impact on education: Were engineering teachers ready to teach online? *International Journal of Environmental Research and Public Health, 18*(4), 2127.

Rodrigues, H., Almeida, F., Figueiredo, V., & Lopes, S. L. (2019). Tracking e-learning through published papers: A systematic review. *Computers & Education, 136*, 87–98.

Romi, I. M. (2017). A model for e-learning systems success: Systems, determinants, and performance. *International Journal of Emerging Technologies in Learning, 12*(10), 4–20.

Sangrà, A., Vlachopoulos, D., & Cabrera, N. (2012). Building an inclusive definition of e-learning: An approach to the conceptual framework. *The International Review of Research in Open Distance Learning, 13*(2), 145–159. https://files.eric.ed.gov/fulltext/EJ983277.pdf

Shahabadi, M., & Uplane, M. (2015). Synchronous and asynchronous e-learning styles and academic performance of e-learners. *Procedia – Social and Behavioral Sciences, 176*, 129–138. https://doi.org/10.1016/j.sbspro.2015.01.453

Triyason, T., Tassanaviboon, A., & Kanthamanon, P. (2020, July 2). Hybrid classroom: Designing for the new normal after COVID-19 pandemic. In *Proceedings of the 11th international conference on advances in information technology* (art. 30, pp. 1–8). https://doi.org/10.1145/3406601.3406635

Valverde-Berrocoso, J., Garrido-Arroyo, M., Burgos-Videla, C., & Morales-Cevallos, M. (2020). Trends in educational research about e-learning: A systematic literature review (2009–2018). *Sustainability, 12*(12), 5153.

Zydney, J., McKimm, P., Lindberg, R., & Schmidt, M. (2019). Here or their instruction: Lessons learned in implementing innovative approaches to blended synchronous learning. *Tech Trends, 63*, 123–132. https://doi.org/10.1007/s11528-018-0344-z

CHAPTER 10

Impact on Teaching Strategies in Saudi Arabian Universities Owing to COVID-19 Pandemic

Maqsood Mahmud, Hoda M. Abo Alsamh, Talha Sarfaraz, Mohd Anuar Arshad, Arshad Mahmood and Bala Raju Nikku

Abstract

The COVID-19 pandemic emerged with an unparalleled emergency in every walk of life. In the area of education, this emergency has led to the massive termination of face-to-face activities. This affected schools and universities in more than 190 countries globally in order to prevent the spread of the virus. The Ministry of Education of Saudi Arabia issued a directive to stop holding face-to-face classes to mitigate the widespread of the novel coronavirus. This directive led to three main areas of action: (1) placement of distance learning modes via a variety of methods and technological platforms, (2) support and deployment of educational workers and communities, and (3) a great concern for the well-being and general health of students. The aim of this chapter is to highlight impacts that these actions had on educational communities. Key recommendations are offered based on student's feedback and training sessions. Students from 14 different universities were sampled including the host university, i.e., Imam Abdulrahman Bin Faisal University, to see pre-training and post-training responses with respect to their experiences and community engagement while learning via online resources. Over 400 responses were received and analyzed to gain the understanding of the current state of how Saudi universities tackled the impacts caused by the COVID-19 pandemic. The training-based research was conducted to measure the actual level of teaching strategies used at Saudi Arabian universities.

Keywords

Saudi universities' role – COVID-19 pandemic – online teaching strategies – training-based research

1   Introduction

Educational systems have been highly impacted by the COVID-19 pandemic internationally. This phenomenon changes have led to closures of schools, colleges, and universities. Most governmental authorities decided to close educational institution provisionally. The main purpose of this action was to reduce the widespread of coronavirus reported by Reuters Staff (2020) (also see Blum et al., 2021; Skulmowski, 2020). As of January 12, 2021, roughly 825 million students across the world were impacted due to school closures as a measure in response to this prevailing pandemic. According to the UNICEF monitoring, 23 countries were applying countrywide closures. Forty countries were applying local closures. This was affecting about forty seven percent (47%) of the world's student populace. One hundred and twelve countries' schools were still open and were not in compliance with international WHO guidelines (UNESCO, 2020a, 2020b; UNESCO Institute for Statistics [UIS], n.d.).

Cambridge International Examinations (CIE) released a declaration on March 23, 2020 to cancel all Cambridge IGCSE, and Cambridge exams including O Level exams, Cambridge International AS & A Level exams, and so on, for May/June 2020 around the world as per report of Cambridge International Examinations 2020. International Baccalaureate exams had also been invalid according to International Baccalaureate in 2020. In addition, Advanced Placement exams, SAT administrations, and ACT administrations had been moved online (Bao et al., 2020). These actions have extensive economic and societal impacts illustrated in reports published by Aristovnik et al. (2020). School closures in response to the pandemic had emerged with various social and economic issues. Those issues include student debt (Jamerson & Mitchell, 2020), digital learning (Aristovnik et al., 2020; Karp & McGowan, 2020), food insecurity (National Public Radio [NPR], 2020), and homelessness (Ngumbi, 2020; Sessons, 2020), as well as access to childcare (Times, 2020), health care (Feuer, 2020), housing (Barrett, 2020), internet (Jordan, 2020), and disability services (NPR, 2021). The influence was more intense for deprived children and their families. This may lead to a disruption in educational life, malnutrition, childcare issues, and financial burden on peoples who could not work due to the pandemic or some other reasons (OECD, 2021; UNESCO, 2021a).

UNESCO suggested the use of remote education mode and install online educational applications and platforms that students and educators could use to reach learners online and alleviate the impact of the disruption of teaching at schools and colleges (UNESCO, 2021b). These types of global measures have also affected Saudi Arabia, which needed to comply with the WHO guidelines and its Ministry of Education, thus, had issued various directives by royal decree to comply with international guidelines. In order to assess the impact of standard operation procedures (SOP) adapted in Saudi Arabian educational institution, a training session with pre- and post-survey has been conducted to measure the involvement of students in community engagement with respect to the COVID-19 pandemic measures. The training sessions included 358 and 468 students respectively in pre- and post-training sessions to assess the level of involvement and their perspective toward community engagement, learning and helping deprived students in communities using technology.

This chapter is divided into literature review, methodology, results, discussion and a conclusion.

2   Literature Review

Social distancing and self-isolation have provoked a worldwide closure of schools, colleges and universities in over 100 countries reported by The Economist (2020)(Also see UNICEF, 2021). Previous pandemics have provoked extensive school closures around the globe, with fluctuating stages of effectiveness. In the work of Barnum (2020), Frieden (2020) and Simon (2020), statistical modelling has revealed that the spread of the novel coronavirus may be delayed by the closures of academic institutions (Jackson et al., 2014). However, this process will be more effective if the contact of children outside school is also kept to a minimum (Cauchemez, 2009; Zumla, 2010). School closures seem effective in lessening cases of deaths, predominantly when enforced in a prompt way (Auger et al., 2020). If academic institution closures implemented late after an outbreak of disease, they are less effective (Barnum, 2020; Simon, 2020), Moreover, it is observed that some academic institutions decided to stay opened and it resulted in increase in infection cases (Jackson et al., 2013). Closure of academic institutions is not the only measure taken to reduce infection cases in a community but there are also some other measures, which were taken to control the virus spread, e.g., ban on public gathering, limiting numbers of people in public areas, such as shopping malls, and wearing of masks in public places (Jackson et al., 2013).

The United States reduced its mortality rate after enacting and implementing legislations and policies on closure of academic institutions in the country during the 1918–1919 influenza (H1N1 virus) pandemic (Barnum, 2020). Cities in the US that observed such policies as a part of public health strategies helped curb the number of deaths (Jackson et al., 2013; Markel et al., 2007). Academic institutions were shut for a median duration of 4 weeks as per a study of 43 US cities' response to the 1918 influenza pandemic (Markel et al., 2007). Also, academic institution closures helped decrease the morbidity rate by 90% during the 1957–1958 outbreak of influenza (H2N2 virus) pandemic (Chin et al., 1960) and reduce it up to 50% during the outbreak of avian (H5N1 virus) influenza 2008–2009 in the US (Wheeler et al., 2010).

Numerous nations positively decelerated the spread of infection through academic institution closures during the 2009 H1N1 influenza pandemic. Academic institution closures in the city of Oita, Japan, were found to have effectively reduced the number of infected students at the peak of the pandemic (Kawano, 2015). Obligatory school closures measures were connected with a 29% to 37% reduction in influenza transmission rates (National Institutes of Health [NIH], 2011). Initial academic institution closures in the United States delayed the increase in confirmed cases during the 2009 H1N1 influenza pandemic. Despite the general achievement of closing schools, a research survey of academic institution closures in Michigan found that "district level reactive school closures were ineffective" (Davis et al., 2015).

A group of researchers and qualified epidemiologists recommended the closure of academic institutions in order to prevent viral transmission. This would also help to reduce further spread and buy time for vaccine development and production. During the swine flu outbreak in 2009 in the UK, there was an article titled, "Closure of schools during an influenza pandemic" published in the Lancet Infectious Diseases (Wardrop, 2009). The article includes a study of previous influenza pandemics including the pandemics occurred in 1918, 1957, and 1968. The researchers observed the undercurrents of the spread of influenza in France over its school holidays during the pandemics. The researchers noted that cases of influenza infection decreased when schools closed but increased again when the French government reopened schools after its school holidays. The researchers also observed that when school instructors in Israel went on strike during the flu season of 1999–2000, a smaller number of patients visited hospitals with a fewer cases of flu infection and respiratory problems. The number of respiratory infection (including influenza) cases was reduced by almost a half (43%) (Walsh, 2009).

3 Methodology

There are two parts in this study. First, designated training programs were conducted in a group of universities in Saudi Arabia. Second, a longitudinal study among sample university students from 14 universities in Saudi Arabia were carried out to achieve the objectives of this research. This study aims at highlighting the impacts that the actions (taken by the government in response to the pandemic) had on educational communities. The purpose of the training program catered for university students is to promote community engagement raising awareness about COVID-19 in local communities and small businesses to perform well in the current COVID-19 pandemic situation. Interviews with sets of survey questions with the student population were conducted before and after the training programs. The selected universities include public and private universities across Saudi Arabia.

In this research, 14 universities were selected. They are (1) Imam Abdulrahman Bin Faisal University, (2) King Fahad University, (3) King Abdulaziz University, (4) King Saud University, (5) Islamic Madinah University, (6) Umul Qura University, (7) Princess Norah University, (8) King Khalid University, (9) Majma University, (10) King Abdullah University, (11) Prince Mohammad Bin Fahd University, (12) Prince Sultan University, (13) Arab Open university, and (14) University of Business and Technology (UTT).

This research, first, applied a quantitative method in the form of survey before and after the community engagement training. Second, longitudinal study method is also applied to help to gather the data from the university students, who were involved in the COVID-19 awareness training programs. As previously mentioned, the sample population spans across 14 universities in Saudi Arabia. The training program aimed to train 1,000 students from those fourteen universities. In other words, approximately 100 students (undertaking such training) from each targeted university were sampled. Two surveys among the students were conducted before and after the COVID-19 awareness training program. There were 358 survey responses of pre-training and 468 responses of post-training were received. An ethical approval for the social experiment/training sessions was obtained from IBR (Institutional Board Review), Imam Abdulrahman Bin Faisal University before conducting this research.

4 Results and Discussion

The results of this research showed significant descriptive and exploratory insights about the students' aptitude toward community services and use of digital technology in academia for their learning and support of the local communities. A training session was organized by researchers of college of business administration, Imam Abdulrahman Bin Faisal University under the supervision of the Deanship of Scientific Research (DSR) in collaboration with Universiti Sains Malaysia (USM), Malaysia, and Thomas River University, Canada. In this research training session, students from the selected 14 universities in Saudi Arabia were invited and trained to gain understanding of community services during the COVID-19 pandemic. They also learned about the use of technology and how to become a change agent for the society. The purpose of the training was to assess the level of change in the students' lifestyle and students' aptitude toward community services. Since the mode of education was switched to online during the training sessions, the researchers also tried to record students' responses on how the students tackled various issues when their academic institutions were closed and how they managed the new challenges of university closure during COVID-19 pandemic. The results included pre- and post-training survey results and they are described in Figures 10.1 to 10.6 in detail.

4.1 *Pre-Training Survey*

How to proceed with the research is based on pre-training and post-training surveys. In the pre-training survey three different results are shown in Figures 10.1, 10.2, and 10.3. Figure 10.1 shows the detailed analysis of universities, which participated in the training-based research. It showed details of universities that took part in the said research. In this part of the research, 358 responses were collected. It was found that most of the trainees in the training could not give their responses in the survey as they could not understand various concepts and terminology of community services.

Figure 10.2 shows student responses toward a set of questions related to technology and community engagement during the COVID-19 pandemic. It was found that the level of understanding of technology and its usage in

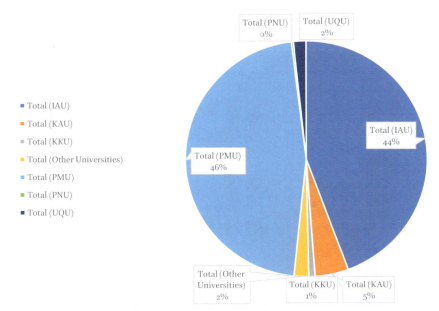

FIGURE 10.1   University students' statistics (pre-training)

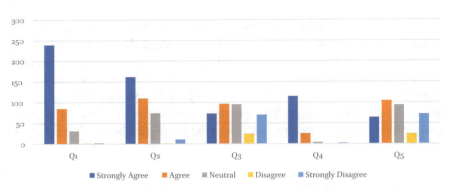

FIGURE 10.2   Technology and community engagement during COVID-19 pandemic (pre-training)

COVID-19 pandemic was limited and they were not able to connect with community engagement or help deprived students. The cause could be lack of knowledge and unawareness of community engagement.

Figure 10.3 shows that how students can be a "change agent" in the COVID-19 pandemic and can contribute toward community engagement in the digital era. Many university students did not know about a plethora of digital applications and online platforms that could connect them with community engagement. Most students could not relate modern digital tools to community service and community engagement. They were not able to realize their importance in the community as how they could be helpful and to the needy students in academia and beyond.

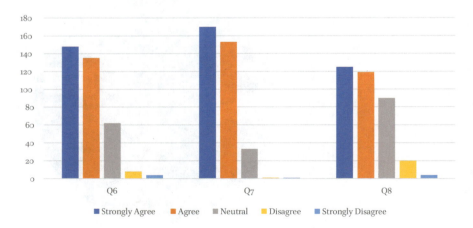

FIGURE 10.3   University community engagement: becoming a change agent in the digital era (pre-training)

4.2 Post-Training Survey

The methodology of this research was based on pre-training and post-training surveys. In the post-training survey three different results are shown in Figures 10.4, 10.5, and 10.6. Figure 10.4 shows the detailed analysis of universities which participated in the training-based research. It also shows details of the universities that took part in our research. In this part of the research, 468 responses were received. The rise in the number of student responses implies that participating students had got more involved in community engagement training sessions with the help of technology (i.e., Zoom). It is perceived that such type of training sessions helped students in their understanding of the survey questions. Thus, there was an increase of 110 (31.70%) student responses from the post-training survey as compared with those from the pre-training survey.

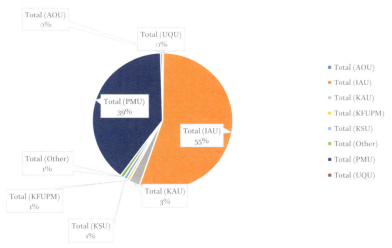

FIGURE 10.4   University students' statistics (post-training)

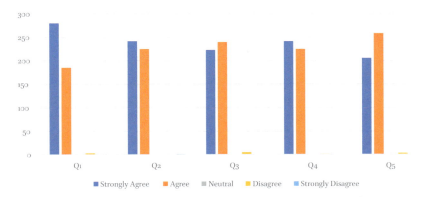

FIGURE 10.5   Technology and community engagement during COVID-19 pandemic (post-training)

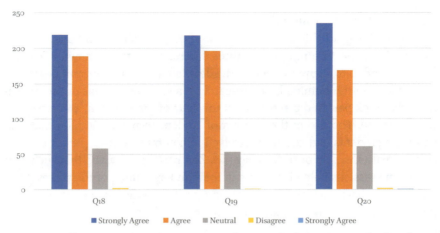

FIGURE 10.6   University community engagement: becoming a change agent in the digital era (post-training)

Figure 10.5 shows student responses to a set of questions related to technology and community engagement during the COVID-19 pandemic after being trained for a few hours. The level of understanding of technology and its usage during the COVID-19 pandemic was improved as depicted by Figure 10.5. The students were now able to think and make use of their capabilities in community engagement with the help of technology used in their daily life and at universities. This training proved that they are now able to help the deprived students, who need help at their academic institution as part of the community service.

Figure 10.6 shows the results of students' level of understanding, and aptitude toward community service at university level. It also assesses maturity level of students in using technology for their learning and helping the community. Students understood how to be a "change agent" during the COVID-19 pandemic with existing capabilities and potentialities. This type of change was beneficial toward community engagement in the modern digital era in Saudi Arabia. The effective use of applications of digital platforms in academic communities and linking them toward community engagement was clarified to students after extensive training. This can be seen from the higher percentage of selecting the "strongly agree" option in the survey. This also shows the importance of training-based awareness of community engagement. Thus, after the training sessions, students would be capable of giving help to those deserving and deprived students as part of community services. This was critical, especially when the Ministry of Education closed academic institutions by royal decree. The Ministry's purpose of doing so was to reduce the infection rate in communities after the peak of the pandemic had been reached. These practices also help the Saudi Arabian government in fighting the new "Delta" variant of coronavirus. Due to these practices in the communities in Saudi Arabia, the number of confirmed cases as of the day when this chapter was written (i.e., September 4, 2021) was 177 showing the effectiveness in the decision of academic institutions closures and in relying on technological platforms to achieve educational goals for the educational communities of Saudi Arabia.

5   Conclusion

To conclude this chapter, a brief overview of the impacts of COVID-19 pandemic on the teaching and learning environment was presented. Academic institution closure strategy was extensively used by various nations of the world to reduce the infection cases of COVID-19. Thus, it would mitigate mortality and morbidity rates in a community. In our research, the Saudi Arabian community contextual scenario was adapted to test the real case scenario. A pre- and post-training-based survey was designed and conducted by College of Business Administration, Imam Abdulrahman Bin Faisal University, in collaboration with Universiti Sains Malaysia (USM), Malaysia, and Thomas River University, Canada. The purpose of the research was to assess the levels of university students' awareness of and engagement with community service and the use of technology during the COVID-19 pandemic for their own learning and supporting their community. An uplift factor in community engagement was evident in the post-training survey, which reflects high importance of training sessions in raising university students' level of awareness of community engagement.

Acknowledgment

The authors of this chapter would like to express their gratitude to the Deanship of Scientific Research (DSR), Imam Abdulrahman Bin Faisal University, Dammam, Saudi Arabia, for the support of Project #COVID19-2020-039-CBA.

References

Aristovnik, A., Keržič, D., Ravšelj, D., Tomaževič, N., & Umek, L. (2020). Impacts of the COVID-19 pandemic on life of higher education students: A global perspective. *Sustainability, 12*(20), 8438. https://doi.org/10.3390/su12208438

Auger, K. A., Shah, S. S., Richardson, T., Hartley, D., Hall, M., Warniment, A., et al. (2020). Association between statewide school closure and COVID-19 incidence and mortality in the US. *JAMA, 324*(9), 859–870. doi:10.1001/jama.2020.14348

Bao, X., Qu, H., Zhang, R., & Hogan, T. P. (2020, September). Modeling reading ability gain in kindergarten children during COVID-19 school closures. *International Journal of Environmental Research and Public Health, 17*(17), 17. https://doi.org/10.3390/ijerph17176371

Barnum, M. (2020, March 9). *Should schools close due to coronavirus? Here's what research says*. Chalkbeat.

Barrett, S. (2020, March 23). Coronavirus on campus: College students scramble to solve food insecurity and housing challenges. *CNBC*.

Blum, S., & Dobrotić, I. (2021). Childcare-policy responses in the COVID-19 pandemic: Unpacking cross-country variation. *European Societies, 23*(Sup1), S545–S563. https://doi.org/10.1080/14616696.2020.1831572

Cambridge International Examinations. (2020, March 23). *Update from Cambridge International on May/June 2020 exams*. Cambridge Assessment International Education.

Cauchemez, S., Ferguson, N. M., Wachtel, C., Tegnell, A., Saour, G., Duncan, B., & Nicoll, A. (2009). Closure of schools during an influenza pandemic. *The Lancet. Infectious Diseases, 9*(8), 473–481. https://doi.org/10.1016/S1473-3099(09)70176-8

Chin, T. D., Foley, J. F., Doto, I. L., Gravelle, C. R., Weston, J. (1960). Morbidity and mortality characteristics of Asian strain influenza. *Public Health Reports, 75*(2), 149–158. https://doi.org/10.2307/4590751

Davis, B. M., Markel, H., Navarro, A., Wells, E., Monto, A. S., & Aiello, A. E. (2015, June). The effect of reactive school closure on community influenza-like illness counts in the state of Michigan during the 2009 H1N1 pandemic. *Clinical Infectious Diseases, 60*(12), e90-e97. https://doi.org/10.1093/cid/civ182

Feuer, W. (2020, March 23). WHO officials warn health systems are 'collapsing' under coronavirus: 'This isn't just a bad flu season.' *CNBC*.

Frieden, T. (2020, March 15). Lessons from Ebola: The secret of successful epidemic response. *CNN*.

International Baccalaureate. (2020, March 23). *May 2020 examinations will no longer be held*. International Baccalaureate.

Jackson, C., Mangtani, P., Hawker, J., Olowokure, B., & Vynnycky, E. (2014). The effects of school closures on influenza outbreaks and pandemics: Systematic review of simulation studies. *PLOS ONE, 9*(5), e97297. https://doi.org/10.1371/journal.pone.0097297

Jackson, C., Vynnycky, E., Hawker, J., Olowokure, B., & Mangtani, P. (2013). School closures and influenza: Systematic review of epidemiological studies. *BMJ Open, 3*(2), e002149. http://dx.doi.org/10.1136/bmjopen-2012-002149

Jamerson, J., & Mitchell, J. (2020, March 20). Student-loan debt relief offers support to an economy battered by coronavirus. *The Wall Street Journal*.

Jordan, C. (2020, March 22). Coronavirus outbreak shining an even brighter light on internet disparities in rural America. *TheHill*.

Karp, P., & McGowan, M. (2020, March 23). 'Clear as mud': Schools ask for online learning help as coronavirus policy confusion persists. *The Guardian*.

Kawano, S., & Kakehashi, M. (2015). Substantial impact of school closure on the transmission dynamics during the pandemic flu H1N1-2009 in Oita, Japan. *PLOS ONE, 10*(12), e0144839. http://doi.org/10.1371/journal.pone.0144839

Markel, H., Lipman, H. B., Navarro, J. A., Sloan, A., Michalsen, J. R., Stern, A. M., & Cetron, M. S. (2007). Nonpharmaceutical interventions implemented by US cities during the 1918–1919 influenza pandemic. *JAMA, 298*(6), 644–654. doi:10.1001/jama.298.6.644

NIH. (2011, June 6). *Flu pandemic study supports social distancing*. NIH Research Matters, National Institutes of Health.

Ngumbi, E. (2020, March 17). Coronavirus closings: Are colleges helping their foreign, homeless and poor students? *USA Today*.

NRP. (2020a, March 20). *Schools race to feed students amid coronavirus closures*. National Public Radio.

NRP. (2020b, March 23). *Education Dept. says disability laws shouldn't get in the way of online learning*. National Public Radio.

OECD. (2020, August 11). *Combatting COVID-19's effect on children*. Organisation for Economic Co-operation and Development.

Reuters Staff. (2020, March 5). *Coronavirus deprives nearly 300 million students of their schooling: UNESCO*. Reuters.

Sessons, B. (2020, March 23). *Homeless students during the coronavirus pandemic: 'We have to make sure they're not forgotten'*. Statesville.

Simon, M. (2020, March 16). Children's coronavirus cases are not as severe, but that doesn't make them less serious. *CNN*.

Skulmowski, A., & Rey, G. D. (2020). COVID-19 as an accelerator for digitalization at a German university: Establishing hybrid campuses in times of crisis. *Human Behavior and Emerging Technologies, 2*(3), 212–216. https://doi.org/10.1002/hbe2.201

The Economist. (2020, March 21). How covid-19 is interrupting children's education. *The Economist*. https://www.economist.com/international/2020/03/19/how-covid-19-is-interrupting-childrens-education

Times. (2020, March 23). Coronavirus forces families to make painful childcare decisions. *Times*.

UIS. (n.d.). *COVID-19 education response: Dashboards on the global monitoring of school closures caused by the COVID-19 pandemic*. UNESCO Institute for Statistics. https://covid19.uis.unesco.org/global-monitoring-school-closures-covid19/

UNESCO. (2020a, March 4). *290 million students out of school due to COVID-19: UNESCO releases first global numbers and mobilizes response*. UNESCO.

UNESCO. (2020b, March 24). *COVID-19 educational disruption and response.* UNESCO. https://en.unesco.org/news/covid-19-educational-disruption-and-response

UNESCO. (2021a). *Adverse consequences of school closures.* UNESCO. https://en.unesco.org/covid19/educationresponse/consequences

UNESCO. (2021b). *Distance learning solutions.* https://en.unesco.org/covid19/educationresponse/solutions

UNICEF. (2021, March 2). *COVID-19: Schools for more than 168 million children globally have been completely closed for almost a full year, says UNICEF.* UNICEF.

Walsh, E. (Ed.). (2009, July 20). *Closing schools won't stop pandemics: Study.* Reuters.

Wardrop, M. (2009, July 21). Swine flu: schools should close to halt spread of virus, ministers told. *The Telegraph.*

Wheeler, C. C., Erhart, L. M., & Jehn, M. L. (2010). Effect of school closure on the incidence of influenza among school-age children in Arizona. *Public Health Reports, 125*(6), 851–859. https://doi.org/10.1177/003335491012500612

Zumla, A., Yew, W. W., & Hui, D. S. (2010). *Emerging respiratory infections in the 21st century, an issue of infectious disease clinics* (p. 614). Elsevier Health Sciences.

CHAPTER 11

It's Time to Rethink Teaching!

Bloom's Pyramid of Higher Order Thinking Skills Revisited

Randa Hariri

Abstract

This chapter discusses the status of teaching and learning during COVID-19 with a focus on the challenge courageously accepted by the education sector to not interrupt the learning-teaching process, based on the great technological support provided to primary, secondary, and tertiary education. Significantly, this chapter calls for a new era of post-COVID-19 education! It focuses on inviting educators and education institutions' leaders to "Rethink Education" and adopt Blended Learning-Teaching Approach. This approach integrates the learning and teaching technologies into the physical classroom settings while incorporating improvements based on education stakeholders' perspectives about their children's learning. More importantly, this chapter makes a revisit to the "Pyramid" of Bloom's Higher Order Thinking Skills and suggest changing it to a "Ladder" that comprises learners' engagement in a "Learning Challenge" in every step of this "Ladder." It also suggests changing the "Remembering" and "Understanding" levels into "Find" and "Explain" stages respectively.

Keywords

learning – teaching – Bloom's taxonomy – higher-order thinking skills – COVID-19 – e-learning – blended learning-teaching approach

1 Introduction

Teaching and teacher education during the COVID-19 pandemic have been through continuous changes that are persistent, imposing great challenges on the learning-teaching process (which shifts the focus of instruction from the teacher to the student). These challenges comprise all education stakeholders, including teachers, students, and parents in primary, secondary, and tertiary education. After the myriads of technological advancements that have propelled human civilizations and connected people from around the globe, the COVID-19 pandemic showed the fragility of our world order, causing disconnection and increasing its chances of collapse.

This year, the world's education systems have experienced unprecedented disruption. As a result of the COVID-19 pandemic, most schools and higher education institutions all over the world have closed their doors and halted teaching of students in their physical spaces (Tadesse & Muluye, 2020; Kelly & Columbus, 2020; Alqahtani & Rajkhan, 2020). This decision was made as a response to an emergency call from governments of all concerned countries to all education institutions, to shut down. This call was a serious attempt to reduce the spread of the coronavirus that spread through the entire globe and caused the current COVID-19 pandemic. Consequently, schools and higher education institutions resorted to *online learning* in replacement of the *traditional in-person learning*.

Teaching and learning during the pandemic allowed the emergence of highly advanced and automated infrastructure (Kelly & Columbus, 2020), which paved the way for significant mind and structural transformation in policies, teaching strategies, attitudes, and assessment in all primary, secondary, and tertiary education. One of the most remarkable transformations of post-COVID-19 education, is the strongly escalating trend toward the utilization of advanced technologies, and the creation of more platforms with new tools for all grade levels, after it has proved to be effective and efficient during the time of severe pandemic.

During the COVID-19 pandemic, online teaching was the sole mode of delivery adopted, in which technology with all the relevant tools constituted the infrastructure of teaching, learning, and assessment. Technology was credited for ensuring the continuity of the learning-teaching process with all its components. In terms of its positive results, it seems to be impressive and it yielded great results (O'Keefe et al., 2020).

2   In the Case of Saudi Arabia

The situation of education in the Kingdom of Saudi Arabia was not different from the situation of education in other countries in facing the challenges imposed by COVID-19, which spread to the Kingdom as well. Accordingly, all schools and higher education institutions closed their doors and switched their teaching and learning modes from in-person to online education. In accordance with that decision, the Ministry of Education in the Kingdom responded immediately to the needs of all stakeholders in the education system and succeeded to render the transition from in-person to online learning to run smoothly. This transition necessitated the creation or development of new platforms to attend to the various requirements of the new teaching-learning process to accommodate the different needs of education stakeholders, mainly students, teachers, and parents. During the COVID-19 pandemic, parents proved to be influential stakeholders in the education of their children (O'Keefe et al., 2020).

From another perspective, the learning-teaching process during COVID-19 was criticized of leading to lost learning. Accordingly, leaders of educational institutions as well as teachers, should start rethinking the means and methodologies needed to retrieve the lost learning and accommodate the new situation of students. These situations include training teachers to employing new mode of instruction delivery.

The global COVID-19 lockdowns have impacted the in-person education system of all countries, especially the developing ones. Therefore, all countries should enhance broadcast teaching, online teaching, and virtual class infrastructures (Tadesse & Muluye, 2020). While many countries in the world were affected by the consequences of the pandemic in the past academic year (2019–2020), Saudi Arabia was resisting the idea of depriving students from education to a great extent. This resistance was supported by providing various modern technical tools and relying on supportive infrastructures for the integration of the e-learning system. These technology-based actions comprised the first steps that prompted the Kingdom to tackle these uncertain times with great success. The Ministry of Education's response by activating e-learning was quick throughout the establishment of the e-learning departments that followed the digital transformation in the Ministry. This move was in alignment with the Kingdom's Vision 2030, whereby the ministry administrative organizational structure has enabled planning and supporting the success of this technological progress with the required quality.

To investigate the teaching and learning situation further and deeper in the Kingdom of Saudi Arabia, semi-structured focus group interviews were conducted with teachers, supervisors, principals, and parents in both public and private schools, as well as in selected private universities. These focus groups were made up of teachers in private primary schools, teachers in public secondary schools, principals in private and public, primary and secondary schools, teachers in private universities, and parents of children in both primary and secondary schools, in addition to faculty members from selected universities. The responses obtained from these focus groups were analyzed following the interpretive approach, while investing in my extensive experience as an educator in higher education institutions with more than 25 years in primary, secondary, and tertiary education institutions, while occupying both academic and non-academic leading positions.

2.1 Platforms & Continuity of Learning

During these focus group interviews, all participants agreed that the technological platforms with all relevant technologies that were created or developed and made available during the pandemic were highly supportive. A teacher in a public school expressed her satisfaction from the "different platforms that we could find and use in our teaching… especially the Madrasati platform." The Ministry of Education in Saudi Arabia provided a platform called, "Madrasati" to all public schools, to encompass the various requirements of the teaching-learning process for all teachers and students. This platform allowed the utilization of online teaching strategies and assessment tools possible. Private and international schools also succeeded in finding appropriate platforms as a replacement of the in-person teaching and learning system. All these attempts had the same goal, which is to ensure the continuity of the teaching-learning process and save education from any interruption; thus, avoiding students from delaying a year of their academic journey. A public-school principal, who is also a father of three children in primary and middle schools, applauded such goal and actions. The principal-father expressed his satisfaction about continuing teaching and learning during COVID-19, stating, "The most important thing is that teaching and learning did not stop in any of its aspects, including assessments."

2.2 Transforming Our Homes to Schools

During the COVID-19 pandemic, parents proved to be active and effective stakeholders in the teaching-learning process. Parents willingly and readily changed their homes to classrooms and transformed their home environments to school-like environments. This was emphasized by the parents of children in primary and secondary schools, in both private and public schools, in the focus group interviews. In their reflection about online learning during the national lockdown due to the COVID-19 pandemic, one of the parents reported that "our house was changed into a real school and our rooms were changed into classrooms; every child in a room and I was sitting with my 7-year old child, who needed my assistance most."

2.3 Teachers' Initiatives

In similar vein, teachers, on an individual basis, exhibited great efforts and perseverance in searching for additional platforms with supportive technological tools to utilize. A teacher in a public school indicated, "It was really surprising to see the number of platforms that were created during COVID-19 with multiple features to help teach the different topics in different subject matters." Teachers succeeded in tailoring new teaching strategies and respective learning activities to ensure students' engagement in online learning. For example, a math teacher reported, "I looked for interactive math formulas to help students solve problems online whether in class or while doing their homework independently." Other efforts were made with a focus on diversifying the utilization of additional platforms with new tools. "I've never stopped searching for more and more platforms with additional tools to diversify my teaching strategies," a teacher in a private school added.

2.4 Students and Teachers' Adaptability

During COVID-19, students and teachers showed high adaptability to the new teaching strategies, to the learning activities, as well as to the new assessment methods and tools (Gonzalez et al., 2020). A principal in a public school praised the ability of students to learn independently and said, "students were highly adaptive to the novel technologies and they had high motivation for online learning." A subject matter supervisor reported, "students and parents showed high level of adaptability to the new format of teaching and learning to an extent that some parents are requesting online learning to continue." Teachers did their best to provide supportive, appealing, and interactive learning environment that allows flexibility during the application of online teaching strategies and assessment tools for their learners.

2.5 Online Assessment: Methods, Tools, and Feedback

It seems that assessment methods and tools did exhibit a high challenge to all teachers at schools, as well as in universities (Nguyen et al., 2020). Teachers seriously addressed their concerns about the assessment methods and tools, which measure the extent to which the intended learning outcomes are achieved. This concern is based on the significance of assessment results, which are crucial for identifying the points of strengths and areas that need improvement of students' work and performance. In accordance with this identification, teachers become able to provide feedback to students and develop plans to improve their learning. This goes in compliance with the chief purpose of assessment, which is manifested in informing instruction, as well as learning (Hariri, 2016).

There is no doubt that assessment is one of the essential components in the educational process. An array of assessment tools was developed to be utilized online. In online learning, as well as in personalized learning, teachers need "[t]o assess students' knowledge and skills… teachers need to implement several assessment instruments such as writing test, project, assignment, simulation, portfolio, journal, exhibition, observation, interview, oral exam, and peers' evaluation" (Sulaiman et al., 2019, p. 430). However, the main issue is how effective these tools are and how effective the holistic online assessment is. Unfortunately, exam-based assessment tools that are utilized online have been criticized of promoting cheating among students. In this regard, Meccawy et al. (2021) expressed that the "internet and technology have increased the temptation to cheat; however, on the positive side, there are tools to help combat online plagiarism." Therefore, electronic assessment reliability of measuring the achievement of students' learning outcomes is under scrutiny. Nevertheless, online assessment is still considered significant in providing immediate feedback compared to the paper-and-pencil tests. Detailed and timely feedback in online teaching and learning helps improve learning, foster motivation, and enhance learners' performance (O'Keefe et al., 2020). Further to that, electronic assessment proved to be a powerful tool in providing flexibility to students in terms of where and when they can be assessed. In addition, finding multiple methods of electronic assessment is consistent with the explosion of information and the continuous demand for education.

Electronic assessments provided a variety of tools to assess the diversified types of knowledge, skills, and attitudes. This is made possible through the utilization of different assessment tools such as electronic test programs, audio recording, and video conferencing. Electronic assessment also provided tools for evaluating the knowledge that requires memorization or assessing students' understanding of concepts including the utilization of presentation programs through e-learning platforms or essay exams, and practical skills, which can be evaluated using simulation programs or electronic files.

It is the right time to grasp the prospect and employ new and innovative educational methods to make the COVID-19 pandemic an opportunity that must be looked into and invest in, rather than just treating the pandemic as a historic event. It is also time to consider the importance of analyzing and evaluating the impact of the accelerated digital transformation and technologies on education and societies.

2.6 A Novel Era of Education

Life after COVID-19 seems different from its pre-pandemic perspective. This applies to education as well. COVID-19 affected the world in all aspects, whether it is economic, societal, cultural, or educational. Education was one of the sectors that was affected by COVID-19 causing radical changes in the teaching and learning process. Despite the adverse consequences of COVID-19, we could announce a new promising era in teaching and learning. A new era of education! Teaching and learning after COVID-19 will not and should not be the same as the teaching and learning prior to COVID-19. (Gonzalez et al., 2020; Komolafe et al., 2020; Tadesse & Muluye, 2020).

As the severity of the pandemic is lessening, many countries began to reopen their schools and higher education institutions welcomed back students and teachers, thus, significant transformations should take place. However, these transformations are subject to variations in available technological infrastructure or are subject to whether the technological infrastructure can be established in any education institution. That is in addition to the expected support that education leaders, including ministries of education, can and will provide to their respective primary, secondary, and tertiary education institutions. Therefore, education institutions are invited to develop their own plans in alignment with the plans of their countries to meet the challenges of post COVID-19 teaching and learning as well as becoming active players in the upcoming transformations in the education system.

It is time to rethink the roles that the various stakeholders in the teaching-learning process should take. Rethinking education entails looking for quality transformations to meet the requirements of a new era of teaching and learning, and to face all challenges. Since teachers are at the very front lines of the teaching-learning process and they are the *de facto* leaders; therefore, they must, as always have been, take the lead to initiate and pursue transformations in the education sector at any grade level. Teachers are the providers of learning opportunities and experience and they are continuously thinking and reflecting on their own teaching and on their students' learning (Hariri, 2016).

It is also time to rethink education! This is the time to rebuild better, more equitable and more effective education systems. The goal should not be to return to the way teaching and learning was before the outbreak of the virus. Rather, it should be to fix the flaws in the systems that have long intended yet not succeeded, in order to generate independent and lifelong learners. In every country, its ministry of education, the senior management of higher education institutions, and school leaders should seriously investigate the teaching-learning situation in the post-pandemic era to gain insights and derive lessons learned.

First, leaders in primary, secondary, and tertiary education should develop professional development programs incorporating activities that focus on preparing teachers to meet again with their students in-person after a disconnection or interruption that lasted for more than one and a half years (Borgen & Ødegaard, 2021). This concern was raised by a parent of two children in the primary school who expressed that "teachers should be trained to be coaches for their students and be taught strategies to meet students after one and a half years of being away from school." These professional development activities or programs should not only include teachers, but also address the development of students, as well as parents or guardians who proved to be effective players in the teaching-learning process. Moreover, these outreach activities or back-to-school campaigns should be thoroughly encompassing to welcome children and young students who missed out on education when schools were forced to close.

Second, COVID-19 unleashed an array of new skills that teachers and students have acquired through teaching and learning online. These skills include technical and intellectual skills as well as study skills and teaching, and learning strategies. Therefore, a new era of education should commence while taking into consideration all the lessons that have been learned from teaching and learning before and during COVID-19. That is in addition to reconsidering the roles of the education institutions' management, teachers, students, parents as well as the whole learning environment. Adopting new technologies is escalating; new technologies would promote online teaching and learning, provide adaptive learning software and research tools that allow students to interact almost instantly, benefit from available information, and acquire skills. This brings into discussion the mode of delivery that will be adopted in teaching and learning in all primary, secondary, and tertiary education.

2.7 *Integrated or Blended Learning-Teaching Approach*

It is time to rethink the mode of delivery. It is time to think about adopting an integrated or blended learning-teaching approach and stimulating the method of delivery, which proved to be effective and preferred by students during the COVID-19 pandemic (Ananga, 2020). Ananga (2020) adds that employing blended learning-teaching approach necessitates effective collaboration between education and technology. This collaboration entails educators to specify the technological tools and techniques they need in teaching and learning as well as to smartly invest in the existing and emerging technological innovations.

Furthermore, the integrated or blended learning-teaching approach seems to be increasingly appealing to teachers as well as leaders at schools and universities in different countries. This can be referred to the significance of this approach in raising the level of skills for both students and teachers, and for being ideal for facing the increasing number of students enrolled and enhancing the quality of the educational process (Alqahtani & Rajkhan, 2020). Blended, integrated, or also called the hybrid learning-teaching approach, is increasingly preferred by teachers and students. Nevertheless, teachers must be provided with all types of support to empower them in employing various types of technology-based and pedagogy-informed teaching (Müller et al., 2021). In accordance with that, and with the vast and fast advancements in technology, schools and higher education institutions are invited to establish well-developed technological infrastructure to enhance the hybrid learning to persist and flourish in the post-COVID-19 periods. Hence, teachers at schools and in higher education institutions must be supported and well trained, since they are key players in making e-learning a major element of primary, secondary as well as tertiary education (Müller et al., 2021). UNESCO has emphasized the importance of integrated education as an approach that promotes learning and pushes toward achieving the fourth sustainable development goals, included in the UN report,[1] known as Education 2030.

Integrated learning promises to benefit students' progress in their educational path, promote active education, help distressed students, and assesses factors influencing a student's success. However, the effective integration of these new technologies into the curriculum requires good planning and resources (Ananga, 2020). A parent of a student in a primary school expressed her daughter's relief from bullying and harassment. The child improved her academic achievement as a result of online learning. Thus, helping distressed students is being emphasized and the parent said, "my daughter's academic achievement and emotions were better during online learning." The education sector will see new situations in many countries of the world in general, including social life at school. Accordingly, a sharp focus should be given to the social life at school in terms of access to the classroom which should be gradual, and the principle of social separation should be seriously considered (Komolafe et al., 2020).

The advancement of technology made the application of artificial intelligence (AI) into education possible. In recent years, educational AI tools and robotics have been made available. The adoption of robotics in teaching and learning has gained its importance in educational institutions. The success of the experimental use of robots teaching languages and basic subjects has become apparent in countries, such as China and some Scandinavian countries, such as Sweden (Stojkovic, 2017).

2.8 *From Teaching First… to Learning First*

It is very well-known that teachers in primary, secondary, and tertiary education work throughout the academic year to support the students in achieving the intended learning outcomes. These learning outcomes have been changed from being called "course objectives" to "learning objectives" or "learning outcomes" in response to the change in the focal point of the what was called the teaching-learning process. For a long time, teachers have taken the center stage of the teaching-learning process and they have been considered as the sole source of knowledge. Nevertheless, "technologization" with all its never-ending advancements, succeeded in diverting the focus back on the students themselves; thus, rendering it a learning-teaching process instead of a teaching-learning process. With this major change, learning is foregrounded rather than teaching, and students have become more responsible of their own learning and begun to increasingly engage in their own learning. Consequently, the authority over learning has also changed from teachers to students. This major change took place in response to changing the sole or main source of "knowledge." In the teaching-learning process, the teacher is almost the sole provider of knowledge, whereas in the learning-teaching process, the students become the active constructor of knowledge. This radical shift in learning and teaching necessitates two major types of transformations involving the "what" and the "how" to implement such these transformations.

2.9 The "What" and "How" of the Transformation

The first type of transformation that should take place is at the level of the "what" teachers need to teach; thus, at the level of the leading component of the learning-teaching process which is at the level of learning outcomes. The second type of transformation is at the level of the "how" or the way teachers, students and other educational stakeholders should think about learning and teaching related processes. A change in the mindset of educators should take place to move from thinking about teachers as knowledge providers, to focusing on students as knowledge constructors. For this to occur most effectively, educators must begin rethinking the curriculum and its essential components: learning outcomes, teaching strategies, learning activities, teaching aids, and most importantly assessment and assessment tools. Therefore, educators are invited to rethink what the learning outcomes really are.

Learning outcomes include the knowledge, skills, attitudes, and values that students need to achieve at any point. These learning outcomes constitute the main guide of teachers, based on which they identify the topic of study, as well as design or select the teaching strategies and learning activities. Moreover, based on the learning outcomes and topic of study, teachers design or select the learning activities and teaching aids in alignment with the teaching strategies. Finally, teachers develop assessment tools to measure whether the students have achieved the identified learning outcome or how far the students are from achieving the learning outcome.

Technology, as a momentous factor of the 21st century, is considered as the chief factor behind the radical shift in the learning and teaching processes. Technology was able to make an unprecedented amount of information readily available. This renders finding the information via search engines or databases even easier and faster than retrieving it from one's own memory. Consequently, teachers should invest in this feature and render it the starting point of students' learning. Here is where and how the learning-teaching journey should start and develop.

Based on that, in primary grade levels, the first significant and essential skills that students should master are related to the utilization of search engines in "finding information." Students need to realize that the various available search engines and databases provide enormous amount of information about indefinite topics from unlimited sources and perspectives. This comprises the very basic and essential skills needed for learning to occur. Accordingly, educators need to rethink the existing learning outcomes in all grade levels. Hence, we need to revise the order of higher levels of thinking skills that was proposed by Benjamin Bloom, in the year 1956.

2.10   *Bloom's Taxonomy Revisited*

Based on the availability of information in the various resources provided by the various search engines, teachers are invited to start the learning-teaching journey by providing a learning opportunity for their students. This opportunity comprises the starting point for independent learning whereby students are entitled to collect information and data about a given topic, or find answers for a given question, or a solution for a given problem, and so on. Nevertheless, for this to be effective, students need to be able to explain the available information, and then evaluate it. This means that teachers need not to spend time and exert efforts on providing the information anymore. Rather, students have access to information available from unlimited resources offered by the various search engines. These efforts and time should be made and spent on higher levels of thinking skills in relevance to learning outcomes that should be developed starting from Bloom's level of understanding (Bloom et al. 1956). With reference to that, the Bloom's Taxonomy Pyramid of Higher Order Thinking Skills should be revised as presented in Figure 11.1.

Based on Figure 11.1, I argue that the learning journey should start when the teachers provide a learning opportunity to their respective students. Then, students are encouraged or invited to "Find" the relevant and needed information, which is made readily available through different sources provided by the various research engines and databases. This stage of finding or collection of information or data comprises a stage of independent learning that students can undertake without scaffolding from their teachers. This is because such kind of intellectual task falls within the zone of the students' proximal development (ZPD) as explained by Vygotsky (Ormord, 2019). Nevertheless, the

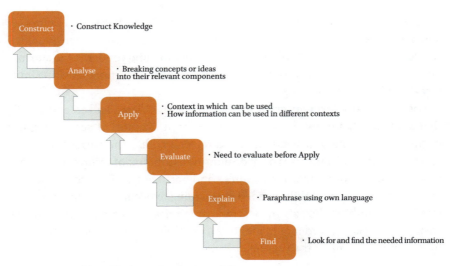

FIGURE 11.1   Ladder of higher order thinking skills

learning experience that students engage in the "Find" stage, falls within their zone of proximal development and accordingly they do not need any kind of scaffolding from their teachers or any other adult, yet they do engage in or face a Learning Challenge manifested in selecting the most relevant information in alignment with the intended learning outcome(s). At this point, students need to take on this Learning Challenge to be able to step up the Ladder of Higher Order Thinking Skills to the next stage, which I suggest be called "Explain" stage.

In the "Explain" stage, teachers are requested to provide suitable scaffolding for students and guide them to explain and define the information they have collected in the "Find" stage. During this stage, students engage in or face another Learning Challenge, which they need to complete successfully to make another step up on the ladder to the "Evaluate" stage. In the "Evaluate" stage, teachers should support students by facilitating the evaluation of the explained information in terms of relevance or through identifying the kind of relationships that exist either among the collected pieces of information or between the collected information and students' previous knowledge. Also, in this "Evaluate" stage, students engage in another Learning Challenge manifested in assessing the relevance of the explained information to the intended learning outcome and the potential of the information that can contribute to achieving this learning outcome. Again, students need to engage in and successfully pass this challenge to make one more step up the Ladder. After the "Evaluate" stage, students engage in a Learning Challenge, which ends up with students becoming able to apply the understood information in new and relevant contexts. Moreover, after the "Evaluate" stage, students engage in another

Learning Challenge until they become able to identify the components of the collected information and discuss the reasons and types of the relationships that exist among these components, hence the "Analyze" stage. Finally, after reaching the "Evaluate" stage, students can construct their own knowledge after successfully completing a Learning Challenge that entails building new concepts or ideas and thoughts based on the collected information. The learning will be relevant to their previous knowledge and learning experiences as well as a result of all the Learning Challenges they have engaged in or successfully accomplished in alignment with the intended learning outcome.

At this point, it can be inferred that learning occurs only when students engage in a Learning Challenge at any stage of the Higher Order Thinking Ladder whereby, they need to successfully complete every Learning Challenge to be able to move up to the next stage. It can also be concluded that the first thinking stage initiates independent learning by facing the commencing Learning Challenge, whereas the other thinking stages may include teachers providing scaffolding in the form of guidance or facilitation.

This new understanding of Bloom's taxonomy pyramid entails two major changes that need to be further discussed. The first change is related to the first level of Bloom's pyramid, which I suggested to change from the "Remembering" level to "Finding." From remembering the information into finding the information. Nowadays, students need not to memorize or in other words, teachers need not to work on supporting the students with achieving learning outcomes at the remembering level, because students can "find" information independently as it falls within the students' zone of proximal development. Learning outcomes in the new era of education should not include the actions in the remembering level of Bloom's Taxonomy. Therefore, essential transformation has to be made in the learning-teaching process to convert the Remembering related actions into independent Finding actions. Following the Find stage, explaining the collected information is needed to demonstrate the student's understanding of the information he or she has gathered.

The second change is related to the third level of higher order thinking, which entails the necessity of students to evaluate the comprehended information, in terms of its relevance and other related criteria. Following evaluation, students can perform any higher order thinking or cognitive skill manifested in the various levels of Applying, Analyzing and Constructing knowledge.

In the reference to the previous discussion, students are rendered information finders and knowledge constructors. Knowledge cannot be found; it is rather constructed. Therefore, it can be said that the enormous number of sources provided through the various available resources can only provide information and data, but can never provide knowledge. Learners or students need to actively engage in thinking and processing the collected information and data to construct their own and unique knowledge and understanding. Nevertheless, teachers' proper scaffolding can enhance the construction of knowledge. The teachers should provide students with appropriate learning opportunities. Appropriate learning opportunity means that the learning opportunity should match the chronological age and cognitive level of students. "Appropriate" means that the learning opportunity should be challenging in a way that can be achieved by students while scaffolding is provided to students to lift them from their actual level of intellectual development to their potential level of intellectual development, as explained by Vygotsky (Ormord, 2019). "Challenging" also means that it is achievable by students when the needed scaffolding is provided; thus, leading to success which acts a strong motive for learners to engage in learning to gain more and more success; thus, creating continuous and even lifelong learners. In addition, the Learning Challenge that learners engage in, suits the curious nature of students as Piaget expressed (Ormord, 2019) and increases their motivation for learning independently.

To summarize, this transformation in the order of various stages of the Higher Thinking Skills and the role of the learners in each stage, emphasizes the role of learners as constructors of knowledge, and teachers as providers of learning opportunities. The Ladder of Higher Order Thinking Skills entails that learners should engage in a Learning Challenge in every higher order thinking stage of the Ladder, whereby learners cannot move up from one stage to another unless they have successfully completed the Learning Challenge in the previous stage. Based on the Ladder of Higher Order Thinking Skills, the learning-teaching process generates independent information finders and knowledge constructors. In turn, this learning-teaching process emphasizes the facilitator role of the teacher through providing the appropriate scaffolding to their students. Accordingly, teachers must work hard to perceive their role in the learning-teaching process, develop their own attitudes, and be committed to becoming intrinsically motivated to provide the appropriate scaffolding to students to achieve the intended learning outcomes (Alqahtani & Rajkhan, 2020).

2.11   *The "How" of Transformation*

The second type of transformation that should be incorporated is at the level of the "how" teachers should teach; in more specific term, how teachers should guide the students to achieve the intended learning outcomes. In this era, and in response to the COVID-19 challenges and consequences, educators and leaders of education institutions are encouraged to consider the blended or hybrid learning-teaching approach in teaching and learning.

Educators, teachers, leaders of education institutions and other stakeholders in education including Ministry of Education in every country, should set a solid foundation for "a transformative learning environment" while integrating virtual platforms with traditional physical settings. This would both improve the learning experience of students and ensure achieving and improving the learning outcomes (Komolafe, 2020). Blended Learning-Teaching Approach integrates the face-to-face practices with the online practices in the physical setting of the classroom. Smartly investing in technology should not be overlooked in an era when technology is influential (Hariri, 2016). During COVID-19, teachers and students acquired a lot of technological skills that they should be encouraged to keep using after the COVID-19 pandemic. Teachers are invited more than ever to diversify their teaching strategies to meet the changing interests of students. Teachers must rethink the examples they utilize in their teaching to make them more relevant to the students' daily life experiences; thus, creating lifelong learners.

Accordingly, teachers are encouraged to diversify the teaching strategies that they employ in the classroom with a greater focus on integrating online strategies and utilizing computer-based methods in their teaching. Technologies have increasingly proved to enhance the learning of students as well as the teaching of teachers. Both comprise the core of students' learning experiences in the classroom in all grade levels starting from pre-school to tertiary education (McEwen & Dubé, 2015).

2.12   *Transformation in Assessment*
In accordance with the suggested changes in Bloom's Pyramid of Higher Order Thinking Skills to become the Ladder of Higher Order Thinking Skills, assessment should start when teachers are actively engaged in guiding students through their learning journey. Teachers should assess students' achievements of the intended learning outcomes at the "Explain" stage and upward.

From another angle, to measure students' achievement of the intended learning outcomes in fulfilment of the Blended Learning-Teaching Approach, teachers are invited to transform the assessment methods they employ in their classrooms from traditional exam-based assessment to "authentic assessment." Authentic assessment tools include journals, reports, reflective papers, case studies, projects, and so on. This was highlighted by parents of students in primary and secondary education during the focus group interviews, whereby they requested "teachers to give our children assignments or tasks that they can do in a longer period of time rather than one-off exams." Nevertheless, extending the time for accomplishing tasks is reasonable considering students' attention span that varies with age. In this regard, McEwen and Dubé (2015) emphasize that teachers must consider the attention span of their students in the different grade levels and provide transitions between tasks in an attempt to avoid overwhelming the working memory of their students (McEwen & Dubé, 2015). This was also highlighted by parents of children in primary grade levels who asked teachers "to consider our children's ability in staying focused on any one task for a long period of time."

3 Conclusion

Education stakeholders are called upon to RETHINK education and more specifically to RETHINK the learning-teaching process. Educators are encouraged to consider making changes that encompass all components of the learning-teaching process starting from the learning outcomes, and ending with the assessments. Essentially, these changes should include revisiting the development of the learning outcomes and consequently the type of knowledge students need to construct, skills they need to acquire, attitudes they need to have, and values they need to hold. Educators are invited to adopt the Blended Learning-Teaching Approach that provides great opportunities for diversification in teaching strategies and learning activities.

Hence, efforts exerted by teachers in designing or selecting teaching strategies, tailoring learning activities, selecting teaching aids, and measuring students' achievement of learning outcomes at the "Find" stage would be lessened. At this point, educators or teachers may still need to include in the outlines or syllabus of the courses or subject matter they teach the learning outcomes at the "Find" stage of the Ladder of Higher Thinking Skills. Yet, this should be done through an independent learning opportunity that teachers must provide and students are rendered accountable for. This transformation will set the cornerstone for generating independent and autonomous learners and knowledge constructors who are able to construct their own understanding about any topic. This understanding has been proven unique in nature due to the difference in the previous knowledge that students have already constructed (Ormord, 2019).

Note

[1] https://en.unesco.org/themes/education2030-sdg4

References

Alqahtani, A. Y., & Rajkhan, A. A. (2020). E-learning critical success factors during the COVID-19 pandemic: A comprehensive analysis of e-learning managerial perspectives. *Education Science, 10*(9), 216. https://doi.org/10.3390/educsci10090216

Ananga, P. (2020). Pedagogical considerations of e-learning in education for development in the face of COVID-19. *International Journal of Technology in Education and Science, 4*(4), 310–321.

Bloom, B. S., Engelhart, M. D., Furst, E. J., Hill, W. H., & Krathwohl, D. R. (1956). *Taxonomy of educational objectives: The classification of educational goals. Handbook I: The cognitive domain*. David McKay Company.

Borgen, J. S., & Ødegaard, E. E. (2021). Global paradoxes and provocations in education: Exploring sustainable futures for children and youth. In J. S. Borgen & E. E. Ødegaard (Eds.), *Childhood cultures in transformation: 30 years of the UN Convention on the Rights of the Child in Action towards sustainability* (pp. 274–296). Brill. http://www.jstor.org/stable/10.1163/j.ctv1sr6k8f.21

Gonzalez, T., de la Rubia, M. A., Hincz, K. P., Comas-Lopez, M., Subirats, L., Fort, S., & Sachaet, G. M. (2020). Influence of COVID-19 confinement on students' performance in higher education. *PLoS ONE, 15*(10). https://doi.org/10.1371/journal.pone.0239490

Hariri, R. (2016) *Understanding teaching excellence in higher education in an Arab country: The case of Lebanon* [PhD thesis]. University of Sheffield. https://etheses.whiterose.ac.uk/14343/

Kelly, A. P., & Columbus, R. (2020, July). *College in the time of coronavirus: Challenges facing American higher education*. American Enterprise Institute. http://www.jstor.org/stable/resrep25358

Komolafe, B. F., Fakayode, O. T., Osidipe, A., Zhang, F. Y., & Qian, X. S. (2020). Evaluation of online pedagogy among higher education international students in China during the COVID-19 outbreak. *Creative Education, 11*, 2262–2279. https://doi.org/10.4236/ce.2020.1111166

McEwen, R., & Dubé, A. K. (2015). Engaging or distracting: Children's tablet computer use in education. *Journal of Educational Technology & Society, 8*(4), 9–23. https://www.jstor.org/stable/10.2307/jeductechsoci.18.4.9

Meccawy, Z., Meccawy, M., & Alsobhi, A. (2021). Assessment in 'survival mode': Student and faculty perceptions of online assessment practices in HE during Covid-19 pandemic. *International Journal for Educational Integrity, 16*(17), 24. https://doi.org/10.1007/s40979-021-00083-9

Müller, A. M., Goh, C., Lim, L. Z., & Gao, X. (2021). COVID-19 emergency eLearning and beyond: Experiences and perspectives of university educators. *Education Sciences, 11*(1), 19. https://doi.org/10.3390/educsci11010019

Nguyen, J. G., Keuseman, K. J., & Humston, J. J. (2020). Minimize online cheating for online assessments during COVID-19 pandemic. *Journal of Chemical Education, 97*(9), 3429–3435. https://dx.doi.org/10.1021/acs.jchemed.0c00790

O'Keefe, L., Dellinger, J. T., Mathes, J., Holland, T. L., & Knott, J. (2020). *The state of online learning in the Kingdom of Saudi Arabia: A COVID-19 impact study for higher education.* Online Learning Consortium.

Ormord, J. E., Anderman, E. M., & Anderman, L. (2019). *Educational psychology: Developing learners* (10th ed.). Pearson.

Stojkovic, A. (2017, November 17). *The use of robotics in education.* Novak Djokovic Foundation. https://novakdjokovicfoundation.org/

Sulaiman, T., Abdul Rahim, S. S., Hakim, M. N., & Omar, R. (2019). Teachers' perspectives of assessment and alternative assessment in the classroom. *International Journal of Innovative Technology and Exploring Engineering, 8*(7), 426–431. https://www.ijitee.org/wpcontent/uploads/papers/v8i7s2/G10730587S219.pdf

Tadesse, S., & Muluye, W. (2020). The impact of COVID-19 pandemic on education system in developing countries: A review. *Open Journal of Social Sciences, 8*, 159–170. https://doi.org/10.4236/jss.2020.810011

UNESCO. (2021). *Leading SDG 4 – Education 2030.* https://en.unesco.org/themes/education2030-sdg4